METABOLIZING CAPITAL

METABOLIZING CAPITAL

Writing, Information, and the Biophysical Environment

CHRISTIAN J. PULVER

UTAH STATE UNIVERSITY PRESS
Logan

© 2020 by University Press of Colorado

Published by Utah State University Press
An imprint of University Press of Colorado
245 Century Circle, Suite 202
Louisville, Colorado 80027

 ASSOCIATION of UNIVERSITY PRESSES The University Press of Colorado is a proud member of
the Association of University Presses.

The University Press of Colorado is a cooperative publishing enterprise
supported, in part, by Adams State University, Colorado State University,
Fort Lewis College, Metropolitan State University of Denver, University of
Colorado, University of Northern Colorado, University of Wyoming, Utah
State University, and Western Colorado University.

∞ This paper meets the requirements of the ANSI/NISO Z39.48–1992
(Permanence of Paper).

ISBN: 978-1-60732-967-1 (paperback)
ISBN: 978-1-60732-968-8 (ebook)
DOI: https://doi.org/10.7330/9781607329688

Library of Congress Cataloging-in-Publication Data

Names: Pulver, Christian J., author.
Title: Metabolizing capital : writing, information, and the biophysical environ-
    ment / Christian J. Pulver.
Description: Logan : Utah State University Press, [2019] I Includes bibliograph-
    ical references and index.
Identifiers: LCCN 2019056178 (print) I LCCN 2019056179 (ebook) I ISBN
    9781607329671 (paperback) I ISBN 9781607329688 (ebook)
Subjects: LCSH: Rhetoric—Philosophy. I Rhetoric—Study and teaching. I Ecol-
    ogy in literature.
Classification: LCC P301 .P85 2019 (print) I LCC P301 (ebook) I DDC
    808.06/6577—dc23
LC record available at https://lccn.loc.gov/2019056178
LC ebook record available at https://lccn.loc.gov/2019056179

Cover illustration credits. Top, left to right: © BNMK 081/Shutterstock;
used with permission from the British Museum; © vkilikov/Shutterstock).
Background illustration by Stephen Salmon (https://steve-salmon.tumblr.com).

To my parents, sisters, brothers

CONTENTS

ACKNOWLEDGMENTS

There were many times while writing this book I thought I might not complete it. Then I'd think of all the help I had received during the project and it would remind me of why I had to carry through. Such a little section could never fully acknowledge the innumerable willing acts of kindness and sacrifice, advice, and guidance that I've received during this journey. The people I acknowledge here—and some I'll inevitably forget—are people I feel the deepest gratitude towards for their support through a project that I eventually came to experience as a sort of *purgatorio*, at times oscillating wildly between heaven and hell.

I want to start by thanking my mentors and advisors who helped guide the inception and development of this work: Donna LeCourt, Charlie Moran, David Lenson, and Eleanor Kutz. Your guidance and support have humbled me greatly—I hope the ideas in this book live up to the standards you set in your own scholarship—I am deeply indebted to you. Thanks to David Toomey and your understated sagacity; Martha Langer for your design skills and visual imagination; and Stephen Salmon for allowing me to use your visionary art for the book's cover. To my parents, siblings, and closest friends—I might be able to keep up with groups chats now, but I make no promises:) To Holly, my better half, for your lucid, loving criticisms of my more grandiose ideas. To Denise Paster, my long-time friend and writing colleague. To my friend Terence Lynch whose support never wavered, even after I stopped responding to your texts. To Ata Moharerri and our late-night problem-solving sessions.

To my patient colleagues at Roger Williams University (RWU) in the Department of Writing Studies, Rhetoric, and Composition—thank you for creating a space for new faculty to succeed. Likewise, this work could not have been completed without the generous support of the Foundation to Promote Scholarship and Teaching at RWU and the timely course releases that freed up valuable thinking and writing time. Many thanks as well to the team at Utah State University Press, especially the support of Michael Spooner, Rachael Levay, Laura Furney, and Daniel Pratt; Karl Yambert and his sharp-eyed copyediting; and the anonymous readers whose feedback was critical in helping me re-envision this book. Finally, I want to thank the hundreds of scholars from across time and discipline who have inspired and informed this work. Without the cumulative and sustained labor of their efforts, this little book would not exist.

METABOLIZING CAPITAL

Introduction

TOWARD A MATERIALIST ECOLOGY OF WRITING

Since life evolved by natural selection, we might surmise that life is assembled from common elements that are easy and cheap to find. Indeed, life's chemical formula mimics in broad strokes the chemical proportions found in seawater and soil. (Kaspari 2012)

We've all had this experience—we overpay for a lackluster dinner at a restaurant, or we buy a product, often electronic, that starts to slow down or stops working. We wonder why we don't cook at home more or why we didn't buy the two-year warranty. In a pre-Web world you might have filled out a customer-service card or called the company to complain. Today, however, we do what any disgruntled customer would do and post an online review.

For those of us who study writing and rhetoric, we might approach the writing situation of a mundane text like an online review by first considering its purpose. At first glance, this seems fairly straightforward: share your experience of a product or service in a way that readers find credible and informative. Upon further study, we could increase our scope and consider the rhetorical relationships between writer, audience, and topic. We could ask questions about the composing process, the time and place of the exchange, and the social relations involved in the transaction. And certainly, this kind of contextual, socially situated approach to studying writing has been a hallmark of writing studies as a discipline.[1]

However, when we start to consider the profuse *materiality*[2] in place for a text like an online review to exist, it's clear there is much more to consider in this writing situation beyond the

DOI: 10.7330/9781607329688.c000

human symbolic activity that happens there. The sheer material abundance overwhelms the mind—the phones, computers, keyboards, screens, wires, cables, routers, telephone lines, cell towers, and data centers—to name a few. On a more micro level we might consider the hundreds of parts that make up the innards of our electronic devices—the microchips, circuits, transistors, and computer processors. Or, on a more macro level, we might consider the global labor force that mines the raw materials used to make electronics and the men, women, and children who assemble and break them down once they are, ostensibly, "obsolete."

Then, of course, there is the stuff that flows through this materiality: the words, texts, information, and data we produce 24 hours a day, seven days a week. With the global online population surpassing four billion people (over half of the humans on the planet), it's been estimated that every minute in the United States over 180 million emails are sent, 18 million texts are sent, 4 million Google searches are made, and 4 million videos are watched on YouTube (Internet Live Stats 2019; Domo 2019). Data management and analytics company Domo estimates that in 2020 "1.7MB of data will be created every second for every person on earth," pushing global production of data by citizen-consumers[3] to 2.5 zettabytes a day (Domo 2018).[4]

Though we are all becoming more accustomed to such numbers, growing flows of texts and data greatly complicate our understanding of contemporary writing situations. Underneath the reviews, posts, texts, tweets, and comments we produce each day exists a vast system of interconnected platforms, networks, and inscription technologies that span the globe, from the bottom of every ocean, to the outer exosphere of the planet, all designed to collect, process, and commodify the streams of data churned out daily by human and nonhuman agents alike. While the information technology industries[5] refer to these flows of data and the material infrastructure necessary to make them flow as "the cloud," we shouldn't be fooled by the slick metaphor. A more fitting name for the modern internet and the material abundance that makes online texts possible is the *global networked infrastructure of inscription*. It's a mouthful for sure, so

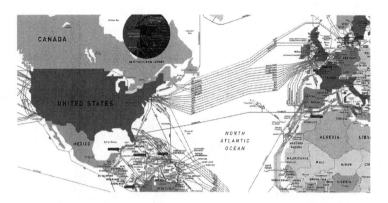

Figure 0.1. Submarine-cable map from data company TeleGeography, documenting all the active domestic and international fiber-optic internet cables that connect the Americas with Europe and Africa. (Image used with permission from TeleGeography Inc.)

I'll often abbreviate and refer to it as the *global archive*.[6] Despite its clumsiness, the phrase is meant to capture the copious materiality in place for online writing to occur more so than the specious metaphor of the "cloud." The submarine-cable map of the internet released annually by the communications company TeleGeography provides a more realistic image of the internet and the more than 700,000 miles of underwater fiber-optic cable that make it a reality (figure 0.1).

In light of this material abundance, it feels constraining to think about writing and rhetoric as simply the human symbolic communication that happens online. Though it's common to think about writing as a tool for rhetoric and communication, one of the great affordances of writing is its ability to record and inscribe the world, helping us quantify and materialize our lived experience. Despite the obviousness of this fact, our research and theories on writing tend to background the inscriptive aspects of writing for a greater focus on its symbolic and rhetorical aspects. And yet, the global archive that currently envelops us suggests that the inscriptive facets of writing technology can tell us a great deal about what writing is and how it changes in the twenty-first century.

I explore the concepts of inscription and the archive more in the next chapter, but a few thoughts here will help me introduce how I'll be thinking about these challenging concepts. I argue throughout this work that, in order to develop our new materialist theories of writing, we need to grapple more with the inscriptive affordances of writing. As writing studies scholar Jodie Nicotra points out, writing-as-human-communication is just one kind of writing and part of the more general use of writing as a recording technology. She describes the ubiquitous use of digital writing tools to record every kind of human and nonhuman activity as "listening inscription" (Nicotra 2017b). While the metaphor is an apt one, I'm thinking of writing-inscription more materially as a form of *datafication*, a term I borrow from Viktor Mayer-Schönberger and Kenneth Cukier, authors of the book *Big Data (2013)*. As they define it, "to datafy a phenomenon is to put it in a quantified format so it can be tabulated and analyzed" (Mayer-Schönberger and Cukier 2014). Digital writing's enhanced capacity to inscribe all experiential phenomena (e.g. movement, growth, color, sound, speech, images, ideas, etc.) into computable binary code not only "listens" and records human activity, it radically changes every facet of our lived experience of materiality.

Inscription as datafication, as well as the material infrastructure of the global archive, both signal a qualitatively new informational environment, one that marks a transition from a Web 2.0 world that celebrated user-generated content and social media,[7] to a world that has been called Web 3.0 by many—a maturing digital environment of escalating data collection by corporations and governments and their relentless pursuit to capture, control, and commodify flows of information.[8] While Web 2.0 has generally been embraced by writing studies scholars, the movement into the more capital-driven Web 3.0 is presenting all kinds of conundrums for our materialist theories of writing. The intensification of inscription and data collection on citizen-consumers is raising troubling questions about labor and automation, surveillance and privacy, data security, the spread of misinformation, search-engine bias, and artificial intelligence, as well as troubling ecological questions about the growing energy demand of the global archive and the growing stream of electronic waste that gets created as a byproduct of our disposable, digital culture. In the transition from Web 2.0 to Web 3.0, we are living through an accelerating process of ubiquitous inscription—a process of incessant datafication not only of our exchange relations with each other, but with the rise of the internet-of-things and the billions of nonhuman devices now connected to the internet, the datafication of any kind of activity that takes place in the phenomenal world. As will become clearer as this work unfolds, I define *data* as the building blocks of *information*. *Information* is the umbrella term and *data* is both a type of information in basic form *and* the building blocks for different kinds of information, both semantic and physical in nature.

The acceleration of data collection we are experiencing in Web 3.0 radically challenges our conventional assumptions about writing, inscription, information, and materiality in writing studies. Indeed, the rate at which digital writing and inscription technologies evolve and spread is greatly testing our abilities to theorize what writing and textuality become in the growing complexity of Web 3.0. Because these changes are so disruptive and potentially harmful to the natural and social systems they are a part of, there's an urgent need in writing studies to develop our critical, materialist, and ecological theories of writing to grapple more rigorously with the social and economic impacts of intensifying datafication and information production.

While new materialist theories of writing are starting to recognize the radical changes spurred by Web 3.0, the predatory nature of twenty-first-century informational capitalism demands a more direct engagement with the two primary agentive forces we consistently background in our materialist theories of writing: (1) the forces of capital circulation and (2) the basic biophysical laws of energy and matter. Without directly confronting these basic material agencies and how they entangle with writing and inscription, our materialist theories of writing will continue to underestimate the virulent nature of neoliberal, informational capitalism and the ways writing and inscription get leveraged for capital circulation. This book is my attempt to fill this need and contribute to current new materialist work by starting to articulate a critical materialist framework designed to help us theorize the larger socioeconomic implications of writing and inscription in Web 3.0.

EXPANDING NEW MATERIALIST AND OBJECT-ORIENTED THEORIES OF WRITING

In order to lay out the basic materialist framework for theorizing digital writing that sits at the heart of this book, I want to begin by unpacking some basic assumptions about materiality and agency that persist in writing studies and consider how new materialist theories of writing are rethinking these assumptions. Historically, whenever radical changes occur to our writing technologies and the quantity of texts produced, scholars in writing studies return to fundamental questions of materiality. Inevitably, questioning the nature of materiality leads us to revisit the concept of agency and who, or what, can enact it. The last wave of materialist theorizing about writing emerged in the early to mid-1990s with the cultural changes prompted by the spread of personal computing, word processing, and the World Wide Web (Bolter 1991, 2001; Haas 1996; Faigley 1999; Selfe 1999; Moran 1999a, 2005). Around the same time, other scholars were invoking the concept of *ecology* to think more materially about how networked, digital technologies changed the ways we produced and circulated texts (Cooper 1986; Syverson 1997; Edbauer 2005; Spinuzzi 2003). While these earlier waves of materialist thinking made important strides in our understanding of writing and its inherent technological and ecological qualities, they also made two key assumptions that continue to hinder our materialist theories today. Assumption one: only humans (and not nonhuman things like nature or technology) can enact agency. Assumption two: the primary site for studying and theorizing writing resides in socially situated, local contexts.

Though it may seem passé these days to claim that only humans can possess agency, it wasn't so long ago that to suggest a nonhuman writing technology could enact some form of agency was patently false—a type of technological determinism that obscured human agents and the diversity of situated writing practices. The critique of technological determinism has long been invoked by writing studies scholars to dismiss materialist analyses of writing that claim that writing technologies can have determining effects on the local scene of writing and human agency (Street 1984; Walters et al. 1990; Faigley 1999; Daniell 1999; Trimbur 2002; Lunsford and Prior 2008).[9] What may have seemed obvious in a pre-Web 2.0 world about who and what could possess agency, in the Web 3.0 world of the global archive, a qualitatively new informational and textual environment has emerged in which our tools for inscription take on greater agency.

In light of such changes, writing studies scholars have turned again to questions of materiality and agency. Work that draws on new materialist cultural theory (Barad 2007; Coole and Frost 2010; Bennett 2010) and Bruno Latour's object-oriented, actor network theory is significantly expanding our materialist theories of writing to better understand how algorithmic, automated, and ubiquitous inscription technologies thoroughly disrupt our lived, ontological experience of agency and writing (Lynch and Rivers 2015; Barnett and Boyle 2017; Dobrin and Jensen 2017; Gries and Brooke 2018). Broad in their sweep and depth, new materialist and object-oriented theories of writing argue that, due to the destabilizing effects of digital media and expanding flows of information, we need to reconfigure our basic assumptions about materiality, writing, rhetoric, and agency (Hess and Davidson 2018; Lynch and Rivers 2015; Barnett and Boyle 2017; Gries and Brooke 2018; Dobrin and Jensen 2017). Taken together, such work emphasizes four fundamental concepts for guiding our materialist theories of writing in the digital contexts of the twenty-first century: *distributed agency, embodiment, flow/circulation,* and *neoliberal capitalism.*

Distributed agency: In a world of automation, algorithmic computing, and ubiquitous inscription, we can no longer assume that agency resides only in human actors. Rather, with our writing environments greatly mediated by digital writing technologies and the profuse textuality it fosters, agency is not something to be possessed by either human or nonhuman, but something distributed across actor networks that include human and nonhuman actants (Gallagher 2017; Reyman 2018; Zappen 2018; Nicotra 2017a; Andrejevic 2013; Hess and Davidson 2018; Barnett and Boyle 2017; Lynch and Rivers 2015; Gries and Brooke 2018; Rickert 2013; Hirsu 2018).

Embodiment: In the hypercirculatory contexts of Web 3.0, where writing technologies take on greater agency, the relationship between our physical bodies and growing digital textuality is radically changing our felt experience of writing and reading. To understand these changes, we must learn to tap the full sensorium of our bodies to become more attuned to affect, corporeality, and mutual accommodation with those human and nonhuman agents we are entangled with (Cooper 2017; Nicotra 2017b; Pflugfelder 2015; Zappen 2018).

Flow/circulation: The material contexts of digital writing are inherently dynamic and thus demand a more posthuman and ecological orientation toward writing and textuality that foregrounds physical matter, intra-relational activity, flow, circulation, complexity, self-organization, contingency, and emergence (Barnett and Boyle 2017; Gries and Brooke 2018; Dobrin and Jensen 2017).

Neoliberal capitalism: With the rise of digital networks and the global archive, neoliberal, informational capitalism is intensifying. As transnational corporations continue to expand and solidify a global economy, they also continue their assault on citizen-consumers and the natual environment by tearing down government regulations, avoiding taxes, and further privatizing more aspects of US socioeconomic life. New materialist theories of writing argue that in theorizing writing today we must grapple with the neoliberal motivations driving the development of digital networks and wide-scale data collection (Chaput 2010; Nicotra 2017b; Trimbur 2000; Dingo 2018).

These four fundamental concepts lie at the heart of new materialist and object-oriented theories of writing. The focus on flow and embodiment reminds us that, as permeable, living organisms, we inevitably assimilate the effects of persistent, ubiquitous inscription, both in the ways we use digital tools to inscribe the world and how those same tools are used to inscribe and datafy our lives.

To be sure, scholarship on writing that draws on new materialist and object-oriented theories is astute, and it is building new and creative frameworks for theorizing the radical changes unfolding in Web 3.0. At the same time, however, we see a familiar pattern emerging in this work that continues to undermine the clarity and explanatory power of new materialist thinking— the stubborn tendency to background the two basic agentive forces that influence all actor networks and the writing that takes place there: the persistent demands of capital circulation and the causal, natural laws of the biophysical environment.

Pulling such forces into the foreground of our materialist theories of writing is, undoubtedly, a difficult endeavor. But we don't have to venture far theoretically to begin this process. For starters, we should acknowledge that many of the basic assumptions of "new" materialism aren't really new. They grow out of the long tradition of materialist thinking known as *organicist materialism*. Organicist materialism conceives of materiality as dynamic, intra-active, self-organizing, and ceaselessly in motion. Its development can be traced through time from pre-Socratic atomists like Democritus and Heraclitus, to Aristotle, Epicurus, and Renaissance thinkers like Spinoza and Leibniz, on to the work of materialists like Karl Marx and Friedrich Engels. I note this history as a reminder to all of us who invoke new materialism that, when we do so, we are invoking a long tradition of materialist thought that conceives of the natural world and physical laws as the ontological fiber of our existence. This tradition vitally includes the historical and dialectical materialism of Marx and Engels and their critical analysis of industrialization and the ways capital circulation exploits both social and natural processes to speed up profit. While current new materialist theories of writing acknowledge the impact of neoliberal capitalism on the shape of writing in Web 3.0, they rarely mention, let alone grapple with, Marx's foundational critique of capital that sits at the heart of new materialist thinking.

By better acknowledging and exploring the fundamental influence of organicist materialism and Marxism on new materialism, we can open up new ways to think about the materiality of digital writing and ubiquitous inscription, and how such forces inevitably intertwine with capital circulation and the natural environment.

INTEGRATING THE BIOPHYSICAL ENVIRONMENT INTO OUR THEORIES OF WRITING

Writing studies has long endeavored to integrate the natural sciences into our social and materialist theories of writing. To capture a more systemic, organic understanding of writing over the decades, we've invoked terms like *ecology, kinesis, emergence, saturation, flows,* and *circulation* to describe writing. Despite our best efforts though, we tend to use these terms more metaphorically an continually pull up just shy of actually integrating the discourses and methods of the natural sciences into our study of writing.

Unsurprisingly, writing studies is not alone in this. As critical sociologist John Bellamy Foster argues about the social sciences,

> Social science today is crippled not only by its growing failure to confront the historical specificity (and thus the hegemonic structures) of present-day society, but also by its repeated refusal to engage critically with the reality of the natural world. Thus the social sciences and the humanities . . . are all characterized to varying degrees by their radical separation from nature—from the concerns that preoccupy natural science, and more particularly from notions of natural history or evolution. (Foster et al. 2011)

It's a strong indictment, and something I think we are starting to address as more colleges and universities develop interdisciplinary programs in environmental and sustainability studies. One of the main reasons for this ongoing separation between the social sciences/humanities and the natural sciences has to do with the extensive practical challenges of doing such crossover work—deep differences in methods, assumptions, discourse, terminology, and what counts as knowledge are all substantial barriers to doing interdisciplinary work. Nevertheless, new materialist theories of writing are certainly moving in this direction, and Foster's critique is a healthy reminder that there is still a lot of theoretical work to do in bridging the gap between writing studies and the natural sciences, in particular ecology, biology, and physics. In light of the environmental and economic problems we are facing in Web 3.0, we cannot miss the opportunity in our recent turn to new materialism to undo this habit of backgrounding capital and the basic laws of the biophysical environment in our critical theories of writing.

We can begin this process by addressing some of the basic assumptions of new materialist theories of writing and key theoretical concepts like *matter*, *information*, and *circulation*.

Matter

How we define and understand the concept of matter will inevitably determine how we might theorize about writing and rhetoric. As Gries emphasizes, new materialist and object-oriented rhetorics wholeheartedly embrace an organic definition of matter as a "productive, dynamic, and resilient force" (Gries 2015, 7). Scott Barnett and Casey Boyle echo a similar idea when they write that, "things are rhetorical . . . vibrant actors, enacting effects that exceed (and are sometimes in direct conflict with) human agency and intentionality" (Barnett and Boyle 2017, 1). To theorize the vibrant agency of material, nonhuman things, new materialists argue that human and nonhuman agents don't just interact, they *intra-act*. As Karan Barad explains in *Meeting the Universe Halfway*:

> The neologism "intra-action" signifies the mutual constitution of entangled agencies. That is, in contrast to the usual "interaction," which assumes that there are separate individual agencies that precede their interaction, the notion of intra-action recognizes that distinct agencies do not precede, but rather emerge through, their intra-action. (Barad 2007, 33)

Intra-action is a useful concept for explaining how nonhuman agents, both living things (like animals) and nonliving things (like writing technologies), come to enact agency by the sheer fact of their existence as living matter and energy. A simple example can be seen when we pick up a hot cup of coffee. Agency emerges in the intra-action between the human who picks up the cup and the transfer of heat as it moves to the hands, then the mouth, of the person who drinks the coffee.

While intra-action is widely invoked in new materialist theories of writing, the focus on how agentive, nonhuman things come into contact with human agency is often interpreted more like *interaction* rather than intra-action. That is to say, though new materialist theories of writing argue that nonhuman things are agentive and rhetorical, such things are generally seen as discrete and separate entities from human agents rather than as "mutually constitut[ed]" of the same substance and beholden to the same physical laws that humans are. Thus, though a new focus on rhetorical "things" has been critical for denaturalizing our preference for humanist agency, intra-activity suggests there aren't individual agencies or things that interact in an actor network but, rather, the basic *modus operandi* of all things, as composed of matter and energy, is fluid, dynamic exchange as energy and matter circulate *through* agents and actor networks. When it comes to understanding intra-action then, and theorizing the agency of a nonhuman thing like a writing technology, we must also consider how all human and nonhuman things are manifestations of how matter and energy circulate, and how they intra-act with another vital circulatory flow, the flow of *information*.

Information

In unpacking our assumptions about matter and how a writing technology enacts agency, we need to revisit our assumptions about *information*—what it is and how it entangles and circulates with energy and matter. I say more about the concept of information and its history in writing studies in the next chapter, but here I briefly introduce how I will be thinking about the term throughout this work.

The term is just starting to appear again in writing studies after a hiatus of about a decade, though our understanding of the concept remains general and vague. I believe the concept has a lot to offer our materialist theories of writing and our understanding of the broader material social effects of ubiquitous inscription. Because of its dialectical relations with energy and matter, information as concept and thing provides a critical interdisciplinary bridge to the natural sciences that will help us further develop of our materialist theories of writing.

New materialist theories of writing generally tend to think of information as the symbolic, meaningful stuff we exchange with each other (the semantic kind), but this is only a partial understanding of a term whose meanings range widely across fields as diverse as biology, ecology, computer science, and mathematics. In these other fields, information is something inherent in all living systems and a basic component of life, along with energy and matter. For natural scientists and mathematicians alike, information is the basic signaling, communicative force that all life and matter exchange in, from the organic sequencing of DNA, to the process of photosynthesis, to the flow of binary and semantic information circulating through the internet. Information then, at its most basic level, is the intrinsic signaling and communication abilities of all matter and biological life, which includes the semantic information we produce via our writing *and* the layers of data and metadata this writing produces.

In a way, it's arguable that *information* is a more useful term than *agency* at this point for theorizing writing. Distributed, intra-active agency means that agency is a given. Human and nonhuman things alike, by the pure fact of their existence as matter and energy, are intrinsically agentive. If we can agree that all things, human and nonhuman, are agentive and networked, then, from a theoretical standpoint, we're ready to make distinctions between different kinds of agency. That is to say, *rhetorical agency* should always be distinguished from a more general, *informational agency*. To use the wonderful example of the dragonfly from Marilyn Cooper's article "Listening to Strange Strangers, Modifying Dreams" (Cooper 2017), a dragonfly is not, unto itself, a rhetorical agent. It's certainly deserving of our respect and acknowledgment, but it isn't rhetorical. It is, however, *informational*. To be rhetorical is to deliberately use (and misuse) complex, symbolic, and semantic information, something a dragonfly doesn't do.[10] Thus, a dragonfly is not a rhetorical agent, though it still communicates with us. Likewise, water is not, intrinsically, a rhetorical agent, but it is always informational, constantly signaling to us through our vital connection with it. Once we put water into a plastic bottle and try to sell it, then it becomes rhetorical. While any human made thing could be considered rhetorical, when we "attune" to living, nonhuman actors and organisms (and they to us) we don't do so through rhetoric, but through the innate communication and informational capabilities of all living matter.

Thinking about information beyond it's more obvious semantic and human aspects is essential for integrating the natural sciences into our study of writing and inscription. In doing so, we can develop our new materialist theories of writing in ways that will help us articulate the dynamic relations among writing, information, energy, matter, and capital. I pursue this idea more in the next chapter, when I dive deeper into the various kinds of information produced in Web 3.0.

Circulation

In revisiting information and its intra-relations with writing, matter, energy, and capital, we invariably must revisit another key concept in new materialist and object-oriented theories of writing—*circulation*. Historically, scholars have used circulation to theorize how texts, genres, and media move through culture (Trimbur 2000; Yancey 2004; Edbauer 2005; Eyman 2007; Porter 2010). But the concept takes on new salience in Web 3.0 with the rise of the global archive and networked, algorithmic computing. More recently, Laurie Gries and Colin Brooke have argued that the theoretical robustness of circulation makes it a *threshold concept* for writing studies. They define circulation studies, "in the most general and simplest sense, as the study of writing and rhetoric in motion," with a focus "on how bodies, artifacts, words, pictures, and other things flow within and across cultures to affect meaningful change" (Gries and Brooke 2018, 201). The authors argue that, because writing is at the heart of how all things, human and nonhuman, circulate in culture, understanding how writing circulates will help us understand other kinds of circulating phenomena.

I find Gries and Brooke's call for circulation studies compelling and I agree that *circulation* should be considered a threshold concept in the field. At the same time, as promising as circulation studies is for expanding our new materialist theories of digital writing, we see, again, in Gries and Brooke's edited collection *Circulation, Writing, and Rhetoric* (2018) the same tendency to background capital circulation and the biophysical laws of matter and energy.[11] This can be seen in the afterward where Gries proposes several research questions for future work in circulation studies:

- How does circulation help us further understand the ontological dimensions of rhetoric and the rhetorical nature of nonhuman things?
- How does circulation studies help us understand how public life assembles and reassembles?
- How does circulation shape identity?
- How do we integrate circulation into our classrooms? (Gries and Brooke 2018, 326)

These are all excellent questions that hold great promise for developing new materialist theories of writing. But it's hard not to notice the same pattern of omission I've been tracing in this introduction. Neither capital circulation or the physical flows of energy, matter, and information are mentioned.[12] I don't mean to single out any particular work here, and I commend Gries and Brooke's push to develop our use of circulation—something I hope this book contributes to. However, in the contexts of Web 3.0, informational capitalism, and environmental crisis, there is a dire need in our new materialist theories of writing to foreground and articulate how circulatory writing gets conditioned by the forces of capital circulation and intertwines with the causal laws of the biophysical environment. From a critical, Marxian perspective such as new materialism, circulation is never simply about tracing written artifacts, rhetorics, or other material flows as they circulate through actor networks. Rather, it's about understanding the circulation of texts and information *in dialectical relation with the circulatory demands of capital* and how this process inevitably conditions *all* other circulatory processes.

FROM CIRCULATION TO METABOLISM

From an ecological perspective, when we background circulating flows of capital, energy, and matter in our materialist theories of writing, we are essentially abstracting our understanding of writing from both the material realities of our socioeconomic lives and the fundamental laws of the natural world. Doing so doesn't mean we can't theorize effectively about writing in culture, but it does significantly limit what it tells us about its materiality. Of the many ways this kind of abstraction limits how we study writing, perhaps the most troubling is how it conceals our understanding of how material things circulate and flow. The basic laws of matter and energy tell us that there is always a material cost for things to move. Circulating writing is no different—there is a material cost for it to circulate that comes in the form of energy used, energy lost, and the inevitable production of waste. This dialectical relation between writing and circulating flows of energy means that we can't fully understand how texts and nonhuman things circulate outside of basic physical and biological laws.

Moreover, we should remember that energy, matter, and information not only *flow and circulate* through all living systems, they also pool and create *stocks*—material spaces where energy, matter, or information slow down and accumulate within the ecosystems they are a part of. A stock of energy can be seen in the oil reserves of a country; a stock of matter can be seen in a lake where water has pooled at the lowest point of a valley. Stocks of information include things like libraries and databases. Exponentially accelerating computer processing, data compression, and networked computing have led to the cheap and bottomless data storage that makes ubiquitous inscription feasible and stocks of data valuable. But both bottomless data storage and ubiquitous inscription pose a serious threat to the finite flows and stocks of energy and matter they intra-act with. Thus, whether we are talking about the energy necessary to circulate information or how to deal with the waste created by information production (CO_2 emissions, electronic waste), there is always a material cost for storing and circulating writing.

To reiterate, my goal in this introduction is to offer a fair critique of new materialist theories of writing so we can more clearly articulate writing's dialectical relation to the natural world and capital circulation. What I see in new materialist theories of writing that invoke words like *ontology, thingness, circulation, flow, ecology, ambience, kinesis, intra-action,* and *agency* is an effort on the part of scholars to find new, interdisciplinary ways to conceptualize digital writing in culture, ways that are more organic, more ecological, more *material.* While the concept of circulation certainly moves us in this direction, what is needed is a complementary term, one that not only recognizes the inherent motion of texts and writing, but one that also foregrounds the intra-active exchange and transformation of energy, matter, information, and capital as they entangle and circulate through *all* ecosystems. I believe that concept is *metabolism.*

I say more about metabolism in the next chapter, but an introduction to the term and how I'll be using it will help introduce the critical, materialist framework for theorizing writing that forms the basic argument of this book. Etymologically, metabolism comes from the Latin word *metabole,* meaning to "change" or "transform." In the popular imagination, metabolism is usually associated with eating and how efficiently our bodies burn calories. However, this is just one aspect of the vital, universal process that all biological systems must undergo in their ongoing need to turn food into energy and process the waste that occurs during this process. As ecologists Jim Brown, Richard Sibly, and Astrid Kodric-Brown explain about the universal process of metabolism that continually flows through every ecology:

> Interactions between organisms and their environments involve exchanges of energy, materials, and information. These fluxes are all part of metabolism in the broad sense. They are all dependent on metabolic rate, because energy powers and controls the exchanges. So, for example, the primary [energy] production of an ecosystem is the sum of the carbon fixation of all the autotrophic organisms [e.g., plants, algae]; the growth rate of a population is the rate of incorporation of energy and materials into new individuals; and the information conveyed by birdsong is generated by the singer transforming metabolic energy into sound waves. (Brown et al. 2012, 3)

The authors go on to emphasize the inherent scaling properties of metabolism and that "all interaction between organisms and their environments involve the fluxes, transformations, and storage of these three basic currencies [energy, matter, and information]" (Brown et al. 2012, 5). *Metabolism,*[13] then, as I use it throughout this work, is the basic, ceaseless circulation of energy, matter, and information that all life depends on at every scale, from DNA, to bacteria, to mammals, to human ecosystems, to the planet's biosphere and beyond (Brown et al. 2012; West 2018).

Metabolism works well alongside concepts like *circulation, flow,* and *network,* but it's even more fundamental. There can be no circulation of anything without the tireless process of metabolism that drives all ecological systems. Moreover, metabolism provides a way for theorists to scale outwards in our materialist analyses to understand how the metabolism of individual human writers metabolizes with the larger ecosystems we are a part of. This ability to scale is one of metabolism's greatest theoretical attributes. When combined with terms like *circulation* and *flow,* we have a potent framework for theorizing how flows of writing and information affect how energy and matter circulate through all biological systems.[14]

My use of *metabolism* is similar to how Thomas Rickert defines *context* in his article "The Whole of the Moon: Latour, Context, and Holism." Rickert argues that, in understanding how context affects an actor network, we need to think of context as "the undergirding logos from which things and language emerge in their meaning and bearing" (Rickert 2015, 141). For Rickert, context is more than a static backdrop for actor networks. He uses the example of a human agent drinking wine (a nonhuman agent) to make his point. Wine takes on agency within an intra-active context that creates the "hybrid coachievement" of wine-human. When framed metabolically, we can take this observation one step further. The undergirding logos of any context is the basic physical laws of metabolism—the transformation of energy, matter, and information as they circulate through our bodies when we drink wine. The "subtle rhetoric" of wine goes beyond human word and deed—it is the physical experience of our bodies processing alcohol and feeling its powerful effects. It's a simple tweak that, in essence, biologizes Rickert's holistic idea of context. By couching these vital agencies in more humanistic, metaphorical terms, we miss an opportunity to integrate concepts from the natural sciences like *metabolism* and *information* that can help us develop more interdisciplinary, materialist theories of writing. Making such theoretical adjustments is all the more important for the ecological challenges we are facing as a planetary community, both environmentally as we struggle with climate change and waste management, and socially and economically as a globalized, neoliberal capitalism continues to widen wealth disparities across the globe.

Towards this purpose, I introduce a theoretical framework for studying writing in Web 3.0 that is critical and metabolic—a framework I call a *materialist ecology of writing* (MEOW).[15] MEOW is a new materialist approach to theorizing writing based on the premise that digital writing tools, and the informational production they foster, radically displace individual human agency and relocate it amongst the flows and stocks of energy, matter, information, and capital that continually metabolize through every human ecology. Like

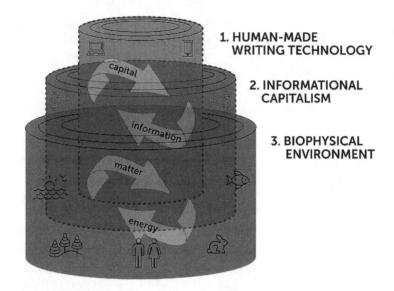

Figure 0.2. Basic diagram of MEOW, composed of three intra-acting material cumuli and flows of energy, matter, information, and capital that continually circulate through each cumulus. (Illustration created by Martha D. Langer, Pear Ink Design.)

other new materialist theories of writing, MEOW assumes that agency resides in collectives of human and nonhuman agents; MEOW, however, specifically foregrounds three fundamental domains, what I call *material cumuli*, that are a part of every actor network that includes human beings: the biophysical environment, informational capitalism, and human-made writing and inscription technologies.

Figure 0.2 illustrates the nested structure of the framework. The arrows represent the metabolic flows of energy, matter, information, and capital that perpetually circulate through and across each cumulus:

First material cumulus: Writing technologies and their embodied history of use; the global networked infrastructure of inscription (global archive)

Second material cumulus: Web 3.0 and twenty-first-century informational, neoliberal capitalism

Third material cumulus: All living, metabolic ecosystems, from the sensorium of the body to the biosphere of the planet

The MEOW framework builds on new materialist trends in the field and the recent "nonhuman" turn in writing studies. Its intent is heuristic—to help writing studies develop our critical materialist and ecological theories of writing in the global contexts of informational capitalism and its growing antagonism with the biophysical environment, including the vulnerable, permeable space of our writing bodies.

The word *cumulus* has been chosen for a few reasons. It's a term that attempts to capture the agency of historical accumulation. One way in which nonhuman things enact agency is through their development and quantitative accumulation over time, what economist Thorstein Veblen called "cumulative causation." Veblen coined the term to draw an analogy between socioeconomic development and the evolutionary process of natural selection (Reisman 2012). In social systems, as in natural ones, when the quantity of something accumulates and reaches a critical mass, it begins to enact qualitative changes within that system. This ongoing process of historical accumulation is an intrinsic part of how both natural and human social systems evolve over time. All matter and living systems could be considered cumuli, products of the accumulative layering of time and biophysical activity, from the billions of years of evolution that have shaped the biosphere of the planet, to the economic structures of capitalism, to the cumulative history of human labor that is embodied in every writing technology we use.

In addition to cumulative causation, MEOW draws on traditional ecological models of human activity that are common in fields like public health and behavioral psychology, including the well-known ecological model of human development outlined by psychologist Urie Bronfenbrenner. In such models, the individual human agent is placed at the center of analysis; the researcher then moves from the local contexts of the individual to study how individuals and their local contexts are influenced by the larger contexts (regional, national, planetary) they are nested within.[16] MEOW borrows this basic structure, but rather than placing the individual human agent as the starting point for ecological analysis, it places nonhuman agents and their embodied history as the starting point. In the MEOW framework, at the level of the first material cumulus, the basic unit of analysis could be any human-made object, thing, or technology. MEOW thinks of all nonhuman, human-made things as living fossils that have evolved over time. As such, any technology and its accumulated history could become the entry point for a critical materialist analysis. In this book, my specific focus is on the accumulated history of writing as a technology, its affordance of inscription, and their co-development over thousands of years to fundamentally condition modern socioeconomic life.

As we move outward from the material cumulus of an individual writing technology to the second material cumulus, we find ourselves, along with every other human and nonhuman actor, ensconced in the cumulative conditions of twenty-first-century informational capitalism and the global networked infrastructure of inscription. The developmental history between writing, economy, and the earliest forms of capital circulation can be traced back to the origins of writing and the development of the first cities in human history (something I take a closer look at in chapter 3). This cumulative relationship between writing and capital is alive-and-well in Web 3.0 and together they fuel an informational capitalism that aggressively leverages inscription to accelerate capital circulation.

These first and second cumuli are, in turn, nested within and dependent upon the third material cumulus, the longer evolution of the biophysical environment that is the living, cumulative history of billions of years of natural selection. Constitutive of this cumulus are the basic physical and thermodynamic laws of energy and matter. I'll say more about such laws in chapter 5, but for now I'll simply mention that I'm referring to two basic physical laws: the concept that neither energy nor matter can be created or destroyed; and the irreversibility of time and one-directionality of all metabolic processes, a process known in thermodynamics as *entropy*. As illustrated in figure 0.2, the perforated borders of each cumulus depict their permeable nature and the arrows depict the flows of energy, matter, information, and capital that metabolize incessantly through all three cumuli.

One of MEOW's primary goals is to displace individual human agents and situated writing practices from the center of our writing theories and foreground instead those aspects of materiality we habitually undertheorize. By doing so, I believe we can further develop our new materialist theories to more effectively study and grapple with the complex metabolic relations between energy, matter, information, and capital. In the chapters that follow I lay out in greater detail how to think through each of these cumuli and how a MEOW framework can be used to theorize writing in Web 3.0. It's still tentative in areas, an initial foray into how we might conceptualize more material, ecological, and metabolic understandings of writing in the twenty-first century.

LOOKING AHEAD

Chapter 1: The Theoretical Roots of MEOW

In chapter 1 I dig deeper into the key concepts I've introduced here and explore a few new ones, in particular *ecology, information, metabolism, inscription, archive,* and *acceleration,* and provide a more thorough discussion of the theoretical roots of MEOW. This includes a discussion of Marxian metabolism and how it's been picked up by modern social and metabolic ecologists who study the relations between the internal (endosomatic) metabolism of organisms and the external (exosomatic) metabolism of the ecosystems we are a part of.

In thinking about the metabolism of human ecologies, I also take a closer look at the concept of information and the uneven, ambivalent relationship writing studies has had with the concept. I argue that, by tying information production to flows of energy and matter, we put ourselves in a better position to theorize the materiality of writing in Web 3.0 and the profound economic and environmental changes brought on by intensifying information and data production. Thus, my primary goal in chapter 1 is to explain the theory informing MEOW and further articulate the role that writing and information production play in accelerating capital circulation and how this acceleration invariably impacts writing's metabolic relations with flows of energy and matter.

Chapter 2: Writing Technologies and their Embodied History of Use

In chapter 2, I theorize the first material cumulus—the developmental history of writing technologies and their embodied history of use. Part of what gives nonhuman technologies agency lies in this embodied history. That is to say, all human-made technologies are the cumulative product of the long, evolutionary process of time and human trial-and-error. The things we call *tablets* today are the living manifestations of a history of use that can be traced back to the origins of one of the first writing systems—the clay-tablet cuneiform of ancient Mesopotamia. Working from Karl Marx's history of money and the origins of capitalist modes of production, I argue that the development of cuneiform presents for us a different economic history than the one Marx conjectured, a history in which writing, not standardized money, is the indispensable technology for giving rise to capitalist modes of production.

Using the history and evolution of cuneiform as my main example, I trace the developmental tie between writing, quantification, exchange, and capital accumulation that emerges in ancient Mesopotamia circa 4000 BCE. While the hundreds of thousands of tablets that have been found in archeological digs vary in form and function, the vast majority of them are records of accounting and exchange: lists, receipts, orders, and ledgers, to name a few (Goody 1986; Powell 1996). This abundance of economic genres tells us two keys things about the history of cuneiform. One, the emergence of writing is also the emergence of textuality; meaning, it's not simply writing, but also *inscription* and *the archive* that account for the diffuse agency that writing enacts. And two, the large majority of these texts, economic in nature, are records of the quotidian exchange relations between ordinary Mesopotamians and the palace and temple complexes. Thus, the historical record we have of Mesopotamia strongly suggests that the technologies of writing and information production evolve in a dialectical relation with money, economy, and power.

Chapter 3: Informational Capitalism and Web 3.0

In chapter 3, I explore the second material cumulus in the MEOW framework, the contexts of informational capitalism and Web 3.0. I argue that, in the shift from Web 2.0 to Web 3.0, there is a need to expand our material and ecological theories of digital writing and engage more with the sub-strata of data and metadata that gets inscribed as a byproduct of this writing.

I begin the chapter with a critique of what I call *Web 2.0 writing theory*, an approach to writing theory that celebrates the growth of online writing and the participatory culture that has emerged with social media. I argue that, as we transition into Web 3.0 and accelerating information production, there's a need to re-conceptualize two basic tendencies of Web 2.0 writing theory that have been carried over into new materialist theories of writing. The first is the tendency to background the *exchange value* of writing for an excessive focus on the *use value* that writers find in it. And the second is its *productivist* tendencies and the assumption that *more writing is intrinsically beneficial* for individuals and the shape of public discourse.

Building on my discussion in chapter 2 and the evolution of cuneiform, I extrapolate into the twentieth and twenty-first centuries to theorize the last hundred years as a pivotal turning point in the transition from industrial to informational capitalism, one driven by computerized, digital, global networks and neoliberal economic policies. At the heart of this transition is the rise of *big data* and the corporate data complex of data platforms, data brokers, and marketers that trade in it. I show how, in the past 30 years, the once publicly owned space of the internet has morphed into a commercialized, global network of inscription designed to produce and collect the flows of consumer-citizen data needed to circulate capital in Web 3.0. I discuss different types of data platforms and focus in on corporate data monopolies like Google, Facebook, and Amazon that manage and control a large portion of how data and information flow in Web 3.0.

Chapter 4: Information Production, Acceleration,
and the Biophysical Environment

In chapter 4, I place the first two cumuli in the larger cumulus of the biophysical environment and focus on how accelerating information production speeds up the human consumption of energy and matter. Drawing on work from the International Geosphere-Biosphere Programme (IGBP), I explore how, starting with the European industrial revolution, and further accelerating in the 1950s with the rise of digital computing, accelerating informational flows intertwine with capital circulation to speed up flows of energy and matter in ways that are harmful to other systems throughout the larger biophysical environment. The acceleration of information production, spurred by the corporate data complex, has led to problematic spikes in energy consumption at all three stages of an electronic device's life: manufacture, use, and disposal (see figures 4.4a–c, for larger infographics depicting these stages).

As I'll show, while efforts to recycle e-waste are improving and the IT industries are taking steps to design more energy efficient technologies and use more renewable sources of energy, corporate business practices like *planned obsolescence* and the *externalization* of e-waste to developing countries continue to undercut the environmental gains of more efficient design. The ecological imbalances caused by acceleration, and the business practices that fuel it have serious implications for the health of local communities and the planet as a whole. In developing our new materialist theories of writing, we must address the ecological antagonisms caused by accelerating information production and the growing energy and carbon footprint of our manufacture, use, and disposal of digital writing tools.

Chapter 5: The Effects of Manufactured Distraction on the Body

In chapter 5, I remain in the third material cumulus of the biophysical environment but shift from the macrosystem of the planet to the microsystem of the body to consider the effects of accelerating information product on the minds, bodies, and spirits of citizen-consumers. I take a closer look at how the corporate data complex aggressively seeks to stimulate the production of data and how such practices interfere with our ability to think and remember, and, as a consequence, to write. Just as accelerating flows of information are harming the metabolic balance of the planet's ecosystems, so too are they harming our bodies in a multitude of ways and contributing to rising levels of anxiety, depression, stress, and suicide in the United States (Lustig 2018; Twenge 2018; Jowit 2016; Horowitz and Graf 2019).

Drawing on work by Kristie Fleckenstein and the concept of *somatic mind*, I explore how we can better attune to our embodied experience of writing in Web 3.0 and develop a deeper understanding of the social and ecological antagonisms that emerge with ubiquitous inscription. I turn to work in writing studies that looks at the popular tropes of "distraction" and "addiction" used by students to describe their experience of reading and writing in digital contexts. While we should always apply such labels with caution, we nevertheless must be careful not to underestimate the relentless nature of corporate data collection. I look at how the corporate data complex draws on research in psychology and neuroscience to design platforms and products that intentionally encourage habit formation in citizen-consumers. One seismic outcome of this push has been to create a continual state of distraction designed to keep us online and producing data. This constant flow of microdistractions is profoundly affecting our somatic minds, and, in particular, our *memory*.

In theorizing distraction's impact on memory, I revisit the field's bumpy history with cognitive theories of writing. I discuss how the field's "social turn" in the 1980s and its critique of cognitivist models of writing obscured the body from our study of writing, creating a schism between social and cognitive approaches to writing that persists today. Citing current research on writing and memory, I show how reintegrating cognitive research into our materialist, embodied theories of writing will help us better understand the harms associated with manufactured distraction and the ways it potentially curtails our abilities to write longer, more complex texts.

Chapter 6: Developing Critical, Ecological Literacies

In the final chapter, I turn to writing pedagogy and suggest ways universities and writing programs can integrate critical, ecological literacies at the university, department, and classroom levels. Drawing on work from Robert Yagelski and Max van Manen, and combining it with work in education, ecoliteracy, cognitive psychology, and environmental science, I introduce four basic ecological competencies that can serve as a guide for developing ecological literacy at all levels of education.

Building from these four competencies, I share a three-part writing sequence intended to help students *defetishize* their lived experience of writing in Web 3.0 and critically explore their embodied awareness of ubiquitous inscription and constant connection. The primary goals behind the sequence are to use writing as a vehicle for helping students develop embodied learning and better attune to the social and environmental problems we are facing in Web 3.0.

* * *

Web 3.0, big data, and the global archive are in their infancy. We must do our best to imagine what our world will look like 10, 20, 30 years down the road. What will be the effects of another decade's worth of data collection on citizens and consumers? How can we ameliorate or avert the devastating environmental imbalances that come with accelerating information production and living beyond the earth's carrying capacity? How can we help usher in a digital future and informational economy that works for more of us and is more sustainable environmentally? Answering such questions and taking appropriate action to address these environmental challenges will depend on how we theorize and teach writing and rhetoric in Web 3.0.

1

THE THEORETICAL
ROOTS OF A MEOW

*The resolution of theoretical antitheses is only possible in a
practical way, by virtue of the practical energy of men. Their
resolution is therefore by no means a problem of knowledge,
but a real problem of life . . . (Marx 1988, 109)*

In the previous chapter I introduced the framework for a materialist ecology of writing (MEOW) for theorizing writing in the
twenty-first century. In this chapter, I extend this discussion and
further develop the key concepts that inform MEOW, concepts
that include *ecology, metabolism, inscription, information, archive,*
and *acceleration.* I begin first with a discussion about the developmental history between the natural science of ecology and the
historical/dialectical materialism of Karl Marx and Friedrich
Engels. Marx and Engels were greatly influenced by discoveries
being made in the natural sciences during their time. Such ideas
would lead Marx to invoke the concept of *metabolism* to theorize
the dialectical relations between capital, human labor, technology, and nature that form the basic conditions of lived experience in capitalist modes of production.

From Marxian metabolism I move into a discussion about
the use of metabolism by contemporary critical ecologists who
study the relationship between the inner metabolism of individual organisms (*endosomatic*) and the outer metabolism we
share with the systems outside our bodies (*exosomatic*). In studying the metabolism of human ecologies, critical ecologists
focus on three fundamental flows—*energy, matter,* and *information.* As I introduced in the last chapter, I see the concept of

DOI: 10.7330/9781607329688.c001

information as a bridge to more interdisciplinary work between writing studies and the natural sciences. I extend my discussion about information in this chapter to explore how other scholars in writing studies have defined and applied the concept. By tying information production to flows of energy and matter, we put ourselves in a better position to theorize the material and ecological implications of intensifying information and data production. As I'll show, accelerating flows of information are destabilizing many of the natural systems of the planet, pushing them past their ecological limits. A primary driver of this acceleration is the corporate and government frenzy to collect data on citizen-consumers. In informational capitalism, accelerating flows of information are dialectically tied to the speed in which capital circulates. Thus, my primary goal in this chapter will be to develop the theory that informs MEOW by elaborating on how writing and inscription metabolize with capital circulation and how these relations invariably accelerate the speed in which energy and matter flow through human ecologies.

ECOLOGY AND MARXIAN METABOLISM

MEOW's theoretical roots grow from a pastiche of disciplines. It combines new materialist and ecological theories of writing with metabolic ecology, information theory, biology, physics, cognitive science, and historical/dialectical materialism. While new materialist theories of writing greatly enrich our understanding of agency and how digital writing circulates, they tend to undertheorize the agentive capacities of capital circulation and the biophysical laws of the natural environment. MEOW foregrounds these fundamental agencies in analysis.

One of the basic tenets of new materialism is the theoretical practice of *historicization*—the process of studying contemporary material social conditions by tracing their historical development over time. The MEOW framework of three intra-acting *material cumuli* (figure 0.1) introduced in the introduction was developed to guide the theoretical practice of historicizing human culture and society as a living expression of the accumulative process of history, where all agents, human and nonhuman, are living expressions of that history.

The accumulation of history is just as true for concepts as it is for material things; concepts are the accumulation of meanings that have come to cohere around a domain of knowledge as it has developed through time and human activity. Unpacking a concept's history of meaning so it can be reimagined in new contexts is the work of theory. In understanding the interdisciplinary roots of MEOW then, a good place to start is by historicizing two primary concepts it draws on from the natural sciences: *ecology* and *metabolism*. I introduced the basic meanings of these terms in the last chapter, but here I explore their historical development to show how they inform MEOW and how they can enrich our new materialist theories of writing.

The term *ecology* first appeared in print in 1868, coined by German naturalist Ernst Haeckel as the study of how organisms interact with other organisms and their surrounding environment. Haeckel is most famous for his stunning drawings of sea life and his vocal support for the work of Charles Darwin. Ecology has long been invoked by writing scholars to study writing, and the history of ecology as a science for studying natural systems has been well documented by other writing studies scholars over the years (Dobrin and Weisser 2002; Dobrin 2012). One aspect that is often overlooked in these histories is ecology's parallel development with another dynamic, relational framework for studying socioeconomic systems: the historical, dialectical materialism of Karl Marx and Frederick Engels. As critical sociologist John Bellamy Foster notes about this parallel development and the emergence of ecological thinking: "This ecological conception of the world of life was itself in many ways reflexive and self-creating, arising out of materialist dialectics, and would give birth to many of the most powerful insights associated with the development of modern ecology. Moreover, it can now be argued more generally, extending Engel's early proposition with respect to nature, that 'ecology is the proof of dialectics'" (Foster et al. 2011, 237). As Foster shows, the science of ecology developed by Haeckel and his contemporary natural scientists wasn't a radically new way of thinking. Rather, it was a new way of applying materialist dialectics to study the biophysical interactions between organisms and their environment.

In like manner, Marx and Engels's materialist critique of industrial capitalism was highly influenced by research then emerging in physics (in particular, thermodynamics) and the natural sciences, especially work by Charles Darwin and German chemist Justus von Liebig. Liebig's work on crop growth and soil composition had an important influence on Marx and Engels's thinking as they watched firsthand the bourgeoisie's aggressive exploitation of human labor and natural resources at the height of England's industrial revolution. The product of this exploitation manifested in ecologically harmful ways including horrendous working conditions (disease, child labor, low wages), soil depletion from over-farming, and the polluting of the Thames River with human and industrial waste (Foster 2010). For Marx and Engels, the excesses of industrial capitalism required a new kind of materialist social science, one that was dynamic enough to capture the motion and complexity of industrial capitalism without abstracting it from its intrinsic relations with the natural environment. The methods they developed as a result of this interdisciplinary work are what we now call historical, dialectical materialism—an organicist model of materialism predicated on the real, observable relations between human labor, processes of capital circulation, and the laws and resources of the natural environment (see page 11 for explanation of *organicist materialism*). For historical, dialectical materialism, "the dialectics of society [are] inseparably bound to the dialectics of nature." (Foster et al. 2011, 238).

While Marx and Engels never use the term *ecology* to describe their dialectical method, in *Capital* (Marx 1990), Marx invokes another biology-based concept to capture the inherent dynamism of socioeconomic change: the concept of *metabolism*.[1] In Marx's time, the understanding of biological metabolism was advancing quickly with the identification of the first enzymes by French chemist Anselme Payen and Louis Pasteur's work on fermentation. Enzymes are necessary for metabolism to take place and for living organisms to process the food and energy necessary for life (Kornberg 2019). Such work in the newly emerging fields of chemistry and biology would greatly influence Marx's understanding of material culture and he would use biological metabolism as a guiding analogy to build a social theory of capitalism based on the metabolic interaction between human agents, technology, nature, and the forces of capital circulation.

In *Capital*, Marx applies metabolism in two ways. He first uses the term to describe commodity exchange as a form of "social metabolism," the generalized social process of commodity circulation in which products and money flow through the market as they are exchanged between buyers and sellers. In his second use of the term, Marx embeds the social metabolism of commodity exchange in the more fundamental, *a priori* metabolic relations between technology, human labor, and the natural environment.

Figure 1.1 illustrates these basic relations. As internal and dialectical, the metabolic exchange of energy and matter that flows between these three agents is bidirectional. When humans use technology to extract the resources from the natural environment, not only is nature changed in the process, the human agent is likewise changed in the interaction. As Marx notes about this fundamental metabolic exchange:

> Labor is, first of all, a process between man and nature, a process by which man, through his own actions, mediates, regulates and controls the metabolism between himself and nature. He confronts the materials of nature as a force of nature. He sets in motion the natural forces which belong to his own body, his arms, legs, head and hands in order to appropriate the materials of nature in a form adapted to his own needs. Through this movement he acts upon eternal nature and changes it, and in this way he simultaneously changes his own nature. (Marx 1990 284)

For Marx, biological metabolism was an apt analogy for developing an organicist materialism predicated on the radical interdependence between human labor, human technology, and the raw resources of nature. Biological metabolism would also help him articulate a theoretical framework flexible enough to

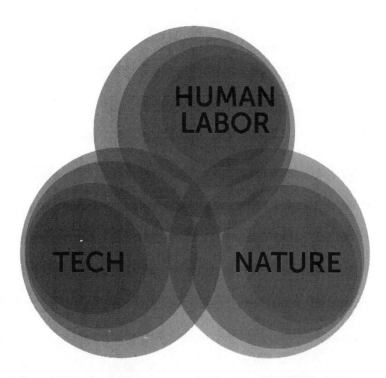

Figure 1.1. The three basic components that form the metabolic foundation of Marx's historical, dialectical materialism: human labor, technology, and the biophysical world. (Illustration created by Martha D. Langer, Pear Ink Design.)

capture the ceaseless emergence of history and cultural development. Although he uses the concept of metabolism sparingly, he makes it clear at the beginning of *Capital* that the metabolic relations between human labor, technology, and the natural environment comprise the indissoluble material backdrop of socioeconomic life.

Defining this relation as metabolic is significant for another key reason. As Marx demonstrates with the rise of industrial capitalism, as economies grow and develop, the metabolic relations between capital, human labor, technology, and nature change in the process, becoming more mediated by technological development. As new power sources like steam and electromagnetism emerged in the eighteenth century, the development of large-scale machinery radically changed the speed of production and, as a result, the speed in which capital could circulate (Foster 2000; Harvey 2019). From the perspective of Marxian metabolism, accelerating capital circulation means the inevitable acceleration of labor, technological development, and the use of natural resources. Foregrounding these basic metabolic relations is critical to understanding Marxian materialism and how we might apply it to theorize the role that modern writing technologies play in accelerating capital circulation.

Thus, there are two key ideas from Marxian metabolism that significantly inform MEOW:

1: All collectives of agency are embedded in the metabolic relations between three fundamental agencies—human labor, technology, natural environment.

2: In industrial, capitalist modes of production, thecirculation of capital depends on the persistent acceleration of this basic metabolism, leading to the reckless exploitation of human labor and the finite resources of the natural environment.

Because of these basic material relations Marx argues that the profit motive creates an inherent "metabolic riff" between human labor and the natural environment, one that "simultaneously undermine[s] the original sources of all wealth—the soil and the worker" (Marx 1990, 638). As internally related, there are repercussions for the system as a whole if any of the three agents grows stronger in size or intensity, leading to potential antagonisms with the other two metabolic agents.

Although Marx acknowledges that communication technologies like the telegraph played an important role in the expansion of industrial capitalism, these take a back-seat in his analysis to the large-scale industrial machinery he saw as dominating his particular era. So, while Marxian metabolism points the way towards more metabolic materialist theories of writing, it's clear that, with the rise of informational capitalism and Web 3.0, writing and inscription technologies take on greater agency in accelerating capital circulation. Because this basic metabolic relation is in every way disciplined by the demands of capital, the metabolic rift between humans and nature that Marx saw as inherent to industrial capitalism has only widened in the informational contexts of Web 3.0.

FROM INDUSTRIAL TO INFORMATIONAL METABOLISM

Today, Marx's use of metabolism to theorize industrial capitalism is resurfacing in the context of twenty-first-century informational capitalism and environmental crisis. Fields such as social ecology, ecological economics, and social and industrial metabolism are expanding his metabolic framework to study how modern informational economies produce, allocate, circulate, consume, and dispose of the energy, materials, and information that flow through them. Like Marx, many contemporary ecologists extrapolate from the basic process of internal metabolism to study how external flows of energy, matter, and information metabolize outside of our bodies in the larger ecosystems in which we are embedded. This distinction between internal and external metabolism has been called *endosomatic* and *exosomatic* forms of metabolism by noted ecological economist Nicholas Georgescu-Roegen. The distinction is useful insofar as it sets up a structural and functional analogue between the internal metabolism of individual organisms and the external metabolism of larger human ecosystems (Georgescu-Roegen 1981).

In drawing on the relation between endo- and exosomatic metabolism to theorize writing, the concept of *information* takes on greater significance. As I argued in the introduction, information can serve as a bridge concept for doing more interdisciplinary work between writing studies and the natural sciences. There I defined information broadly as both a rhetorical and physical phenomenon. In natural sciences like biology and chemistry, information describes the basic biochemical reactions that take place inside and outside an organism, from the enzymatic processes that build DNA to the physical sensations we experience when our bodies interact with the living world. We can think of this kind of information as "biological information"—information that is "*for* something, not *about* something" (Floridi 2010, 79). Biological information is the basic signaling process of life itself that initiates and directs flows of energy and matter as they circulate through a living system.

While related, biological information is different than *semantic* information, which is the symbolic, rhetorical kind of information that circulates through human ecologies. Both endosomatic and exosomatic metabolisms involve flows of energy, matter, and information, but in the exosomatic metabolism of human ecologies, the flow of semantic information takes on greater agency in the system. The emergence of symbolic behavior in human societies, from the development of cuneiform in ancient Mesopotamia, to the rise of the alphabet, on to the binary, digital media of Web 3.0, are clear manifestations of how central the production and circulation of semantic information are to the metabolic functioning of human ecologies.

While most ecologists who study exosomatic metabolism agree that the shape of a human ecology is determined by the way it exchanges and processes energy, matter, and information, they tend to focus more on flows of energy and matter. For example, one method for studying exosomatic metabolism is *material flows analysis* (MFA). MFAs are studies that measure the flows of energy and matter (water, gas, food, etc.) that enter a particular human ecosystem and then compare these quantities against the amount of energy and matter that leave the system in the form of waste (CO_2 emissions, trash production, bodily waste, etc.). MFAs are used to study the resource consumption of human ecosystems of any size, from a small household to a large nation-state (Brunner and Rechberger 2016; Gonzalez de Molina and Toledo 2014; Giampietro et al. 2012). In such analyses, the more abstract informational flows tend to be omitted for the more readily quantifiable flows of energy and matter. It's an understandable omission: energy use and the exchange of matter provide tangible, quantifiable things to measure. Energy can be measured in joules, watts, or calories. Materials and matter, including essential nutrients for life like hydrogen, oxygen, carbon, and nitrogen, can be measured by weight and volume. Flows of human semantic information, on the other hand, are more abstract and unwieldy, and often follow different patterns than do flows of energy and matter.

Though methodologies like MFAs are invaluable for studying how human ecosystems function, without understanding how information flows, such analyses are limited in what they can tell us about how writing metabolizes with flows of energy and matter. As social ecologists Manuel Gonzalez de Molina and Victor M. Toledo note about the role information plays in building the "intangible super-structures" of a culture such as the ideas, beliefs, laws, and customs that give it shape: "[T]he flows of matter and energy that are the material or tangible part of the metabolism between nature and society, are always conditioned, regulated, and articulated by these intangible super-structures that exist and persist by means of flows of information" (Gonzalez de Molina and Toledo 2014, 68). While the health and sustainability of human ecosystems necessarily depend on flows of energy and matter, in studying their exosomatic metabolism, the currency of information takes on a greater agentive role. We are reminded of this fact every month when we receive our electric bill. We can think of the bill as the informational expression of the immense power grid we are networked into. It tells us how much electricity we've used, where it comes from, how much it costs, and it reinforces my agreement with the utility company, an agreement that must be upheld on both ends for electricity to flow. It used to be that customers would send a check to the pay the bill. These days the bill is usually electronically withdrawn from our bank accounts. In either case, for energy to flow from the power grid to my house, several informational agents must be in play, including all kinds of writing technologies, phones, computers, and databases, as well as textual genres like spreadsheets, invoices, and checks.

Granted, it's a simple example, but it doesn't take much to scale outward and start asking questions about the metabolism of a larger human ecosystem: How do nonhuman information technologies and flows of information condition and regulate flows of energy and matter in human ecosystems? What are the material effects of accelerating information production and data collection on the larger metabolic functions of these systems? These questions are central to MEOW and answering them requires us to reconceptualize information in writing studies, the different forms it takes, and how informational flows can accelerate flows of energy and matter in ways that are harmful to the health and sustainability of human ecosystems at every scale.

REVIVING *INFORMATION* IN WRITING STUDIES

Information is the kind of comprehensive concept that spans disciplines and offers great potential for interdisciplinary work. While the term is just starting to appear again in recent new materialist research, its use is still fairly general, and writing studies continue to define information narrowly as the semantic kind that humans are most familiar with. In developing a critical, metabolic framework for theorizing digital writing, it's imperative that we unpack our humanistic assumptions about information so we can more systematically articulate how writing and information production metabolically intra-act with flows of energy, matter, and capital.

I pointed out the difference between semantic and biological information above, but the concept of information has a variety of meanings, from the popular to the esoteric, in fields as diverse as mathematics, biology, communications, and media studies. One shared understanding that most fields agree upon is that we, as a planetary community, have entered a new stage of information production, one that reflects the historical transformation of the industrialized, global economy that emerged in the mid-eighteenth century to the rise of an industrialized *informational* economy in the mid twentieth century. Whereas manual labor and the production of manufactured goods drove industrial capitalism, in informational capitalism it is knowledge labor, information production, writing, and networks of inscription that serve as primary engines of capitalist production. Traditional forms of the information industry include academic and medical research, media and entertainment, marketing and consulting, communications, law, patent and copyright creation, as well as the large-scale informational labor of modern nation-state bureaucracies. More modern actors include the computer and information technology industries. Such work is characterized by intensified research and development through more data collection, from more sources, with the specific purpose of controlling vast flows and pools of information to generate actionable insights and make political and economic decisions (see note 5 from introduction for expanded definition of information technology industries). While estimates vary, many scholars agree that modern informational production and work accounts for 40–70 percent of gross domestic product (GDP) in the United States (Floridi 2010; Fuchs 2012a; Castells 2010; Brandt 2005).

In writing studies specifically, research into information can be found in areas like *information literacy* (Fabos 2008; Perelman 2008), *access to information* (Moran 1999a; Faigley 1999; Selber 2004; Selfe 1999; Hicks and Turner 2013), and *information visualization* (Sorapure 2010), as well as work on the *information economy* from the perspective of situated writing practices (Bazerman et al. 2003; Brandt 2005; Lanham 2007). It is the last group that particularly informs MEOW and my discussion here. These scholars each argued that the use of popular phrases like the "information superhighway" to describe the expansion of the internet in the mid-1990s diverted our attention from the local realities of information labor and the highly collaborative, literate labor force needed for information production. While information in this work is primarily understood as the semantic kind and doesn't consider the different forms that information takes in Web 3.0, it does raise important theoretical questions about how writing and information production entangle with forces of capital circulation.

Despite the fertile ground this work started to sow, information as a theoretical concept fell out of the purview of writing studies just when social media and big data were beginning to take hold of the internet. Scholars like Sidney Dobrin have even gone so far as to dismiss the concept of information as having little theoretical value for writing studies. In *Postcomposition* (2011) he argues that the field's use of information, along with terms like *meaning* and *knowledge*, mistakenly see writing as simply a "mechanism of transfer" for exchanging the semiotic content it carries. In contrast, he asserts that, in our current hypercirculatory writing environments, we need theories of writing that see writing as "a structural component within a general system of discursive circulation" (Dobrin 2011, 4) that affects the shape of all other systems. He urges scholars to "disrupt the metaphoric attachment to information and shift the focus from information/meaning to writing and concentrate on developing ecological understandings of writing instead of on the things that we (incorrectly) assume writing to convey" (Dobrin 2011, 139).

In many ways, Dobrin's call to relax our focus on human agency so we can shift to a more distributed understanding of writing "as an open system" reiterates many of the basic critiques that new materialist theories of writing are raising. This is very much in line with the theoretical goals of MEOW. At the same time, Dobrin's dismissal of information as theoretically useful raises three conceptual problems from a materialist perspective. First is the overly abstract nature of his "writing-as-system" model and its detachment from the biophysical environment. Second is the assumption that information is primarily semantic and representational. And third is the way it closes off an opportunity for interdisciplinary work with the natural sciences.

The "writing-as-system" model Dobrin theorizes draws heavily on poststructuralist ideas of the pervasive *a priori* text and leaves us in a purely discursive world. In place of terms like *information* and *knowledge* to describe what writing creates, Dobrin invokes other metaphors. Writing is a "system of interconnections," as it "saturates" other systems; it is "viscous" and "liquid" and it has "velocity." No doubt, these are compelling ways to describe writing and they have similar meanings to new materialist terms like *flow* and *circulation*. But Dobrin's theorization of these liquid systems remains far removed from the material realities of the writing-as-system that I've been calling the global networked infrastructure of inscription (or global archive). Yes, writing is a kind of system that entangles with all kinds of systems. More precisely though, systems of writing in the twenty-first century are composed of massive amounts of nonhuman agents—the phones, computers, routers, transmission lines, data centers, and electrical grids that make digital, networked writing a reality. The "liquid" that continuously flows through this infrastructure is commodified data and information produced by ubiquitous inscription and our incessant use of digital writing technologies. By abstracting writing and information production from the very real and cumulative materiality of Web 3.0, we miss the opportunity to articulate how flows of informational production profoundly affect the flows of energy and matter they metabolize with. Flows of information, and the human and nonhuman agents that produce them, do not exist outside of physical flows of energy and matter, nor do they exist outside of informational capitalism and the immense value that writing, as the engine of information production, creates.

The second theoretical issue that arises in Dobrin's dismissal of information is his assumption that information exists only in human, semantic form. While the writing-as-system model is certainly flexible enough to theorize other kinds of information beyond the semantic kind, it doesn't consider the various forms that information takes in Web 3.0. One salient example is the massive sublayer of *metadata* that is created as a byproduct of our time and activities online. Metadata is "data about data" (Mayer-Schönberger and Cukier 2014), information that computer networks use to organize and manage data about when we visit a website and what we do there, what geographic location we visit from, the language we use, the numbers we call or text, and the time of day we do it. With the rise of mobile computing, metadata now keeps a record of where we go in the physical world: our morning commute, the restaurants we eat at, the stores we shop at. Bruce Schneier, a well-known expert on network security and author of *Data and Goliath* (2016) defines metadata this way: "One way to think about it is that data is content, and metadata is context. Metadata can be much more revealing than data, especially when collected in the aggregate. When you have one person under surveillance, the contents of conversations, text messages, and e-mails can be more important than the metadata. But when you have an entire population under surveillance, the metadata is far more meaningful, important, and useful" (Schneier 2016, 23). With the emergence of big data and the internet-of-things, the semantic information we exchange online is just one of the many flows of information now being produced by the second. This layered expansion of data production fundamentally alters our relationship to information. Metadata, and data collected by nonhuman devices and sensors connected to the internet, are certainly forms of information, but they aren't semantic or rhetorical, not yet anyway. They're informative, but they're often pre-semantic, the raw resources needed for producing commodified information and knowledge. The rise of the global archive and the collection of metadata provides corporations and governments unprecedented amounts of data on the activities and behavior of large populations of citizen-consumers. In Web 3.0 we've entered an era of ubiquitous inscription, or what I called in the introduction an intensified process of *datafication*—the process of incessantly inscribing both human activity and natural phenomena so it can be saved, quantified, and studied (Mayer-Schönberger and Cukier 2013, 78). It's been estimated that we now generate quantities of data every day at a scale equal to the storage capacity of four thousand Libraries of Congress (Andrejevic 2013; Schneier 2016; Hilbert 2012; Mayer-Schönberger and Cukier 2013). It is the intensification and diversification of informational flows that emerge in Web 3.0 that Dobrin misses in *Postcomposition*.

The last unfortunate outcome of dismissing the theoretical value of *information* is how it closes off an opportunity for interdisciplinary work. In light of the aggressive data collection occurring in Web 3.0 and the social and environmental problems emerging as a result, the shared use of *information* by the natural sciences and writing studies is an invitation for crossover work. By expanding our understanding of information and its metabolic ties to energy, matter, and capital, we can deepen our materialist ecological theories of writing to grapple better with the ways that intensifying information production impacts human and nonhuman ecosystems alike.

INSCRIPTION, THE ARCHIVE, AND ACCELERATION

In understanding the layered nature of information production and the central role it plays in accelerating our lived experience in Web 3.0, we need to develop our theories of information, how information relates to writing, how it's produced, where it flows and pools, and how it entangles with capital. In theorizing these metabolic relations and the phenomenon of acceleration, we can start by looking at writing's primary affordance of *inscription* and its co-development with *the archive* to understand how the cumulative agency of our writing tools, and the textuality they engender, take on new levels of agency in Web 3.0.

Like information, *inscription* and *archive* are emerging concepts in new materialist scholarship. Such ideas have long been a part of our theories of writing, in large part due to the poststructuralist work of Jacques Derrida and Michel Foucault and their theories of writing and discourse as the all-encompassing *text* we live within, what Derrida called *arche-writing* (see note 6 in the introduction). More recently, Jodie Nicotra has argued that, in theorizing the nonhuman agency of writing technologies we need to consider their inscriptive affordances and think of them as "rhetorical listeners," ever-monitoring and recording what we write and do in the world (Nicotra 2017b). The affordance of inscription, as writing's affordance *par excellence*, is certainly a process of recording, but, as I clarified in the Introductory chapter, it is recording as *datafication*—that is, recording human activity and other natural phenomena in order to quantify and study them.

With inscription comes the process of self-augmenting textuality[2] and *the archive*—the general phenomenon of textual accumulation and the pooling of information that emerges with writing and the development of technologies for storing and organizing this information for future use. Both Derrida and Foucault imagine the concept of the archive as a metonym for the systematic collection and organization of information (Derrida 2016; Foucault 2011). Bureaucracies, libraries, bookstores, and databases are all manifestations of the archive. MEOW foregrounds inscription and the archive in analysis (first material cumulus) because of how they fundamentally shape and mediate our lives by controlling how information flows and pools.

As inscription and the now global archive have developed through time, history reveals various efforts to expand and enhance inscription technologies to control information production for purposes of managing and *accelerating* economic activity. The phenomenon of *acceleration* has long been recognized by scholars and journalists alike (Noys 2013; Virilio 2012; Harvey 2000). The basic idea behind my use of the concept is that, as flows of information grow in size and speed, the pace of cultural development speeds up too. Conventional wisdom tells us that our lived experience of acceleration is just a byproduct of technological advances. While there is some truth to this idea, it's not simply technological advances that contribute to acceleration but, more specifically, the use of writing and inscription technologies for the specific purposes of accelerating capital and the turnover speed of profit. To be sure, the cumulative enhancement of inscription technologies over time entails many actors and motives, but it's clear that many of these enhancements have been driven by the push to accelerate capital circulation by controlling and exploiting flows of information. For a metabolic framework like MEOW in which flows of information and capital are intrinsically tied to flows of energy and matter, accelerating flows of information inevitably mean an acceleration in the circulation and use of energy and matter.

In understanding how writing and information production accelerate capital today, we first need to have a basic idea of what capital actually is. Though we often think of money and capital as the same thing, Marx argued that capital is not a thing but a *process*, one that depends on the constant production and circulation of commodities (Marx 1973). Embodied in the finished commodity is capital waiting to be realized. If a commodity stops moving at any point on its journey from production to consumption, the value it carries stops too. As David Harvey puts it, "capital must circulate continuously, or die" (Harvey 2015, 73).

As Marx describes in great detail throughout all three volumes of *Capital*, in order for capital circulation to accelerate in human culture, it will try to break down any barriers that slow its circulation (Marx 1990). Barriers to capital circulation come in many forms—tariffs, government regulations, corporate taxes—anything that impedes how fast capital circulates and accrues. Though such barriers abound, Marx claims there are two fundamental barriers that slow capital's circuit: the physical laws of *time* and *space*. "Thus, while capital must on one side strive to tear down every spatial barrier . . . to exchange, and conquer the whole Earth for its market, it strives on the other side to annihilate this space with time, i.e. to reduce to a minimum the time spent in motion from one place to another" (Marx 1973, 539). In the industrial London of his day, the annihilation of time and space was driven by sources of energy like steam and fossil fuels that gave rise to large-scale machinery. Yet, for production to accelerate as it did, there also needed to be a material infrastructure in place to circulate more commodities—a need that would lead to the development of bigger and faster transportation and communication networks. As I mentioned earlier in this chapter, Marx doesn't spend much time talking about communication technologies, but it is clear today that, in the transition from industrial to informational capitalism, digital writing tools, inscription, and the global archive take on primary roles in accelerating flows of capital by radically shrinking the time and space commodities must travel through.

Accelerating flows of capital may not sound too bad, especially if you benefit from them. But we must remember that, although dialectically tied to flows of energy and matter, flows of information and capital often behave differently. The basic biophysical laws of the conservation of energy and matter tell us this. We know that matter and energy are neither created nor destroyed, but, rather, take on different forms as they cycle through different ecosystems. While information and capital cycle through human ecologies alongside energy and matter, they also flow and pool differently within human ecosystems. Flows of information and capital can be created and destroyed, and they can grow and circulate in ways that overwhelm and dangerously accelerate the flows of energy and matter they metabolize with.

Thus, the phenomenon of acceleration is, in large part, a manifestation of the antagonistic relation between flows of capital and information on one side, and flows of energy and matter on the other. From a metabolic perspective, the incessant push to accelerate flows of capital by speeding up flows of information always entails accelerating how we process and consume energy and matter. And, as we are experiencing in Web 3.0, accelerating flows of information greatly impact the earth's ecosystems in ways that harm their ability to naturally regenerate and sustain themselves. One of the more obvious environmental problems associated with the acceleration of information production is the immense electronic waste (e-waste) streams it creates. Over forty million tons of e-waste are produced every year globally as developers and technology companies continually release new products and new versions of their products, stimulating consumer demand and increasing our waste production in the process. E-waste is the fastest-growing part of the global waste stream and it's highly toxic to the environment when not recycled properly (United Nations 2017).

Electronic waste is just one symptom of a larger, more general pattern of how accelerating flows of information production can negatively affect the natural ecosystems we live within. Research by the International Geosphere-Biosphere Programme (IGBP)[3] shows how human activities in the past 250 years, beginning with the industrial revolution in Europe (circa 1750 CE), have altered the earth's ecosystems so definitively that humans have initiated a new geological phase, the *Anthropocene* (Steffen et al. 2015). In 2015, the IGBP published the consumption rates of 24

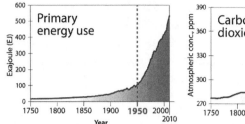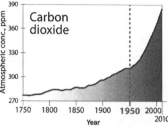

Figure 1.2. Two example graphs from the IGBP study (Steffen et al. 2015) on the "Great Acceleration," depicting the rapid rise in (a) global energy use and (b) atmospheric CO_2 concentration that begins in the 1950s—the same era that digital, networked computing emerges and global information production begins to accelerate. (Permissions by SAGE Publications.)

different planetary systems and resources, including metrics for water usage, population growth, gross domestic product, carbon emissions, and transportation. Figure 1.2 shows two examples taken from the study that chart the steady growth in energy use and CO_2 emissions that begins with the start of the industrial revolution and shoots exponentially upward in the 1950s with the rise of computing and informational capitalism. The report has garnered widespread attention and led to the coining of the term the "Great Acceleration" to describe the generalized process of acceleration occurring evenly and radically across a range of social and natural systems. I take closer look at e-waste and the environmental impacts of accelerating information production in chapter 4.

Acceleration, then, is more than a compelling metaphor. It is the physical, visceral reality of living in a world of alternately accelerating and accumulating flows of energy, information, matter, and capital.

CONCLUSION

My goal in this chapter has been to explore the various theories that inform MEOW and further define the key concepts that shape the framework, in particular *endo-* and *exosomatic metabolism, information, inscription, archive,* and *acceleration.* I believe we have a lot to gain by re-imagining our understanding of these concepts in writing studies one, for the opportunities they present for interdisciplinary work with the natural sciences; and two, to help us theorize how information production entangles with capital circulation to dangerously accelerate the flows of energy and matter they metabolize with.

In the next chapter I look at the first material cumulus in MEOW and the development of one of the world's first writing systems, cuneiform. When writing emerges in ancient Mesopotamia, it develops alongside greater complexity in socioeconomic life and the rise of the first cities, large-scale agriculture, and long-distance trade. The result of this development between writing and culture is the emergence of a kind of proto-informational economy, a society in which writing, information production, and the archive become central technologies for power and capital circulation—a relation that continues into the twenty-first century, embodied in every digital writing tool we use.

2

WRITING TECHNOLOGIES AND THEIR EMBODIED HISTORY OF USE

*The thing about artifacts . . . is that they give us a sense of
who we are in history, so, we may live in the 21st century,
but people came before us and achieved many things. And I
think a sense of our reality, and the permanence of our reality
is solidified by real objects. (Jenkins 2017)*

In this chapter I foreground the first material cumulus of
MEOW: human-made writing technologies and the affordance
of inscription (figure 2.1). I turn to ancient Mesopotamia and
the development of one of the world's first complete writing
systems, cuneiform. Because of the durability of clay and the
aridness of the region, a rich textual history has been preserved,
giving us a unique look into Mesopotamia's experience with
writing and its co-development with socioeconomic activity.
Archaeologists have excavated over four hundred thousand cuneiform tablets from the modern Middle East, specifically Iraq,
Syria, Iran, and Turkey. These texts, dating from as early as the
fourth millennium BCE to as late as the first millennium BCE
represent the oldest and largest corpus of texts from any ancient
civilization (Aubet 2013; Roaf 1990). The widespread informational and textual culture that cuneiform helped produce over
a span of three millennia is a rich example of the role that information production plays in the shaping of economic life—an
economy in which writing, inscription, and archiving become
key agents in processes of capital accumulation.

While historical comparisons are not without their problems,
I believe that one of the keys to developing our new materialist

DOI: 10.7330/9781607329688.c002

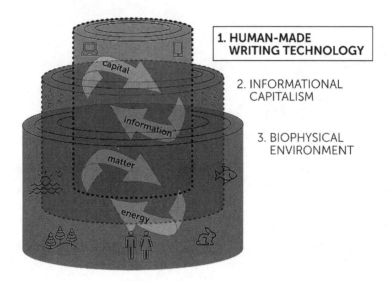

1. **HUMAN-MADE WRITING TECHNOLOGY**

2. INFORMATIONAL CAPITALISM

3. BIOPHYSICAL ENVIRONMENT

Figure 2.1. MEOW framework. The first material cumulus, human-made writing technologies, is represented within the bold dotted outline. (Illustration created by Martha D. Langer, Pear Ink Design.)

theories of writing and agency in Web 3.0 is to pursue more diachronic analyses of writing's technological development as it unfolds over centuries, even millennia. While the field of writing studies excels in synchronic, situated studies of local writing practices, we've likewise tended to avoid more material, evolutionary analyses of writing to consider how local writing situations are always affected by the larger infrastructure of inscription they are a part of.[1] In articulating new materialist theories of writing capable of grappling with the growing complexity of Web 3.0, it is imperative that we open up the local scene of writing to the larger material and historical forces that condition our writing practices.

In MEOW that theoretical work begins in the first material cumulus. For other fields that draw on ecological models to study human behavior like public health and developmental psychology, analysis begins with human individuals in their immediate context and moves outward to make connections with the larger systems (community, country, planet) they are embedded in. MEOW uses the same nested structure for theorizing writing, but rather than placing a human agent at the center of analysis, nonhuman writing technologies and the affordance of inscription become the starting point of analysis. Human agents are still important, but MEOW places us, as embodied, living organisms, within the larger system of the third material cumulus and the biophysical environment (something I explore more in chapters 5 and 6). Writing technologies, like human writers themselves, emerge from specific historical contexts and become living, accumulated embodiments of that history. Just as we study the material evolution of life to understand how different organisms develop over millions of years, a materialist approach to writing should do the same with the historical development of writing and inscription, a history that can be traced back thousands of years to the emergence of the world's first writing systems.

In beginning a MEOW analysis, we can start by historicizing the development of writing and inscription over a time frame of hundreds, even thousands of years. Other researchers could just as easily choose a different time and place than the one I have chosen here. But the basic idea is to consider a more diachronic, less human-centric analysis in which writing technologies are placed at the center and understood as agentive forces that coevolve with human culture as generations of humans adapt and improve the writing tools they inherit from prior generations. With writing comes human history, and wherever writing emerges in the world it becomes an essential component of the human ecosystems it emerges within. To claim a technology embodies a history of use is to think of it as a living fossil. All writing technologies, and the textuality they foster through inscription, are the embodied accumulation of the long, sociohistorical process of adapting and enhancing writing technologies over time. It is this history of embodied use, manifested in every writing tool we encounter, that provides the necessary grounds for theorizing the nonhuman agency of writing and inscription. Our use of the word *tablet* to describe today's touchscreen computers reflects an implicit understanding of this genealogical evolution.

The history of cuneiform is an ideal starting point for a materialist analysis of writing due to its longevity, availability, and developmental history with early forms of capitalist economy. While archaeologists and historians believe that writing developed independently in at least four different times and places—Mesopotamia, Egypt, China, and Mesoamerica—chronologically, cuneiform is the first full writing system to be developed. Moreover, the archaeological record of ancient Mesopotamia shows compelling evidence for an evolutionary history of writing and inscription that spans over eight thousand years of symbolic behavior in the region. From the use of clay tokens for counting and simplifying trade, to the fully developed system of cuneiform capable of accurately representing spoken language, the experience of writing in Mesopotamia reveals a long, historical, and cumulative process of improving and extending the technologies of inscription to meet the growing social and economic needs of the region. Thus, in looking at the development of cuneiform as a writing system, we are returning to the very origins of inscription to understand the beginnings of writing and the radical socioeconomic effects that emerge with it.

The textual record of Mesopotamia is more abundant than other ancient writing systems and its use for over three thousand years provides for us a long textual and technological record. Some estimates put the current number of discovered tablets between four hundred thousand and five hundred thousand, of which around fifty thousand have been deciphered (Van De Mieroop 1999; Watkins and Snyder 2003; Cuneiform Digital Library Initiative 2020). In doing this kind of historicizing, we must always keep in mind that writing technologies and the cumulative effects of inscription have long, uneven histories that cannot be condensed into a simple narrative of progress. In turning to Mesopotamia and the development of writing, we are not trying to "discover" a linear history of development, but rather to see what kinds of historical and theoretical insight we can glean from the emergence of writing at an earlier stage and on a smaller scale. In understanding this cumulative history, we are trying to understand how nonhuman writing technologies and the textuality they foster take on agency as they accumulate in culture alongside the human agents who use them.

Another key reason to look at the evolution of cuneiform is for what it can tell us about writing's developmental relations with economy, exchange, and early forms of capital accumulation. As Denise Schmandt-Besserat and Michael Erard argue, "the function of writing when it came about in 3200 BCE was exclusively economic" (Schmandt-Besserat and Erard 2008; Gabriel 2008). The long history of cuneiform and its developmental relations with economy present for us a rich example of how and when writing emerges in human history along with other notable changes such as large-scale agriculture, the first cities, and long-distance trade. The earliest textual genres we know of—ledgers, lists, receipts, inventories, statements of account, contracts, and titles of ownership—all speak to the developmental tie between writing and economic activity. Figure 2.2 is a map of the Tigris-Euphrates river valley showing the location of ancient Mesopotamian cities/villages and cities in the modern Middle East.

In the context of an ancient Mesopotamian society that was stratified and class-based, writing becomes not just a cornerstone of socioeconomic life, but also a key technological agent leveraged by the ruling elite to acquire more land and wealth by controlling the production and flow of information.[2] The material and textual history of Mesopotamia provides for us an early example of how writing, inscription, and archiving become vital agents in the accumulation and circulation of capital.

With this history in mind, I begin the chapter with the following questions: What can we learn about the metabolic relations between writing, information, and capital circulation by studying the cultural origins of cuneiform? And how can this history inform our current materialist theories of writing and inscription in Web 3.0? To answer these questions I turn to recent work in Near East history, archaeology, and anthropology that looks at

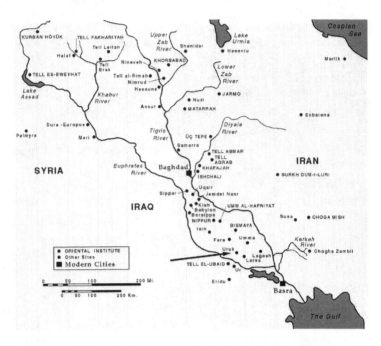

Figure 2.2. The modern-day Middle East, showing the location of both modern and ancient cities in the Tigris–Euphrates river valley. Cuneiform first emerged as a full system of writing in southern Mesopotamia in the city-state of Uruk. (Reproduced with permission from The Oriental Institute.)

the development of cuneiform and its impact on Mesopotamian life (circa 4000 BCE to 1000 BCE). Although conventional wisdom suggests that writing emerges out of a human need to record speech, history, and myth, the history of cuneiform reveals a different evolution, one in which writing emerges from the needs of Mesopotamians to quantify and keep accurate accounts of trade and exchange. The emergence of writing in Mesopotamia offers us a unique perspective on how writing and inscription develop in response to the growing size and complexity of socio-economic life. In our effort to expand our materialist theories of writing, we have much to gain through more diachronic analyses of how writing and economy develop over long stretches of human history. The historical, dialectical relation between writing and economy that begins with cuneiform and Mesopotamia continues to live on, embodied in the shape and use of our contemporary digital writing tools.

WRITING AND MONEY AS TECHNOLOGIES OF CIRCULATION

Since MEOW is grounded in historical, dialectical materialism, I begin my analysis by briefly revisiting Marx's understanding of how and when capitalism, as a mode of production, first appears in history. In *Capital*, Marx argues that capitalism emerges in fifteenth-century Europe with the discovery of the Americas and the rise of the European bourgeoisie (Marx 1990). He conjectures that, for capitalism to emerge as a mode of economic production, certain historical conditions were necessary, conditions that included a greater division of labor, a certain level of technological development, and some kind of "money form." According to Marx, the *idea* of money arises out of the long evolution of labor and exchange relations between early human cultures (he never gives an actual time frame). He explains that, as social and economic trade relations grow in size and complexity, a common commodity begins to crystallize as a basic standard for *value*—a single thing or substance that can represent the value of all other commodities. In modern cultures this standardized form of value takes the shape of coin and paper currency, but in ancient civilizations like Mesopotamia, any common commodity that was widely traded could take the role of a shared money form. Archaeologists and historians who study the ancient Near East have found evidence that barley, cattle, silver, and gold all served as money forms for trade throughout the region (Van De Mieroop 2007). Oddly though, despite having several kinds of potential money forms, most historians believe that a system of standardized coinage never emerged in Mesopotamia, a point I'll take up shortly (Powell 1996; Charpin 2010; Van De Mieroop 1999).

Marx argues that, when a universal money form emerges in a culture, it does so to serve two key economic functions: (1) simplify exchange relations by using an agreed-upon *standard*

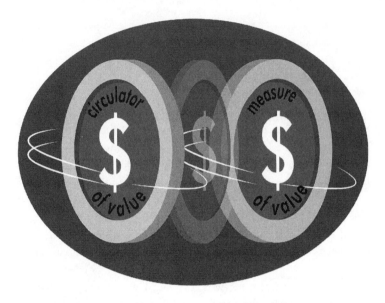

Figure 2.3. Depiction of Karl Marx's concept of the dialectical "money form," shown as two sides of the same coin. For capital to emerge as a socioeconomic agent, Marx argued that something (e.g., gold) in culture had to emerge that could simultaneously function as both a circulator and measure of value. (Illustration created by Martha D. Langer, Pear Ink Design.)

form of value, and (2) act as a tangible *circulator of value* capable of being exchanged by buyers and sellers in the market (Marx 1990, 192). If and when a money form emerges at a specific stage of economic development, it is this dual nature of a money form that helps create the conditions for capital accumulation to emerge. Figure 2.3 is a simple illustration of Marx's concept of the money form as the dialectical expression of the socioeconomic need to measure and circulate value.

Once the concept of value is expressed in a tangible money form (be it livestock, gold, or bitcoin), it is now possible to hoard and accumulate this value. The process of accumulating value through hoarding a universal money form helps create the material conditions necessary for capital to emerge as a cultural agent that begins to mobilize other aspects of culture for the primary purpose of circulating capital and accruing profit. As Marx famously notes of the money form, "by virtue of it being value, it has acquired the occult ability to add value to itself. It brings forth living offspring, or at least lays golden eggs" (Marx 1990, 255). This "occult ability to add value to itself" is Marx's way of describing how a standardized money form becomes capital as it starts to accrue and circulate in the market. In Marx's time a common money form was gold. Gold was used for millennia as a standard of value based on its durability and scarcity. It thus served (and still does) as a universal money form capable of homogenizing the diversity of values in lived experience, making *every thing*, human and nonhuman alike, reducible to its price in gold.

While Marx was certainly on the right track with his ideas about money and capitalist development, we now have the benefit of over a century's worth of archaeological and historical studies on ancient economies that give us a more detailed picture of how and when the earliest forms of capitalist production begin to emerge. Ancient Mesopotamia, in particular, has provided scholars with a large corpus of texts regarding the economic lives of Mesopotamians, a history different than the one Marx conjectured. As I mentioned above, while a variety of money forms were used in Mesopotamia, archaeologists believe that standardized money and coinage never emerged there despite plenty of archaeological evidence showing early forms of capitalist production and profit making (Powell 1996; Allen 1992; Van De Mieroop 2014; Goody 1986).

Modern studies on Mesopotamian economy suggest that, in addition to developing money forms, the technologies of writing, inscription, and archiving play an equal, sometimes greater, role in the emergence of the earliest forms of capitalist activity in human history. As more tablets are deciphered, the history of cuneiform continually rewrites our understanding of Mesopotamian economy, strongly suggesting there is a historical, dialectical relationship between writing and the development of capitalism. While a tangible, exchangeable money form is necessary for simplifying trade and exchange between people, its existence alone isn't enough to initiate the accumulation of capital that emerges in Mesopotamia. What is needed is another technology to coordinate, manage, and keep track of the money form and how it moves through exchange relations and the market. That technology is writing.[3]

Jack Goody emphasizes this point in *The Logic of Writing and the Organization of Society* where he argues that we cannot understand the roots of capitalist development without considering the "means of production" in relation to the "means of communication": "There is another, more basic level at which writing intervenes [in Mesopotamian economic life] . . . Most obvious is book-keeping of various kinds, but there is also the related question of the link between different systems of circulation, of money on the one hand and of the written word on the other" (Goody 1986, 46). While Marx focuses on money as a precondition for capitalism to develop, Goody foregrounds writing, arguing that, in the case of Mesopotamia, it is the development of writing as a technology for inscribing and managing the growing informational needs of the region that becomes the catalyst for the development of early capitalist modes of production. As Goody stresses, it isn't simply the technology of writing that becomes agentive; it's the combination of inscription, information production, and archiving that form the agentive matrix of writing as a technology (see also Bazerman 2006).

This dialectical relation between writing and capital circulation is clearly manifest in the profusion of economic and accounting genres that form the largest percentage of texts from ancient Mesopotamia—statements of account, balance sheets, ledgers, lists, receipts, loans, contracts, property deeds, and tax records (Smart 2008; Charpin 2010; Powell 1996; Goody 1986). Such genres are reflections of a growing bureaucracy necessary for managing burgeoning cities and populations, while at the same time allowing for more elaborate economic transactions, census taking, taxation, tribute, and money lending. Goody concludes that "we find an association between money-lending, banking, and literacy throughout human history" (Goody 1986, 175).

How exactly does writing become a circulator of value in Mesopotamia? The following passage by archaeologist Maria Aubet from *Commerce and Colonization in the Ancient Near East* describes the kinds of problems that had to be solved in order for trade and exchange to happen in Mesopotamia:

> [I]n conditions where communication and transport are difficult, and when state institutions are unable to guarantee the physical and economic security of the merchants, long-distance trade, if it is to function well, *demands a series of solutions and measures* to tackle basic technical problems such as the regular exchange of information about conditions of supply and demand in the target country, safe and effective transport of merchandise—in particular perishable goods—the criterion and maintenance of relations of trust between traders and intermediaries, regularity in the setting up of credit facilities, an efficient arbitration system in disputes and the development and maintenance of a system of authority capable of guaranteeing order and respect for contractual norms and decisions. (Aubet 2013; my emphasis)

As Aubet's description makes clear, Mesopotamia was a growing society with a vast trade network of peoples, goods, languages, technologies, and ideas. For capital to accrue and take flight in a context of risk and insecurity, not only were specific types of written genres useful for keeping track of loans and interest, written contracts would become essential for minimizing risk and for formalizing agreements. While a standardized money form would be necessary for supporting long-distance trade, it is the technology of writing that makes more complex exchange relations possible. Writing is the "solutions" and "measures" for addressing the basic challenges of successful market exchange. As such, contrary to Marx's argument that the conditions for capitalism begin to emerge in early fifteenth-century Europe, we now know that wealth accumulation and early forms of profit-making arose much sooner in ancient Mesopotamia, along with the development of the first large cities, expanding trade networks, and, most notably, the use of writing and archiving by the ruling elite to manage and control flows of information.

EMERGENCE OF INSCRIPTION AND THE ARCHIVE

With this historical context in mind, the next step in exploring the first material cumulus and theorizing how writing

technologies take on agency is to foreground the basic affordance of inscription and the self-augmenting textuality it gives
rise to. To say a technology *affords* something is to assume it has
some kind of agency. All technologies afford humans certain
potentials for use—a chair affords sitting, a car affords transportation, a writing technology affords inscription. Affordances are
those functions a technology is intentionally designed for, as well
as the potential uses human agents may create with it. A focus on
the historical development of inscription provides an entry point
for materialist theorizing by drawing our attention to the cumulative effects of textuality and information production, and how
these effects grow through the evolutionary process of human
use and enhancement.[4] Inscription, of course, is the fundamental affordance of writing. It is fundamentally a process of datafication, a way of materializing and quantifying our experience of
the world and our exchange relations with each other.

But inscription alone is only half the story of how writing
technologies emerge as agents in culture. It is what happens after
inscription that enables us to understand how writing becomes
a powerful agentive force. Once unleashed in Mesopotamia,
writing spreads through the region as texts and information
begin to proliferate, creating what anthropologist Norman
Yoffee calls a "textual tradition" (Yoffee 2015). As inscription is
further used in Mesopotamia, more texts are created, creating
a new material, informational layer in culture that gives rise to
archives for storing and managing the ongoing production of
texts. With inscription comes textual accumulation, and with
textual accumulation we begin to see qualitative changes occur
throughout Mesopotamian culture, in the shape of the religious
and ruling institutions, economic life and trade, labor, education, and law (Goody 1986; Charpin 2010; Van de Mieroop
2007). The accumulation of texts produced by writing takes on
agency through the cumulative causation of self-augmenting
textuality and information production as it feeds back into the
shape of Mesopotamian life.

In turning to Mesopotamia to trace the early history of inscription and information production, we do so to understand how

the earliest forms of inscription emerged and the material social impacts they had on the culture as texts began to proliferate. It's a history that shows us how agency comes to be embodied in a nonhuman writing technology, and it's a useful illustration, on a smaller scale, of how the development of archiving, and the bureaucratic structures that follow, feed back into culture and qualitatively reshape socioeconomic life.

FROM CLAY TOKENS TO CLAY TABLETS

But how do the Mesopotamians arrive at a full writing system, and is it possible to trace some of the material social effects of writing as textuality accumulates in Mesopotamia? It's a history that starts long before the emergence of cuneiform. Early twentieth-century theories on the origins of writing argued that modern writing systems stemmed from earlier pictographic systems (one-to-one representations of things in the world) that evolved into more abstract systems that combined logographic and phonetic signs to represent spoken words. Although there is some truth to this progression, the development of cuneiform as a full writing system capable of expressing all manner of verbal and symbolic communication reveals a different evolution. Today, many archaeologists and historians agree that, rather than emerging from pictographs, cuneiform developed from an earlier symbol system of clay tokens (Castor 2006; Logan 2004; Faigley 1999; Schmandt-Besserat 1996). The earliest clay tokens begin to appear around 8000 BCE, in parallel development with animal domestication and agriculture, while a full system of writing doesn't emerge until five thousand years later with the first cities and the rise of urban life.

As Mesopotamia grew in area and population, the token system evolved along with it (figure 2.4). Tokens like these have been found to exist throughout the ancient Near East. Their presence across a large geographic region suggests there was a type of shared economy and symbol system, even by many who spoke different languages. Such tokens are some of the earliest known forms of human symbolic activity and indications

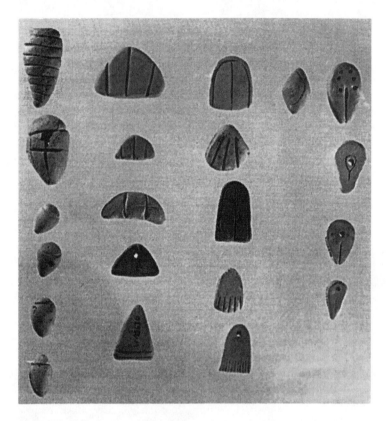

Figure 2.4. Clay tokens used for exchange in Mesopotamia (circa 5000–3000 BCE). Tokens represented basic goods for trade—sheep, wheat, textiles, etc.—and are considered some of the earliest evidence of human symbolic communication, predating both writing and coinage. (Image from How Writing Came About, *by Denise Schmandt-Besserat, Copyright 1992, 1996. Courtesy of the author and the University of Texas Press.)*

of abstract thinking. They represent a point in history when humans began making objects to represent important material things in their everyday lives, things like deities and animals, and especially things that were commonly traded. A token with a cross symbolized a "sheep"; a cone-shaped token symbolized "bread." Tokens were useful for counting and for simplifying more elaborate trade transactions. Over time, as socioeconomic life grew more complex in Mesopotamia, more complex tokens emerged to represent more objects and make finer distinctions between classes of objects.

Clay tokens are significant for many reasons and their existence tells us a great deal about the evolution of writing. When the ancient Mesopotamians fashioned a token, they were making it primarily for purposes of counting and quantification. Or, anachronistically, we could say they were datafying common objects in their phenomenal world to facilitate trade and exchange. With the development of farming and agriculture (8000 BCE), there came the need to manage larger labor forces and food surpluses. As a consequence, the token system evolves to meet the informational and organizational needs of a rapidly growing and changing culture (Schmandt-Besserat 1996, 102). By 3500 BCE, archaeologists find that more kinds of tokens emerge with the first cities and the rise of food and textile manufacturing in southern Mesopotamia (known as Sumer), in one of the world's first cities, Uruk. Such tokens are more elaborate, often with incisions and punched holes, and they represent a greater range of things, especially manufactured goods like textiles, oil, metals, tools, bread, and beer (Schmandt-Besserat 1996, 103). What we witness in the movement from simple to complex tokens is a symbol system that evolves in response to changing informational needs as Mesopotamian culture evolved and expanded across the region.

From complex tokens, the next stage of early inscription technologies appears to be the emergence of what archaeologists call clay *bullae* (sing. *bulla*), or clay envelopes. Clay bullae, like the one pictured in figure 2.5, have been excavated throughout the Middle East, with many found still intact and containing tokens inside. Researchers believe that clay bullae served as an early form of contract, a technology for accounting and ensuring the correct quantity of goods to be delivered or received. Bullae that have been found are often impressed with a seal, an early type of signature that confirmed the validity of the tokens inside. Others have been found with impressed images on their surfaces—images that often match up with the shape and number of tokens in the bullae. Figure 2.5 is a

Figure 2.5. Clay tokens and clay bulla (ca. 8500–3500 BCE, the city of Uruk). The tokens themselves were found inside the bulla and images of the tokens were impressed on the outside of the bulla. (Image used with permission from Art Resource and the Louvre Museum, France.)

well-known image of a clay bulla from the fourth millennium BCE with six impressions and the six tokens found inside.

Schmandt-Besserat and others have argued that these impressed bullae are evidence of a key stage in how writing evolved in Mesopotamia. According to the archaeological record, impressed clay bullae emerge around 3500 BCE, two centuries before the earliest-known clay tablets. As cities emerged and exchange relations spread in southern Mesopotamia, the clay-token system slowly evolved each step of the way, from tokens to impressed bullae to tablets—each stage a response to the changing socioeconomic conditions then taking shape. During this two-hundred-year transitory period from tokens to tablets, the Sumerians were laying the foundation for the full writing system of cuneiform that would unfold over the next thousand years and spread widely through the region (Schmandt-Besserat 1996; Logan 2004).

The first clay tablets, called *proto-cuneiform*, start to appear around 3200 BCE in the city-state of Uruk in southern Mesopotamia (see figure 2.2). Figures 2.6 and 2.7 are examples of proto-cuneiform tablets found in the temple archives in Uruk (3400–3200 BCE). There are two significant points to make here about writing from the proto-cuneiform era. First is the similarities we see between the shapes of the clay tokens and the shapes either impressed or incised on these early tablets, suggesting a transitionary period. And second is the development of two notation systems, one for counting and one more semantic and descriptive. As Schmandt-Besserat explains,

> notched spheres . . . and incised triangles . . . were the prototypes for impressed/incised signs. These signs are very important because they attest to the close relationship between impressed and incised signs. They show, beyond any doubt, that the incised pictographs came as the third and final step of the evolution from tokens to writing. The incised triangle is of particular interest since one can trace it through the following four stages of evolution: (1) complex token, (2) impressed sign, (3) impressed/incised sign, and (4) pictograph. (Schmandt-Bessert 1996)

While the token system continued alongside the early use of clay tablets and proto-cuneiform, there appears to be a chronological transition from impressed bullae to tablets with both incised and impressed signs. Figure 2.6 is an image of a proto-cuneiform tablet with an incised token.

In addition to incised tokens, what also emerges with proto-cuneiform is what scholar Robert K. Logan calls a technological "bifurcation" (Logan 2004). As the token system morphs into a writing system, two forms of inscription take shape: one quantitative and one qualitative. This bifurcation in shown in figure 2.7 where things (barley, beer) are incised and their quantity is represented as impressed spheres and wedges. Of the many things the bifurcation of proto-cuneiform tells us, it strongly suggests that (1) writing in Mesopotamia goes through a long process of accumulative development and (2) it emerges from the human need to quantify and engage in more elaborate economic transactions.

As writing and textuality began to permeate Mesopotamian life, the tools for inscribing and archiving evolved in concert. The nature of clay as a medium encouraged impressions over incisions and a more refined stylus was developed for impressing both numbers and nouns. This move from incision to impression

Token Type		Pictograph	Translation
3: 22		ZATU 452c	type of garment or cloth
3: 24		ZATU 452b	type of garment or cloth[149]
3: 28		ATU 755 ZATU 555	type of garment or cloth[150]
3: 30		ATU 759 ZATU 452c	type of garment or cloth[151]
3: 32		ZATU 452e	type of garment or cloth (fig. 26)[152]

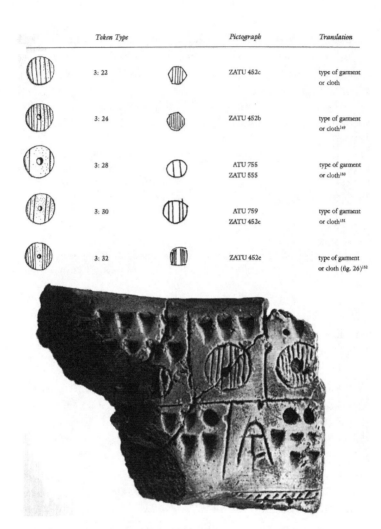

Figure 2.6. Proto-cuneiform tablet from the late third millennium BCE, southern Mesopotamia, with different types of clay tokens drawn above. The two representations of circular tokens (with inscribed vertical lines and central impressed circles) on the upper-right corner of the clay tablet signify two examples of a particular type of garment. (Image from How Writing Came About, by Denise Schmandt-Besserat, Copyright 1992, 1996. Courtesy of the author and the University of Texas Press.)

Figure 2.7. Another example of a proto-cuneiform tablet, with the incised symbol for barley (third symbol from the left, top row) and the amount of barley represented as three round impressions (circa 3500 BCE). (Used with permission from the British Museum.)

was a more pragmatic way to inscribe clay, and the improved wedge-shaped stylus eventually led to a proliferation of symbols that would, over time, become more abstract and removed from the objects they originally represented. From the time of its emergence in the fourth millennium BCE to the last known cuneiform text (75 CE)—a span of about thirty-five hundred years—written cuneiform went through several phases. Figure 2.8 shows the evolution of the signs for "star," "sun," "stream," and "barley." What begins partially as a pictographic script in proto-cuneiform evolves over three millennia into more abstract symbols and a syllabary that combined logographic and phonetic signs. Over that same span of time, the number of cuneiform signs was trimmed from over two thousand to eight hundred symbols (Roaf 1990).

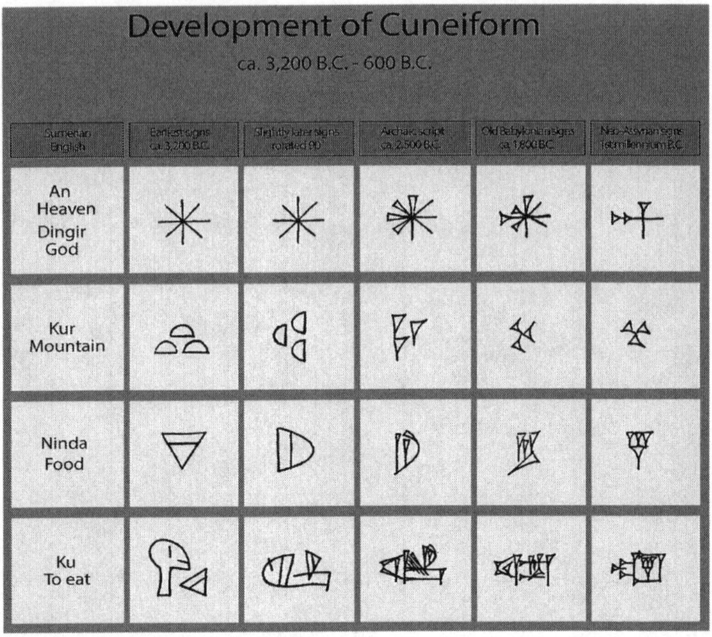

Figure 2.8. Common symbols in the cuneiform script, evolving (left to right) through various stages of abstraction into a mature system of writing as Mesopotamia grew in size and population. (Courtesy of The Oriental Institute of the University of Chicago.)

As cuneiform spreads and is picked up by other groups, we see a process of enhancement and standardization as cuneiform becomes a full-fledged writing system. As this evolution unfolds, tablets get larger, more information gets condensed into the space of the tablet, and the direction of the writing is more aligned and moves more consistently left to right (figure 2.9) (Robinson 2009; Van De Mieroop 1999). With a more developed writing system, what also emerges are new kinds of texts beyond the economic and administrative: myths, hymns, treaties, and legal codes.

The gradual transformation of clay tokens to clay tablets is important for what it tells us about the cumulative agency of writing and inscription, and it tells us a lot about how writing

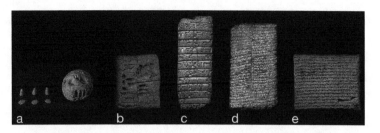

Figure 2.9. Evolution of cuneiform from clay tokens and bullae (ca. 3500) to tablets and a full writing system over three millennia: (a) clay bulla and tokens (ca. 3500 BCE — permissions from the Louvre Museum); (b) proto-cuneiform (3200 BCE — permissions from British Museum); (c) tablet from the Old Ak-kadian period (ca. 2300 BCE — permissions from University of Pennsylvania); (d) tablet from the Middle Babylonian period (ca. 1400 BCE — permissions from University of Pennsylvania); (e) tablet from Achaemenid period (ca. 500 BCE — permissions from University of Pennsylvania). As cuneiform spread throughout Mesopotamia and was adopted by other peoples in the region, tablets become larger, the cuneiform script became more abstract, syllabic, and phonetic, and the symbol system was trimmed from 2,000 symbols to fewer than 800 by the first millennia BCE. All tablets shown are thought to be adminis-trative documents.

and human culture develop together. When cuneiform becomes a full writing system capable of conveying both quantitative and qualitative information, it embodies within it the long evolu-tion of the clay-token system and the human need to inscribe our lived experience and exchange relations with each other. It wasn't simply a few bright Mesopotamians who conjured up a new writing system, and writing didn't emerge to serve just one purpose. It is a history that spans millennia, a slow process of cumulative development as Mesopotamians, generation after generation, enhanced and built on the writing technologies they inherited from those who came before them.

WRITING AND THE WORLD'S FIRST CITY: URUK

In distributed models of agency, the agency that inheres in a writing technology is always dialectically tied to human agency. When we look at the interplay between human and nonhuman agency that unfolds in the development of cuneiform, we must also consider how writing was continually enhanced by the religious and ruling classes and used to organize trade and production, maintain professional armies, collect taxes, and annex land—practices that would give rise to the first monarchies and empires in history. Although writing would lead to other important types of inscription, including mathematics, myth, literature, and law, "cuneiform was invented for the purposes of record-keeping by the public institutions and for its entire history this remained one of its primary purposes. Public administrative documents are common in almost all periods, produced by bureaucracies of palaces and temples" (Van De Mieroop 1999, 13).

The cultural and developmental relation between writing, inscription, archiving, cities, and economic control by a ruling elite can be traced in the clay tablets excavated from what is thought to be the first city in history, the Sumerian city of Uruk in southern Mesopotamia.[5] It is estimated that Uruk, at its height during the Late Uruk period (3500–3000 BCE) grew to six hundred acres within the city's walls and had a population of up to fifty thousand people (Castor 2013). Historians believe that the "Uruk phenomenon" was the product of several historical conditions, including natural changes in the climate that transformed the Tigris and Euphrates river valley into suitable land for large-scale agriculture (Van De Mieroop 2007; Roaf 1990).

While our understanding of this ancient history is still unclear, many historians believe that, at some point before cuneiform developed, there was a long process of land consolidation by powerful families and tribes in the region (Castor 2013). What emerges in southern Mesopotamia around the same time that cuneiform begins to emerge is a hierarchical, class-based social system where powerful, theocratic families controlled large areas of farm land that needed laborers to work the fields. The opportunities for consistent work and food attracted people from across the region, giving rise to greater population density. By the time proto-cuneiform emerges around 3200 BCE, Uruk was reaching a level of food production and population that was outgrowing the clay-token system of exchange. This combination of climate change, migration, and socio-technological development would turn Uruk into a central hub of culture and commerce, driven first by agriculture and then expanded through trade and manufacturing. With such a critical density of people in one area, more specialized labor developed—weavers, metalsmiths, potters, tanners, and carpenters—giving rise to a new division of labor. In these changing material social conditions, the writing system of cuneiform begins to emerge as rulers and priests alike developed new ways for managing the growing complexity that comes with greater concentrations of people and greater levels of exchange.

Figure 2.10 shows the modern ruins of Uruk (located in Iraq) and figure 2.11 is an artist's depiction of what Uruk might have looked like in 3200 BCE.

Archaeologists have excavated over five thousand tablets from the city-state of Uruk. Eighty-five percent of these tablets are accounting documents (ledgers, inventories) and the majority of the remaining 15 percent are word lists that scribes referred to when needing to know a particular cuneiform symbol (Goody 1986; Van De Mieroop 1999). The tablets were found primarily in the remains of a temple for the goddess Eanna, the goddess of fertility and war. This trove of texts is one of the earliest-known examples of bureaucratic administration and the use of archiving. In Uruk, like most city-states in ancient Mesopotamia, the temples played a vital role in managing how information flowed through the city-state and beyond. The earliest priest-leaders of Uruk leveraged writing and archiving to keep track of harvests and manage the laborers who worked the fields. As Near East scholar Marc Van De Mieroop explains, "a robust system of writing had to be in place to manage corvee labor [unpaid labor in which workers work for food or in lieu of taxes] and to keep records of those that fulfilled their obligations, as well as to distribute rations. Tablets from the ancient city of Shuruppak have records detailing the daily barley rations for 20,000 people for a period of six months" (Van De Mieroop 2007, 58). It is estimated that the temple complex of Uruk controlled around six hundred acres of agricultural land during

Figure 2.10. Ruins of the temple at Uruk in modern-day Iraq. (Permissions by Getty Images.)

this time and employed thousands of people in the growing of food as well as the processing of food products and textiles. As Uruk grew in size, ruling elites continually refined and improved the system of writing and archiving to more precisely track the goods and payments that flowed in and out of the temple (Law et al. 2017, 213). Writing would thus aid elites in controlling the flow of information and the economy by keeping track of what was owed to them, as well as the interest that would be charged on loans.

CREATING A TEXTUAL COMMUNITY THROUGH TEXTUALITY

What we see unfolding in Uruk, and eventually all of Mesopotamia, amongst a wide range of cultural changes that emerge with urbanization and population density, is the transition from a region of disparate groups and tribes into a centralized economy pulled together by the systematic use of writing and archiving by a powerful minority of elites to control socioeconomic life.

Because Mesopotamia was primarily an agricultural economy, it lacked other common resources like wood, stone, and precious metals like copper and gold. In order to acquire these

Figure 2.11. Artist's rendition of the city of Uruk, third millennium BCE. (Permissions by Artefacts.)

goods, the rulers of Uruk had to develop long-distance trade networks that reached in all directions, to modern-day Turkey, the Mediterranean, Egypt, and the Persian Gulf. Due to this need to import goods, the Sumerians used cuneiform extensively in their trading and, in the process, created a "textual community" (Yoffee 2015) throughout the region. As Uruk grew in size and economic power, the use of cuneiform by the ruling elite laid the foundation for a shared culture even though it was a region of many different languages and customs. Cuneiform, as a syllabary script, meant it could be easily adopted to convey different spoken languages including Akkadian and Elamite—peoples to the north of Uruk (Yoffee 2015, 291). From around 3000 to 2500 BCE, Uruk and Sumerian culture would use their writing system and their position as a center of commerce to spread their influence across the Tigris–Euphrates river valley (Castor 2013). Archaeological digs have found Sumerian art, pottery, and texts in distant regions of northern Mesopotamia (modern-day Syria) and regions to the east (modern-day Iran).

In addition to trade, cuneiform was further disseminated by the training of Sumerian scribes and the need to govern the regions around Uruk that were under the city's control. As I've noted, while 85 percent of the texts that have been found in Uruk are administrative in nature, the other 15 percent are primarily lexical lists: cuneiform vocabulary and phrases grouped into categories such as cities, gods, foods, animals, and professions:

> These lists were faithfully copied in large quantities over a period of more than a thousand years and held in high esteem . . . This distribution of contents suggests that in the earliest phase of script development in Mesopotamia, the simple word lists used for scribal training were indispensable, in addition to learning the system of administrative control, and not other genres of writing featuring connected discourse. (Law et al. 2017, 220)

Such word lists, like our dictionaries today, served an important function in establishing a shared textual community throughout Mesopotamia. A textual community, in this instance, does not mean there was widespread literacy; writing would continue to be a tool of the elite. However, it does mean that a shared culture was created across the entire region due to the spread of cuneiform and textuality. In this way, the Sumerians and the city of Uruk they founded, would leave an indelible impression on Mesopotamian culture via the script they invented and the model of the city as a form of centralized organization.

FROM URUK TO EMPIRE: KINGSHIP, WRITING, AND POWER

Over the next thousand years after the appearance of the first proto-cuneiform tablets in Uruk, writing, now unleashed, is picked up by other peoples in the region who adapt it to their own languages. As a result, cuneiform is further developed beyond its uses for accounting and quantification to become a full-fledged writing system. During this time, from the peak of Uruk's prominence to its eventual decline (3200 BCE to 2200 BCE), another important cultural shift occurs as the main center of socioeconomic power, the temple, is eclipsed by the rise of kingship and monarchy. To be sure, the early kings of Mesopotamia always shared power with the religious authorities. However, as Mesopotamian civilization developed, and as writing came to be used more extensively, powerful, autocratic rulers start to emerge who amass large armies and extend their control over trade routes, labor, and natural resources. Yet, it wasn't force alone that these aspiring kings used to consolidate power. Just as the temples had done, Mesopotamian kings would enhance and expand the technologies of writing to better manage and control the lands they conquered by controlling the flow of information. Two notable examples of empires leveraging writing in this way are Sargon and the Akkadian kings (2334–2193 BCE) and what is known as the Third Dynasty of Ur (2112–2004 BCE).

The rise of Sargon and the Akkaadian kings is considered one of the first empires in world history. Supported by a scribal elite, the Akkadian kings managed to unite for the first time the southern and northern regions of Mesopotamia, an area of over 300,000 square miles at its peak (Taagepera 1979). This was initially completed through force and a trained military, but power was held through the extensive use of writing and bureaucracy to manage the city-states they brought under their control. While Uruk was the model city-state, the Akkadian kings would become the model of empire and kingship that would dominate the sociopolitical landscape of Mesopotamia for the next 1,500 years. Sargon and the Akkadian kings developed a new system of governance that used writing extensively to coordinate with the governors who watched over their conquered cities. They adapted Sumerian cuneiform to their language, made it more legible, added more syllabic signs to better express the Akkadian language, and established schools to train scribes (Castor 2013; Charpin 2010; Van De Mieroop 1999).

Narum-Sin, Sargon's son, further used writing to develop innovative tax and tribute systems, along with more standardized ways for accounting, planning, weighing, and measuring to facilitate record-keeping and trade. In addition, he used writing more comprehensively to organize labor and build monumental architecture that often required thousands of workers. Narum-Sin also became the first Mesopotamian king to use writing and inscription to seize temple property and represent himself as a deity in ceremonial texts to further establish his family's right to rule (Castor 2013; Charpin 2010). Although Sargon, Narum-Sin, and the Akkadian empire only lasted a little over a century, they would set the precedent for how to use writing and inscription to run an empire. Granted, Mesopotamian city-states were constantly in conflict and always resistant to being conquered by other city-states. But it nevertheless happened time and again that certain city-states would come to control large regions by leveraging new writing technologies.

Another example worth mentioning here is the Third Dynasty of Ur (2112–2004 BCE), an era often noted for the many innovations in writing it developed, especially during the reign of King Shulgi. The Ur III kings took control over a large portion of Mesopotamia a century after the Akkadians. Like the Akkadians, they resorted to military power to take control of land, but they also utilized writing for diplomacy and to craft trade agreements. Over forty thousand clay tablets have been discovered from the ancient city-state of Ur, the largest trove of texts from any ancient civilization (Van De Mieroop 2007, 75). These texts "range from the simple receipt of one sheep to the calculation of the harvest of 38 million liters of cereals" (Van de Mieroop 2007, 75). They provide a detailed account of economic life and the extent to which the Ur III kings used writing to manage and control the economy. The Ur III kings took inscription and archiving to another level, enhancing every aspect of bureaucracy, introducing improvements in accounting, new methods for collecting taxes and tribute, and more efficient communications between the centralized government and the city-states under its control. Such changes would further strengthen the redistributive economy in a way that furthered the accumulation of wealth by the palace complexes. Like the Akkadian kings before them, the Ur III kings intensified the training of scribes to help expand bureaucratic control of their conquered lands. It is also with the Ur III kings that we see the development of the first law codes and the use of inscription to create a codified system of rules intended to mediate behavior and further manage the economy (Yoffee 1995).

My main purpose in tracing the evolution of cuneiform has been to show how a history of use comes to be embodied in each successive iteration of writing and archiving. From Uruk onward, writing and inscription become keystone technologies used by the temples and palaces to organize labor, manage exchange and trade, and accrue wealth and power in the process. Such control was necessary for the ruling elite to ensure that the economy continued to work in their favor. Writing not only helped create a stratified society composed of an aristocracy, administrators, merchants, and laborers, it helped solidify unequal class divisions that would come to define the basic class structure of Mesopotamian society. As Schmandt-Besserat explains,

> writing, therefore, bestowed on the ruler effective control over the input of assets. By making the administration accountable for the goods received, the written receipts also conveyed mastery over the redistribution of these commodities. In other words, writing endowed the third-millennium kings with full control over communal resources. Writing was the backbone of the economy of redistribution—an economy that brought prosperity to Sumer. (Schmandt-Besserat 1996, 105)

While certainly not all wealth and land were owned by the temples and palaces, they always owned a significant portion of the economy and had a large influence on how it functioned. Records show that, at certain times in Mesopotamian history, the level of debt owed to the palace was high, and laborers frequently could not meet their daily quotas and would have to borrow to pay off their debts. The level of indebtedness was especially high for those who worked in the fields or in the textile factories where loans for silver have been estimated at 20 percent interest and loans of grain at 33 percent interest (Van De Mieroop 2007, 94). That being said, we should keep in mind the limitations of the clay-tablet archives. The great majority of cuneiform tablets that have been recovered are from temple or palace archives, so we don't have as detailed a record of how writing was used by Mesopotamians not directly engaged with the central authorities. While the temples and palaces played a central role in the shape of the economy, "their efficiency depend[ed] on private entrepreneurs and the state interacting with the private sector in the framework of some very centralized structures" (Aubet 2013, 155). As more cuneiform tablets are deciphered, our understanding of writing and economy in Mesopotamia continues to evolve.

CONCLUSION

So, what can we take away from this evolution of cuneiform as one of history's first writing systems? First, it helps us articulate how nonhuman writing technologies can enact agency and how this agency is dialectically tied to the socioeconomic development of human ecologies. The human need to inscribe and manage information for economic exchange is manifested in the clay tokens and the gradual development of cuneiform as it gets borrowed and adapted by each successive generation. The cumulative history that unfolded five thousand years ago in the early economies of Mesopotamia illustrates, in embryo, the vital metabolic relation between inscription, quantification, information production, and capital that continues to greatly determine how we use our modern digital writing technologies today.

A second takeaway from the history of cuneiform is the developmental connection between inscription and city life that emerges in southern Mesopotamia around 3500 BCE. With cities came a greater abundance of texts and information that enact agency through their cumulative force and the archives to store and manage them. The emergence of textuality, along with the bureaucracy necessary for managing it, is a perfect example of how a technology like writing, and the inscription it affords, qualitatively changes culture via the accumulation of texts. Moreover, the developmental history of cuneiform tells us that more advanced writing and archiving technologies are often used by privileged groups to consolidate wealth and power. What takes shape in ancient Mesopotamia and the emergence of writing is a form of *information hegemony* and *asymmetry* where those who had access to and knowledge about the most advanced inscription tools of the era used them to manage the economy and direct it towards their advantage.

While I don't want to overstate the relevance of this history to our modern writing tools, I find it useful for understanding how a nonhuman technology like writing, and the inscription it affords, takes on agency. Of the many insights I think Mesopotamia's experience with writing suggests about our contemporary digital environments, it raises some interesting questions about who controls information production and how that information is used to control behavior. With the rise of Web 3.0, ubiquitous inscription, and what has been called *big data*, we've entered a new stage of information production and with it, a new stage of information hegemony and asymmetry. The intensification of data collection we're experiencing now, along with the valuable flows of information it creates, are the latest iteration of the same dialectical relations between writing, inscription, the archive, and capital that first emerged in the city of Uruk over five thousand years ago.

As we continue to develop our new materialist theories of writing, we must continue to ask how (and by whom) writing and inscription technologies get leveraged to control information production and, in the process, perpetuate unequal economic relations and environmental degradation. Just as writing, inscription, and the archive were used as forms of power in ancient Mesopotamia, their use and reach by governments and corporations have only escalated in Web 3.0 and informational capitalism—the second material cumulus in the MEOW framework to which I turn to in the next chapter.

3

WEB 3.0 AND INFORMATIONAL CAPITALISM

A new commodity spawns a lucrative, fast-growing industry, prompting antitrust regulators to step in to restrain those who control its flow. A century ago, the resource in question was oil. Now similar concerns are being raised by the giants that deal in data, the oil of the digital era. (The Economist *2017*)

In this chapter I focus on the second material cumulus in the MEOW framework: the historical and ecological conditions of twenty-first-century informational capitalism. I take a closer look at the shape of writing in Web 3.0 and explore the rise of *big data* and the emergence of the global archive, the planetary networked infrastructure of inscription that ceaselessly records and collects data churned out by both human and nonhuman agents. The torrent of informational flows we are currently living through in Web 3.0, ignited by the corporate and governmental hunt to collect data on the activity of all citizen-consumers,[1] should be understood as a new phase of neoliberal, informational capitalism in which flows of data take on greater agency as the vital resource that drives capital circulation.

While it's not news that corporations and governments have long collected data on citizen-consumers, Edward Snowden's 2014 revelations about the reach of such data collection exposed the mutually beneficial relationship between the federal government and the information-technology industries[2] in the United States. Such widespread data collection and surveillance on citizen-consumers has reached unprecedented levels, and both governments and corporations have a stake in keeping

DOI: 10.7330/9781607329688.c003

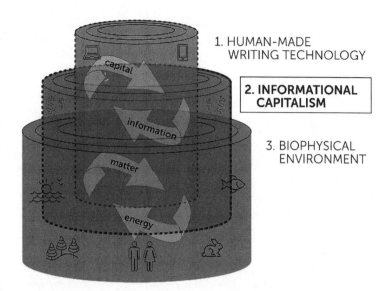

1. HUMAN-MADE
   WRITING TECHNOLOGY

**2. INFORMATIONAL
CAPITALISM**

3. BIOPHYSICAL
   ENVIRONMENT

Figure 3.1. MEOW framework, with the second material cumulus represented within the bold dotted outline. (Illustration created by Martha D. Langer, Pear Ink Design.)

such activities obscure and unregulated. In Web 3.0 we find ourselves in a world of pervasive data collection by governments worried about terrorism and by corporations determined to commodify every aspect of our lived experience through persistent datafication.

While theorizing wide-scale data collection is fairly new terrain for writing studies, scholars are starting to explore some of the ways in which ubiquitous inscription challenges our basic understandings of writing and rhetoric. Work that looks at the rhetoric of algorithms (Gallagher 2017; Reyman 2018), the internet-of-things (Zappen 2018; Pfister 2018), cookies and tracking (Beck 2015; Vie and Dewinter 2015); recording and inscription (Nicotra 2017b), and augmented publics (Boyle and Rivers 2018) have started to lay the groundwork for developing more critical, materialist theories of writing in the informational economies of Web 3.0. MEOW draws on this scholarship to theorize specifically how flows of data and information, produced by our writing and activities online, intertwine with flows of capital, and how those flows metabolize with flows of energy and matter.

The information technology industries have labeled the massive influx of data production we are currently living through *big data*. As concept and ethos, big data represents the latest stage in the long development of the global archive and pervasive data collection on citizen-consumers that begins in the United States at the end of the nineteenth century. I explore this history in this chapter to contextualize the roots of our current data environments and the central role that data collection on citizen-consumers has played in the emergence of twenty-first-century informational capitalism. The rise of big data is just one expression of the ways our modern writing and inscription technologies take on greater agency in the circulation of capital. The intensifying relation between information production and capital, in turn, metabolizes with flows of energy and matter in ways that are manifestly harmful to human ecosystems at every scale, from the permeable systems of our bodies to the endangered biosphere of the planet.

In theorizing big data as a form of writing and inscription, I begin this chapter by taking a critical look at what I call *Web 2.0 writing theory*. I trace how writing studies scholars have historically theorized data production and argue that we must reconceptualize some of the basic theoretical tendencies of Web 2.0 writing theory in order to develop more robust materialist theories of writing in Web 3.0. The first tendency is to overemphasize the *use value* of online writing while glossing over its economic *exchange value*, and the second tendency is a *productivist ethos* that assumes *more* writing in culture is intrinsically more valuable than *less* writing. Such tendencies reflect the same pattern of backgrounding the agentive forces of capital and the biophysical environment in our study of writing that I've been critiquing throughout this work.

When we start to trace where digital writing goes, along with the flows of data and information it generates, we find that a large proportion of such flows are controlled and owned by private corporations, not only by obvious ones like Google, Facebook, and Amazon, but a multitude of actor networks, all part of what I call in this chapter the *corporate data complex*—the thousands of companies that collect and commodify data on citizen-consumers. This includes the data platforms that collect the raw data (e.g., Google, Facebook, Amazon), the data brokers who combine it with other flows of data they collect from sources like public records and health data (e.g., Acxiom, Experian), and the marketers who purchase the insights gleaned by data brokers to better target citizen-consumers. The rise of big data and the corporate data complex has created a new era of information hegemony and asymmetry where private corporations leverage ubiquitous inscription tools to own and control the global production and flow of data created by the citizen-consumers who use these tools.

In light of this large network of actors and in exploring the second material cumulus, in this chapter I trace the history and current shape of the corporate data complex and take a closer look at how growing flows of data, fed by the semantic information and data/metadata we produce, metabolize with flows of capital.

WEB 2.0 WRITING THEORY

To be sure, I don't want to overstate the significance of the shift from Web 2.0 to Web 3.0. While aspects of this shift are certainly radical, in a cumulative, historical framework like MEOW, the present is continually emerging from the cultural conditions that have evolved over time. Nevertheless, in the transition from Web 2.0 to Web 3.0, we are living through a turbulent period of change as our digital writing tools mature and the production of data and information accelerates.

The concept of Web 2.0 is now around twenty years old.[3] It was originally coined to describe the shape of the Web at the turn of the twenty-first century, what many have called the *social Web*—a global computer network built on interactive platforms that encouraged sharing, collaboration, connection, and writing between users. The participatory ethos of Web 2.0, along with the infrastructure of the global archive that makes it possible, have spurred tremendous growth in the amount of writing and rhetorical activity we now engage in every day. For the most part, the textual fecundity of Web 2.0 has been embraced by writing studies scholars as signaling a qualitatively new public sphere where we write more than ever—leading to a particular way of thinking about digital writing that I call *Web 2.0 writing theory*. Web 2.0 writing theory foregrounds the social aspects of writing and makes the tacit assumption that a more accessible public sphere, enabled by social media and digital networks, translates into higher levels of civic participation and more opportunities for realizing individual human agency (Porter 2010; Clark 2009; Dilger 2010; Wolff 2013).

Work that exemplifies Web 2.0 writing theory is captured well in the Stanford Study of Writing (2001–2006) (Lunsford et al. 2019). Andrea Lunsford and colleagues analyzed over fourteen thousand pieces of student writing, written in and out of class, over a five-year period. In referring to the study's results in a 2009 interview with *Wired* magazine, Lunsford refutes the popular myth that Web 2.0 writing technologies are ruining students' abilities to write thoughtful, academic prose. In fact, she argues, "we're in the midst of a literacy revolution the likes of which we haven't seen since Greek civilization" (Thompson 2009). As Lunsford emphasizes, digital writing tools aren't "killing our ability to write"; rather, they're "reviving it—and pushing our literacy in bold new directions" (Thompson 2009).

Others have voiced similar excitement. J. Elizabeth Clark argues that, in Web 2.0, we are entering "a new era of digital rhetoric where, more than ever before, people are becoming authors every day, constructing digital profiles, public commentary, and using publicly available resources to research and inform their opinions" (Clark 2010, 27). James Porter argues that the companies that thrive in Web 2.0 are the ones that help writers build "productive and pragmatic knowledge about how to create information products that will matter to people—that is, be usable and useful" (Porter 2010, 174). Perhaps Kathleen Blake Yancey best captures the excitement that Web 2.0 evokes in writing and rhetoric scholars when she writes about the kinds of value students receive when writing in Web 2.0: "Whatever the exchange value may be for these writers . . . it's certainly not grades. Rather, the writing seems to operate in an economy driven by use value" (Yancey 2004, 301). Throughout all of this excellent scholarship there is an explicit emphasis on the *growth* of textual production in Web 2.0 and the valuable *use* that writers receive from it. As Porter stresses, "the secret of the Web 2.0 dynamic" is not the economic value we receive from using online platforms, but rather the social and emotional benefits we receive from greater participation on such platforms (Porter 2010, 176).

I too embrace this excitement. Many of the cultural changes that have emerged in Web 2.0 are cause for celebration and Web 2.0 writing theory rightly emphasizes the democratic potential of these technologies. At the same time, in light of big data and some of the social and environmental problems that are emerging in Web 3.0, we must be careful in our new materialist theories of writing not to detach the *use value* we receive from online writing from the larger economic systems of informational capitalism and the lucrative *exchange value* of the data that is produced by this writing and our other online activities. As Marx theorizes in *Capital*, commodities emerge when an object takes on two types of value simultaneously, a *use value* and an *exchange value*. In informational capitalism, writing and information are keystone commodities. As such, their high use value for citizen-consumers is dialectically tied to their high exchange value for corporate data platforms. As I argued last chapter in my discussion on the origins of writing in ancient Mesopotamia, the long evolution from clay tokens to clay tablets presents a compelling case for a cumulative and developmental relation between writing, economic development, and capital circulation through history. Those same dialectical relations continue apace in Web 3.0 where the high use value of online writing propels the lucrative exchange value of the data/metadata it produces.

We've seen this history unfold as we've moved from Web 1.0 to Web 2.0 and now to Web 3.0, in which the use value of our online writing initially preceded its exchange value. The Web 2.0 companies that made it through the Web 1.0 bubble had done so because they prioritized *use* and *functionality* in their platform designs. The goal of attracting an audience was the same, but by prioritizing *use* Web 2.0 companies could build a critical mass of users whose data production could potentially be exploited for profit at a later point. In 2005, when Web 2.0 was establishing a foothold in American culture, though most companies didn't know exactly how to monetize the data they were collecting, the potential value of the data was never a question. In Facebook's initial public offering (IPO) in 2012, the company was valued at $104 billion, the largest IPO for a technology company to date. On paper, Facebook only owned $15 billion in assets. The other $89 billion of the valuation was based on the speculation that Facebook's tentacular reach and growing troves of data on the behavior, likes, and dislikes of citizen-consumers would eventually reap huge profits (Cukier and Mayer-Schonberger 2013). Today, Facebook is valued at close to $600 billion (Facebook Market Cap 2009–2019). Thus, the "secret of the web 2.0 dynamic" (Porter 2010), embedded in the contexts of twenty-first-century neoliberal, informational capitalism could never be *just* about the use value we receive from online writing; it also lies in the continual development of writing and inscription technologies to stimulate and expand our production of commodified data and information.

In understanding the second material cumulus and the materiality of writing in Web 3.0 then, we must grapple with the immense exchange value of digital writing. This shift in theoretical perspective begins by tempering the *productivist* assumptions of Web 2.0 writing theory. I borrow the concept from critical sociologist Anthony Giddens. For Giddens, productivism is the belief that *growth and productivity* in human ecosystems are more important than other measures of ecosystem health like equal access to resources or the effective management of waste production (Giddens 1994, 247). For productivism, the phenomenon of *growth itself* is the standard for assessing the health and value of a system, be it human or nonhuman. Web 2.0 writing

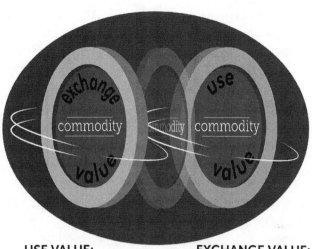

USE VALUE:
The social value we receive through our "free" use of an online platform

EXCHANGE VALUE:
The monetary value of the data/metadata produced by our activities and writing online

Figure 3.2. Graphic depicting a spinning two-sided coin to illustrate the dialectical relation between use value and exchange value that defines the basic value of a commodity. In Web 3.0, the use value we receive from using online writing tools exists via the lucrative exchange value of the data/metadata we produce as a result of our use of these tools. (Illustration created by Martha D. Langer, Pear Ink Design.)

theory is productivist because it assumes that more textual production is *intrinsically positive* for individuals and human ecosystems alike.

From a materialist, ecological perspective like MEOW, productivism is problematic because real biophysical ecosystems have limits on their size and growth based on their environmental surroundings and the natural limits of metabolism itself. For living ecosystems to function and survive, they must perpetually enact the metabolic cycles of producing, consuming, and excreting energy, matter, and information. Such cycles go through different phases, but they are not designed to continually grow; they are designed, instead, to find the optimal balance for sustaining the metabolism of the ecosystem under conditions that are continually emerging. All ecosystems have limits to their growth and they run into trouble when any particular metabolic flow outgrows the others, unbalancing and putting a strain on the system. The most obvious example of this is climate change and the productivist forces of neoliberal capitalism. As we burn more fossil fuels that have remained dormant in the earth for millions of years, we release more CO_2 into the active metabolism of the planet. This increase of CO_2, driven by the global demand for oil, is overloading the natural cycles of the planet and destabilizing how flows of energy and matter metabolize through it. The same holds true for human ecosystems in Web 3.0 where accelerating flows of commodified information are dangerously accelerating the consumption of natural resources and energy, and, in the process, contributing to growing social and environmental antagonisms around the globe.

By recoupling the use and exchange value of the writing we do and questioning the implicit productivism in Web 2.0 writing theory, MEOW explicitly foregrounds how growing textuality and accelerating information production dangerously accelerate the metabolic relations between capital, energy, and matter as they circulate through human ecosystems. MEOW makes two key theoretical adjustments by explicitly foregrounding how growing textuality and information production are metabolically tied to (1) capital circulation and (2) the biophysical environment.

BIG DATA: FROM DATA SCARCITY TO DATA ABUNDANCE

In understanding how our writing and online activities get entangled with flows of capital, we need to have an understanding of how data flows and accumulates in the global archive of the internet. At the heart of the global archive sits the data center. Data centers around the globe are essential nonhuman agents for collecting and circulating data, and their size, location, and ownership tell us a lot about how information flows and who controls it. As I mentioned earlier, the information technology industries have labeled the data deluge we are living through *big data*. While surely big data is another marketing catch phrase to sell servers and software, as data collection expands into every aspect of socioeconomic life, we are learning quickly that the phenomenon of big data, and the global archive it flows through, radically challenge both our social and materialist theories of writing and inscription.

As a concept, big data describes the exponential growth in data production that has emerged in the past two decades in tandem with faster computer processing, greater data compression, bottomless data storage, and the global buildout of the internet. Big data is different from conventional understandings of data as carefully collected and managed through hierarchical, relational databases. In contrast, the escalating growth of data now being produced by our online activities is of such volume and speed that relational databases are ill-equipped to process it. Making sense of big data requires networked servers and algorithmic modeling to process the petabytes of data that flow in from multiple sources, churned out by both human activity and the billions of nonhuman agents (sensors, chips, cookies, scripts, beacons) that are connected to the internet (see also Mayer-Schönberger and Cukier 2013; Beck 2015; Stephens-Davidowitz 2017; Zappen 2018). As Danah Boyd and Katie Crawford describe it, big data is a new "model of intelligibility" (Boyd and Crawford 2012) where the unprecedented growth in the production and collection of consumer-citizen data ruptures our standard research methods and the traditional search for *causation* in carefully curated data sets. Big data places new emphasis on finding *correlations* and statistical relationships across large data sets using unstructured data bases and algorithms.

In their book *Big Data: A Revolution That Will Transform How We Live, Work, and Think* (2013), Victor Mayer-Schönberger and Kenneth Cukier explain that, before the rise of big data and the development of the hardware and software that make it possible, scientists and marketers developed the research technique of *sampling* in the "data scarce world" of the twentieth century (Mayer-Schönberger and Cukier 2013, 30). Sampling was developed as a way to get around the cost and difficulties of collecting data in a data scarce world by using small, random

samples of data from larger potential data sets to make infer-
ences and hypotheses about the larger data set. In Web 3.0,
however, we are living in new era of *data abundance*. For data
corporations in the business of making profit, big data means
the size of the sample grows exponentially. By collecting data
on millions of citizen-consumers, corporations have a much
larger representation of people, with more data points on each
person, and a more continuous flow of data, often in real time.
It is the unprecedented breadth, depth, and speed of big data
that make it a new "model of intelligibility." Larger, more precise sampling through intensified data collection means new
and more accurate patterns and correlations can be discovered
at the micro level of the individual, as well as the macro level of
a region or country. In a world of data abundance, correlation
analysis becomes more extensive and precise at the same time,
greatly enhancing a corporation's abilities to surveil and study
consumer patterns across several streams of data. In Web 3.0,
corporations routinely leverage big data for making business
decisions and developing predictive models to better anticipate
the behavior and purchasing habits of citizen-consumers.

While the term big data didn't initially invoke associations
with other corporate monoliths like "big oil" and "big tobacco,"
the predatory nature of pervasive data collection now puts the
data and information technology industries in a similar category as the oil and tobacco industries—industries monopolized
by a few companies that wield their power to limit competition
and continually expand their control over the economy, often
in ways that harm citizen-consumers and the natural environment. Emerging problems with privacy violations, surveillance
overreach, data breaches, misinformation campaigns, racial and
political bias in search algorithms, and the normalized selling of
our personal information are clear examples of how the largely
unregulated corporate data complex, and its zealous effort to
colonize more streams of data, are having profound socioeconomic effects across the globe. In Web 3.0 and the internet-of-
things, big data has become the coveted raw material that powers
twenty-first-century informational capitalism.

In May 2018, the European Union enacted the first substantial regulatory laws for corporate data collection and privacy protections called the General Data Protection Regulation (GDPR). All European citizens are protected under the law, and American corporations will have to abide by the regulations or face costly fines. Under the GDPR, corporations have to be more transparent about their data-collecting practices and citizen-consumers have more control over what data is collected about them and are given the option of opting out of data collection completely.

As of early 2020, the United States has not enacted any federal laws regulating data collection, though there are several bills currently under discussion that offer stronger data protections for citizen-consumers and more stringent regulation over the data industries. Twenty nine states now have consumer data protection laws of varying degrees in place (Singer 2019; Beckerman 2019). Passing and upholding such laws will be vital to the protections and rights of citizen-consumers. With the European GDPR leading the way globally towards more oversight and transparency in the data industries, such regulation will be an ongoing struggle as the tools for inscription continue to aggressively develop and expand.

THE CUMULATIVE DEVELOPMENT OF THE CORPORATE DATA COMPLEX

In understanding the socioeconomic implications of big data and how data abundance challenges our materialist theories of writing, we need to parse the different kinds of corporate data collection underway. We can start by distinguishing the different kinds of platforms that have emerged in Web 3.0. Nick Srnicek in *Platform Capitalism* (2017) breaks them down into five types: *advertising platforms* (Google, Facebook, LinkedIn); *cloud platforms* (Amazon, Apple, Cisco); *industrial platforms* (General Electric, Siemens); *service platforms* (Spotify, Adobe Creative Suite, Zillow); and *lean platforms* (Uber, Air BnB). All of these categories fall under the umbrella term of big data, and while each platform uses data in different ways, collecting, analyzing, and commodifying it is the foundation of their business model. As Srnicek cogently describes, the business model of the data platform emerges early in the twenty-first century, formed out of the crucible of Web 1.0 and the need for internet companies to process the massive amounts of computing data being generated as a normal byproduct of hosting a networked, digital platform on the internet—data on network traffic and functionality of the site, users IP addresses, usernames, passwords, zip codes, language, etc. Pioneers like Google, Yahoo, Facebook, and Amazon all developed new ways to collect, handle, store, and analyze this operational data, and, in the process, developed the algorithms that could turn this data into valuable information about users. Due to the immense success and reach of these companies and their innovations in data management, the data platform has become a basic corporate tool for doing business in Web 3.0 (Srnicek 2017, chapter 1).

Thus, platforms are much more than simple free online tools. More precisely, they are "an extractive apparatus for data" (Srnicek 2017, 85). Platforms are designed to organize and facilitate human and nonhuman activity *by collecting as much data as possible about these activities.* Facebook organizes social connections; LinkedIn organizes business relationships; Match.com, dating. Our use of the platform creates large flows of data and metadata about who we are and how we use the platform—data that provides unique and valuable insight into our behavior. In terms of the internet-of-things, data platforms extract data produced by devices and sensors that monitor every kind of natural and phenomenological activity, from delivery companies collecting continuous data on vehicle performance, to wearable tech monitoring heart rates, to farmers gauging when to plant their crops.

Most relevant to my discussion here are advertising platforms. Advertising platforms like Google, Yahoo, Facebook, and Amazon are the prototypes of the platform business model. Not only has their model of organizing and managing human activity through extractive data collection led the way in showing the value of big data, their extensive experience with large-scale data processing has given them a head start in developing the most advanced and sophisticated inscription tools in existence. Their intense experience with data collection over the last two decades has, in turn, led to their monopoly control over the way data flows and pools in Web 3.0. Along with the entire corporate data complex, corporate advertising platforms like Google, Facebook, and Amazon own and control large flows of information about citizen-consumers. Because they were in the data game early, they have continued to grow by aggressively buying out start-ups and expanding their abilities to control how data and information flow. This living history is a fundamental part of the second material cumulus and it provides context for us to understand the emergence of Web 3.0 and the power that comes with corporate control over the platforms and networks that information flows through.

As I pointed out in the last chapter in my discussion of cuneiform in Mesopotamia, there is a developmental pattern that begins early in the history of writing that shows that those groups who control the most sophisticated writing and inscription tools available often leverage these tools to control how information is produced and flows. This same pattern has emerged in the transition from Web 2.0 to Web 3.0. Google, Facebook, and Amazon dominate where and how information and data flow on the internet. All three were in the twelve most-visited sites in the United States in 2019, with Google and its subsidiary, YouTube, ranked number one and two respectively. Facebook came in at number four, and Amazon at number twelve ("The Top 500 Sites on the Web" 2020). Google owns 90 percent of the search market around the world (outside of China) and Facebook currently boasts over two billion active users—up from eight hundred million in 2012. It's been estimated that the two platforms together have some level of influence on over 70 percent of internet traffic (Staltz 2017) and take in over 80 percent of global spending on internet advertising due to their massive market share and reach in data collection (Giles 2018).

To be sure, Amazon is becoming an entirely different behemoth. In 2019 it handled almost 50 percent of all ecommerce transactions in the United States, generating over $50 billion in sales ($40 billion more than its nearest competitor, Walmart). In 2018, Google, Apple, Facebook, and Amazon—often referred to as GAFA—were four of the five wealthiest internet corporations in the world with an estimated market value of $2.9 trillion—a figure larger than the GDP of India, the seventh largest economy in the world (Statista 2017; Galloway 2018; Montasell 2019).

In understanding the historical conditions that have given rise to informational capitalism and the central role that advertising data platforms play in Web 3.0, we need to place them in the longer evolution of the *corporate data complex:* the industry of platforms, brokers, and marketers who tirelessly collect and mine data on citizen-consumers. Advertising data platforms are just one vital piece to a larger data-collection industry that began to take shape in the United States over a century ago.

In *The Control Revolution* (1986), James Beniger argues that the roots of modern data collection on citizen-consumers can be traced to the industrialization of the US economy during the mid-nineteenth century. He explains that the explosive growth in commodity production during this era created a "crisis of control." By "control," Beniger means any "purposive influence on behavior" (Beniger 1986, 8). With new forms of steam power and the growing use of electricity across the country, the manufacturing capacities of US businesses began to accelerate, creating for the first time in American history a national economy in which the production of commodities outstripped demand. In such a new environment of excess, corporations and governments scrambled to move surplus product. What emerges, alongside developments in telephony, printing, and the railroads, are the nascent glimmers of mass culture and the earliest forms of mass advertising to control demand and stimulate consumption (Beniger 1986, 18). To jumpstart the stagnating flows of products, companies started to give them a push by giving them a voice—a catch phrase or a logo—to distinguish themselves from other commodities, a practice we call "branding" today. The practice of commercial branding arises at the same time as mass consumer culture does in the United States, at the beginning of the twentieth century. This response by American culture to industrialization (1880–1940) marks the general period when the United States begins to transition from an industrial-based economy into an informational one.

It is during this transition that flows of information, much of it produced and disseminated by marketing and advertising agencies, begin to play a larger role in the economy and the circulation of capital. As all good rhetors know, the more you know about your audience, the more you are able to craft the right appeals. To come to know their audience in an age of mass culture, advertising and marketing agencies invented new ways to learn about consumers by creating new ways to collect data on them—their habits, preferences, and behaviors. New genres like opinion surveys and questionnaires, new sampling methods, and new ways to store and analyze this data, helped create the first networks and archives for inscribing mass consumer culture in the United States (Beniger 1986, 20). What emerges in the United States in the early twentieth century is the first wide-scale data collection efforts on citizen-consumers for the deliberate purpose to stimulate and influence consumption. With the rise of industrialization and mass production, the forces of capitalist production began laying the technological and semiotic groundwork for pervasive data collection on citizen-consumers that would help create the material social conditions for the emergence of computer networks, informational economies, and the eventual development of the entire corporate data complex.

DATA AND INFORMATION AS RHETORICAL WEAPONS

Web 3.0 is the current culmination of this ongoing development, a process of data collection that is accelerating as the corporate data complex further infiltrates more aspects of our daily lives. In understanding how this corporate-data complex functions in Web 3.0, we can start by looking at how consumer-citizen data is collected, processed, and turned against us through algorithmic and predictive modeling. Even though we are all getting use to the targeted ads that stalk us online, it's worth exploring some of the technological and automated processes behind the ways ads find us and how our data is used to influence and control our behavior.

A useful tool for visualizing how consumer targeting works is Firefox's browser add-on "Lightbeam."[4] With Lightbeam, users can "track the trackers"—that is, visibly track which companies are placing cookies on their computers and tracking their every move, click, like, and purchase they do online. When you visit a site online, Lightbeam records the number of tracking devices that are installed and displays them in a kind of network graph.

Figure 3.3 is an example of such a graph showing what happens when you visit a common news site like Huffington Post Online. One visit to Huffpost and a computer is assailed by over thirty different tracking technologies (cookies and beacons).[5] Many of these technologies are used by the hosting site for basic site analytics and other functions like remembering your password or what you put in the shopping cart. However, the majority of cookies placed are by third parties (25 in this case). Third parties are other data companies who have agreements with the host site to install their own cookies on visitors' computers. As internet regulation stands now in the United States, for many sites, just by visiting we agree to the collection of any data we create while there. We also agree to let third-party companies they have agreements with place their own tracking technologies on our computers and devices. These third-party companies can range from marketing and advertising firms to data aggregation firms that package and resell the consumer insights they glean about us by recording our click stream as we move through the internet.

Huffington Post isn't unique in this case. According to the *Wall Street Journal*'s series "What They Know," "the largest U.S. websites are installing new and intrusive consumer-tracking technologies on the computers of people visiting their sites—in some

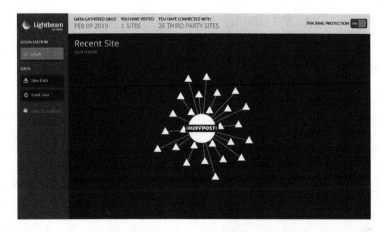

Figure 3.3. Screen capture of Firefox add-on "Lightbeam," showing 26 different third-party sites that install tracking devices (cookies and beacons) on users' computers when they visit a standard-content site like Huffington Post Online. (Permissions by the Mozilla Foundation.)

cases, more than 100 tracking tools at a time" (wsj.com 2012). Though news sites tend to have the most trackers, research from Princeton's Web Transparency and Accountability project has identified over eighty thousand different types of third party data trackers, with an average of twenty trackers present for the majority of sites we visit online (Englehardt and Narayanan 2016). Cookies, of course, are just one technology that facilitates data collection. Because cookies don't function on mobile devices, the data industries have developed new ways to track consumers without them. By cross-referencing the times we go online and what we do there on different devices, companies triangulate these different flows of data to "fingerprint" our identities and build an even more accurate picture of who they think we are, all while capturing more flows of data in the process.

Although data platforms like Google and Facebook have come under more scrutiny in the past few years by the mainstream press, government, and academics,[6] most of us rarely consider the thousands of third-party companies that are involved in the data industry. It isn't simply Google and Facebook that accumulate data about us—it's actually thousands of companies. Third-party data brokers are powerful, mostly unregulated, and often obscure actors in Web 3.0 who actively collect and commodify flows of citizen-consumer data. Their services entail gathering and analyzing data from every available source, both online and off, from web searches, likes, emails, and reviews, to pharmacy prescription lists, government census data, and employment records we produce in the physical world. According to a 2014 study by the US Federal Trade Commission (FTC), it's estimated there are over four thousand such companies in existence, with some like Acxiom and Experian holding data on almost every American consumer and millions of others around the world. Acxiom claims to have over three thousand different data points on the majority of Americans (Acxiom 2019), while many others claim to have at least 1,500 data points on every American consumer (FTC 2014). Such pervasive tracking and surveillance has only intensified in the past five years as more consumers access the internet using mobile devices.

I realize I'm not saying anything that the majority of citizen-consumers aren't already aware of. Americans, at least, seem to have quietly acquiesced to rampant data collection and targeted advertising as a fair exchange for content and convenience. But is this really all that is being traded, and how fair of a trade is it? What are some of the less obvious costs associated with ubiquitous inscription and corporate data collection? If it was only targeted advertising we had to worry about, that might be acceptable, but targeted advertising is only one of many ways our data is put to use, for and against us. In addition to predatory, targeted advertising, the corporate data complex uses our data to control and personalize our content and searches, adjust prices on the fly based on past purchasing history, and do credit and background checks. Such uses of data, for both good and ill purposes, remind us that wide-scale data collection permeates our society, and it is a very lucrative source of socioeconomic power.

Much of this power comes from *information asymmetry*—owning and controlling flows and pools of privatized information that is unavailable for use by the majority of citizen-consumers.[7] One of the greatest sources of power that comes from controlling flows of information is its use in building predictive models of human behavior and consumption. Predictive modeling is the process of developing computerized models based on the analysis of large data sets and finding correlations across these data sets. In his book *Predictive Analytics*, data scientist Eric Siegel argues that the term *predictive analytics* is preferable to "big data" or "data mining" because it better describes how businesses put data to work through predictive modeling. The shift in emphasis from data production to machine learning highlights the critical role that automation and algorithms play in turning data into actionable insights. The value in predictions, Siegal notes, is in the *persuasion effect*—a phrase that should catch the attention of writing and rhetoric scholars (Siegel 2013, 27). The persuasion effect is another way to describe the primary purpose of corporate data collection—to influence citizen-consumers by predicting their future behavior based on their previous actions and the correlations discovered through the algorithmic analysis of other large data sets on citizen-consumer behavior.

This persuasion effect is vividly depicted in an infographic created by the Interactive Advertising Bureau (IAB), a leading professional organization for the online advertising industry (figure 3.4). The "Engagement Continuum Metrics" graphic comes from the IAB's annual public report from 2014. The report covers the current economic health of the industry and helps codify industry standards for the use of data and online advertising. The playfulness of the model belies a subtle rhetoric. One of the explicit goals of the group is to articulate a broad consensus on the meaning of "engagement" and develop a core set of thirty metrics to accurately measure the impact of online advertising and whether or not it influences the purchasing behaviors of citizen-consumers.

On the outer rim of the graphic, the arrows show different phases of *pre-engagement* to *consumer/brand,* and *attention plus* to *consumer/brand* again. What these cryptic terms describe is the persistent process of reminding consumers about products they

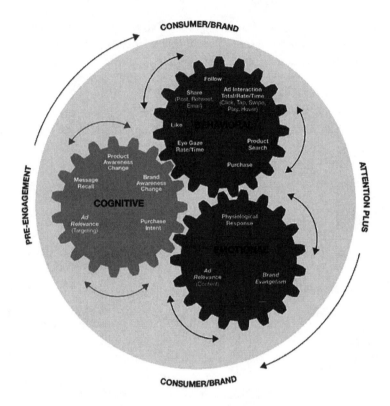

Figure 3.4. Graphic from the Interactive Advertising Bureau's report on how best to stimulate "engagement" with consumers based on collecting behavioral, cognitive, and emotional data on our interactions with ads and digital devices. (IAB 2014; permissions by IAB.)

may be interested in. The three cogs in the middle—cognitive, behavioral, and emotional—describe the rhetorical "targets" that internet advertisers aim for in their relentless drive to engage consumer attention. This is a strategy of persuasion that goes beyond enticing users with ads; it is a more systematized and psychologized approach designed to influence purchases and produce larger, more precise, and perpetual data flows on the personal and emotional lives of citizen-consumers.

I'll say more about such methods in chapter 6 when I take a closer look at how the corporate data complex uses brain science and behavioral psychology to take advantage of our natural responses to environmental stimuli. I introduce the graphic here to provide a basic understanding of the persistent and multifaceted process of data collection and how the corporate data complex amasses detailed profiles of us based on the data we create every second of the day. As more and more data is collected and combined, the more thorough these profiles become, often containing thousands of different data points combed from online data and offline data from public records, medical records, loyalty cards, and credit card purchases. This data is then analyzed and used to categorize us into marketing demographics. A 2016 study by ProPublica.org found that Facebook had developed over fifty-two thousand different "categories of interest" that they used to parse citizen-consumers, categories ranging from general terms such as "millennial" or "frequent traveler" to more specific categories based on income and education level, and groupings with names like "Pretending to Text in Awkward Situations," or "Breastfeeding in Public" (Angwin 2016). Finer-grained data collection allows them to develop more detailed profiles that can be sold for more precise and targeted advertising.

In addition to targeting consumers through detailed categorization, Experian, one of the country's largest data brokers, sells consumer profiles based on "life-event triggers." Experian monitors citizen-consumers through persistent data collection to predict when someone is nearing a major life event like having a child, buying a house, or getting married ("Consumer View" 2018). Marketers purchase this data to develop more timely ways to intervene and influence the purchasing decisions of citizen-consumers. It's the kind of rhetorical practice that gives *kairos* new meaning. Such real-time information about us is continuously sold on one of the many data exchanges that exist. Further concerns arise on these data exchanges with how citizen-consumers are categorized and sifted, exposing them to systematic and algorithmic discrimination based on race, gender, and income (Turow 2013, 158–160; Devlin 2016).[8] Despite growing public awareness of such practices, business is good.

Research from the Interactive Advertising Bureau (IAB) shows that revenue from online advertising has grown no less than 10 percent a year since 2000. In 2018, online ad revenue surpassed $100 billion.[9]

Such trends are troubling and they raise serious questions about the potential long range material and social effects of intensifying data collection and amassing detailed portfolios on hundreds of millions of citizen-consumers. While our current informational economies have their roots in the U.S. industrial revolution, today we are witnessing the maturation of corporate data collection as the cumulative, living embodiment of more than a century's worth of enhancing data collection technologies and expanding the global archive. The radical effects of intensifying data collection on human and nonhumans ecosystems goes well beyond the petty "creepiness" of targeted advertising. In fact, the popular use of "creepy" to describe how we feel when targeted ads follow us online grossly underestimates the manipulative and predatory nature of the corporate data complex in Web 3.0. We should make no mistake, big data is the next stage of informational capitalism, a squeezing of the invisible hand of the market through wide-scale surveillance and data collection on citizen-consumers and the use of pervasive inscription technologies to manage, ever finely, our socioeconomic lives.

SELF-AUGMENTATION AND PERPETUAL FLOWS OF INFORMATION

In making sense of intensifying data collection and its relation to our modern experience of writing, it's vital we understand the processes behind how consumer-citizen data is produced and commodified. From the perspective of the second material cumulus, we need to identify the corporate data platforms that own and leverage the most sophisticated inscription tools. Such platforms are designed to datafy and colonize large swaths of human and nonhuman activity through inscription. Huge corporate data platforms like Google, Facebook, and Amazon have, for all intents and purposes, monopolized large sectors of human activity and the data that comes along with it. They therefore play a central part in how commodified data flows. For these monopolies to persist, and for them to maintain their hegemonic control over information, *the data must continue to flow.* To ensure that this process continually reproduces itself, corporate data platforms aggressively collect consumer-citizen data to not only influence citizen-consumers' decisions and behaviors, but also to stimulate *more* flows of data in the process.

Figure 3.5 illustrates the self-augmenting process of data and information production in Web 3.0. The process is self-augmenting because it is designed to continually reproduce the flows of data needed to keep the cycle going and achieve its ultimate end—accelerate capital circulation. The writing and activity we do online, as well as the data churned out by the internet-of-things (stage 1), produces large flows of data that are inscribed and collected in the archive of the corporate data platform and data center (stage 2). This data is then analyzed and correlated using machine learning to categorize citizen-consumers and develop algorithms that can be used to predict future behavior (stage 3). The data is then mined for correlations and insights on citizen-consumers (stage 4) and then packaged and sold to marketers who develop the rhetorical strategies to engage consumers and, ideally, keep the data cycle going by continuing to stimulate more data production by citizen-consumers. From the perspective of the individual human agent, this cycle of predatory data collection is particularly virulent for the ways it turns Web 3.0 writers into "double objects of commodification" (Fuchs 2012a, 57)—where the data we create is doubled back upon us through targeted ads and an "intensified exposure to commodity logic" (Fuchs 2012a, 57; Turow 2013). By continually amassing data about individuals, the corporate data complex can better predict our future spending behavior *and* keep the production of data flowing simultaneously.

Likewise, we must keep in mind that, while the impact that corporate data collection has on individuals is important, of

*Figure 3.5. Self-augmenting data flows in Web 3.0. The production of commodi-
fied data moves through five fluid stages from the moment we go online and
engage the global Internet. The data we create (stage 1) is archived and stored
(stage 2) until it is fed through algorithmic models and predictive analytics
(stage 3) to find valuable correlations and insights (stage 4) that can be packaged and sold to marketers, who turn the data into engagement strategies with
consumers (stage 5) to sell products and, ideally, continue to reproduce the
data that will keep the system regenerating itself (back to stage 1). (Illustration
created by Martha D. Langer, Pear Ink Design.)*

equal concern is the immense amount of socioeconomic power
that comes with data in the aggregate. We often miss this larger
point when we focus too narrowly on the privacy and data rights
of individuals. It isn't the individual's data alone that is worth
our critical attention; it's also the insight and power that comes
with understanding consumer behavior at the macro level. At
the scale of big data, the corporate data complex has unprecedented insight into the lives and behavior of millions of citizen-
consumers. As such, the "intensified exposure to commodity

logic" we experience in Web 3.0 isn't simply the creepy advertisements that follow us around the web; it is also, more problematically, the constant exposure to suggestive selling and the micromanagement of human behavior, from the level of the individual to the level of the global. As computer science professor and early Web pioneer Jaron Lanier explains it, the corporate data platforms "have not built a profile of you alone, they've built a behavioral model that is predictive. That's the crucial difference" (Lanier 2014). By continually amassing data about individuals, and correlating this with data collected about millions of other individuals, the reach and depth of the corporate data complex effectively permeates every aspect of our lives, from influencing an individual's buying decisions, to persuading large populations on how to vote in national elections.

CONCLUSION

As we move deeper into Web 3.0 and informational capitalism, our new materialist theories of writing must grapple with big data and accelerating information production. In the context of ubiquitous inscription and the global archive, we must acknowledge that we have forfeited control of a large part of our computing environment to the corporate data complex. We find ourselves ensconced in an automated world in which nonhuman inscription systems take on more agentive force than individual human agents. What has emerged is a relentless cycle of data collection that is creating several social and ecological antagonisms as a result. Understanding these antagonisms is more urgent than ever. Problems with misinformation, illegal use of voter data, and the dozens of data braches that occur every day at U.S. corporations (Green and Hanbury 2018; Fraud.org) further erode citizen-consumer privacy and information rights.

Moreover, we must come to understand the real value of the data our writing and online activities create, something we have greatly undervalued in our focus on the use value of digital writing. Not only is value created through the insights gleaned by the data and meta data produced by citizen-consumers, another layer of value is created when our data is used to develop machine learning and artificial intelligence tools like facial recognition, natural-language processing, and driverless cars. This kind of innovation, and the information asymmetry that it engenders, helps corporate data platforms strengthen their monopoly control over how information is produced and flows in Web 3.0, and it gives them immense advantages in controlling human activity, innovating new products, and cornering new markets.

In addition to these socioeconomic antagonisms that are emerging in Web 3.0, accelerating information production is having radical impacts on the biophysical environment. In the productivist ethos of the corporate data complex, there can never be a limit to the amount of writing and data that flows. From a metabolic perspective this presents a problem. For data platforms with bottomless storage capacity, there doesn't appear to be technical limits on the amount of information that can be produced—the faster data flows, the better. But for finite flows of energy and matter, accelerating information production dangerously accelerates the natural metabolism of the planet in harmful and unsustainable ways. As a result, accelerating flows of information are having detrimental effects on human ecosystems and our ability to sustainably process the accelerating amounts of waste that come with information production.

It is to these concerns I turn to in the next two chapters when I dive into the third material cumulus in the MEOW framework—the biophysical environment. I explore some of the more troubling ecological issues that are emerging with ubiquitous inscription, including the profound effects of acceleration on the natural environment, the toxic problem of electronic waste, and the felt impact of big data on our permeable bodies, our memories, and our abilities to write.

4

INFORMATION PRODUCTION, ACCELERATION, AND THE BIOPHYSICAL ENVIRONMENT

Information is not tangible; it is not a solid or a fluid. It does not have its own particle either, but it is as physical as movement and temperature . . . Information is incorporeal, but it is always physically embodied. Information is not a thing; rather, it is the arrangement of physical things. (Cesar Hidalgo 2016)

In the two preceding chapters I sketched out some ways to think about the first two material cumuli of the MEOW framework: writing technologies and their embodied history of use, and the historical conditions of Web 3.0 and twenty-first-century informational capitalism. In this chapter I take a closer look at the third material cumulus and consider the radical impact of accelerating information production on the biophysical environment. I look specifically at the larger ecosystem of the planet and trace how accelerating information production, propelled by corporate practices like *planned obsolescence* and the *externalization* of waste, dangerously accelerates how energy and matter metabolize across several environmental indicators.

By *biophysical* I mean the all-encompassing, *a priori* domain of the natural environment and the physical and thermodynamic laws of energy and matter that form the basic biological processes of all living systems. The science of thermodynamics is a sub-field of physics that studies heat and it's relation to energy, work, and matter. The term stems from a combination of the ancient Greek words *therme* ("heat") and *dynamis* ("power") to

DOI: 10.7330/9781607329688.c004

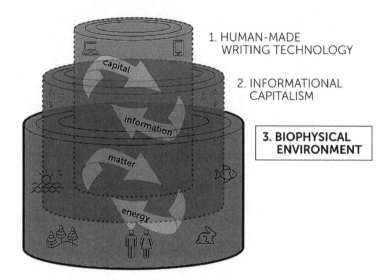

1. HUMAN-MADE
WRITING TECHNOLOGY

2. INFORMATIONAL
CAPITALISM

3. BIOPHYSICAL
ENVIRONMENT

Figure 4.1. MEOW framework, with the third material cumulus represented within a bold outline. (Illustration created by Martha D. Langer, Pear Ink Design.)

mean "heat in motion." The formal science of thermodynamics emerged in the mid-nineteenth century with the rise of the European industrial revolution and the push to engineer more efficient steam engines. Today, thermodynamic laws form the bedrock assumptions of how energy and heat do work and are converted from one form to another as they move through a system.[1] Because the fundamental laws of thermodynamics describe the basic properties of energy and the ability of heat to do work, it "makes them applicable to all physical and biological systems" (Drake 2018). Metabolism is a thermodynamic process that all living systems cycle through as they exchange and convert flows of energy, matter, and information.

There are four basic thermodynamic laws that describe how heat and energy move through a system.[2] For the purposes of my discussion here, it's the first and second law of thermodynamics that are most relevant. The first law states that energy is neither created nor destroyed, only transferred from one system to another; and the second law states that the production and use of energy is irreversible.[3] That is to say, in any living or non-living system, flows of energy and matter perpetually emerge, converted from one form to the next in a ceaseless process of conversion that cannot go backwards in time. This one directionality of energy is known as *entropy*. The concept of entropy has many meanings and is used in both thermodynamics and information theory. I use the term in a general way here, as a fundamental physical law of life that all metabolic processes are continually emerging and those processes can only ever move forward in time—what the science of thermodynamics calls the *arrow of time*.[4]

Of the many material and metabolic implications we can derive from the first and second laws of thermodynamics, they tell us that all systems, big and small, invariably lose energy through waste heat and waste production as they metabolize. While we have an intuitive understanding of how systems process energy and produce waste based on our everyday, sensual experience of the biophysical world, capitalist modes of production tend to treat waste production as an afterthought in their drive to intensify energy use and accelerate capital circulation. The laws of thermodynamics tell us that ignoring, or not properly handling waste, is problematic for any ecosystem, and as ecosystems grow in size and more energy is used, more waste is created. Though modern corporations have taken strides to be better stewards of the environment, many corporations still fight to obscure the basic truth of waste production and the challenges of handling it in environmentally sustainable ways. Like all thermodynamic processes, there is an energetic cost for information to flow, especially in human ecosystems where flows of information take on greater cumulative agency.

In Web 3.0, our use of digital, networked writing technologies and the escalating hunt to collect citizen-consumer data, is contributing to serious ecological problems, from the energy-intensive manufacture of electronics, to energy-hungry data centers, to the massive amounts of electronic waste created in the process. Such energy use and waste production by the IT industries has grown exponentially in the past twenty years.

While both governments and corporations are currently grappling with such concerns, these developing trends are the product of a larger, more systemic, and global metabolic problem that arises with intensifying information production: the process of *acceleration* itself. Accelerating flows of data and information are playing a central role in what the International Geosphere-Biosphere Programme (IGBP) has called the *great acceleration*, a term that describes the immense growth in human consumption and energy use that began during the European industrial revolution in the eighteenth century and has further accelerated with the rise of electronic computing in the 1950s (Steffen et al. 2015). From the perspective of the earth's biosphere, there is compelling evidence that shows how accelerating information production by humans is speeding up other social and natural systems on a global scale in problematic and unsustainable ways.

INFORMATION ACCELERATION AND OTHER
SOCIAL AND NATURAL SYSTEMS

Over the past century, several scholars have theorized the phenomenon of *acceleration* (Keller 2014; Castells 2009; Harvey 2000; Virilio 1986). James Beniger lists over one hundred different phrases coined to describe the human experience of acceleration in the past century. Writing in 1986, he voiced a concern we still hear today: "If social change has seemed to accelerate in recent years . . . this has been due in large part to a spate of new information-processing, communication, and control technologies like the computer, most notably the microprocessors that have proliferated since the early 1970s" (Beniger 1986, 6). Big data, along with the parallel development of the global archive, faster computing, greater bandwidth, better data compression, and bottomless data storage are the most recent examples of how information production has steadily evolved since the late nineteenth century and accelerated into the twenty-first. Work by information scientist Martin Hilbert affirms the profound impact more advanced inscription technologies are having on our socioeconomic lives. He argues in his research that "the world's technological capacity to store and telecommunicate information has grown at a compound annual growth rate of 25–30% during the period from 1986 to 2007" (Hilbert 2012, 9), while our "capacity to compute information has grown even faster—by 60 to 85 percent. That is 10 times faster than our economic capacities" (Hilbert 2012, 9).

The quickening pace of information production in Web 3.0 corresponds to the advancements made in microchip design described by *Moore's law*. Named after Gordon E. Moore, cofounder of microchip pioneer Intel Corporation, Moore estimated in a 1965 paper that the processing power of integrated circuits (industry name for microchips) doubled every two years by doubling the number of transistors that could fit on an integrated circuit. Transistors are the switching apparatus on microchips that enable computers to process binary code. One transistor switch can either be a 0 or 1. Placing more transistors on a microchip helps computers store more information and process it faster. The first commercial microchips sold in 1971 had 2,300 transistors. Microchips today contain over a billion transistors and have 400,000 times more power. Though Moore's law appears to be slowing down as silicon-based microchips reach their physical limits in the number of transistors they can carry, the trend has remained consistent for the past fifty years (Levermore 2017). The law has since been used to forecast the rate at which other aspects of computing will advance such as memory capacity, data compression, screen resolution, and video and sound card development.

In light of such technical developments, the phenomenon of acceleration is more than just a catchy metaphor. Social change and the pace of life feel faster in Web 3.0 because our technological capabilities to produce, store, and process information are growing exponentially. As our capabilities to process information speed up, we invariably accelerate the metabolic rates of how energy and matter flow through both social and natural ecosystems. In 2004, the IGBP published research showing evidence that human activities in the past 250 years have

profoundly accelerated the use and consumption of earth's natural resources. Using twenty-four different social and environmental measures, the IGBP argued that humans have initiated
a new geological phase, the *Anthropocene* (Steffen et al. 2015, 2),
where human made technology and waste production is fundamentally altering the planet's biosphere. As I mentioned above,
one of the distinguishing characteristics of the Anthropocene
era is the phenomenon of the *great acceleration*—a process of
metabolic acceleration that is occurring at the global level and
across a range of social and natural systems. In 2015, the IGBP
published updated versions of all 24 metrics.[5] Figure 4.2 shows
six of the indicators (primary energy use, water use, use of
telecommunications, atmospheric CO_2, surface temperature,
and atmospheric methane). The trends you see in these charts
are consistent across all twenty-four indices, with each system
exponentially surging around 1950—the same time period
when the modern computing era begins and the United States
begins to shift from an industrial economy to an informational
one (Beniger 1986; Drucker 2017; Hayles 1999). The IGBP's
research shows a clear association, on a planetary scale, between
the rise of informational capitalism in the 1950s and the problematic acceleration of other natural and social systems.

Several ecological antagonisms are emerging as a result of
accelerating information production, including the greater
production of CO_2 and methane gas. Moreover, the growing
energy demands of data centers and the global archive contribute greatly to primary energy use. According to Greenpeace,
the total consumption of energy by the IT industries is currently
around 7 percent of annual global energy use, a number pre-
dicted to grow to 13 percent by 2030 as more devices and servers
are added to the global archive. This projected rise in energy
use by the IT industries is double the average growth rate of
energy used globally (Cook et al. 2017). In 2012, the global
archive alone (device use, data centers, and network operations) consumed the equivalent energy output of forty nuclear
power plants—more energy used than France, Germany, Brazil,
and Canada combined (Cook 2012; Glanz 2012—see figure

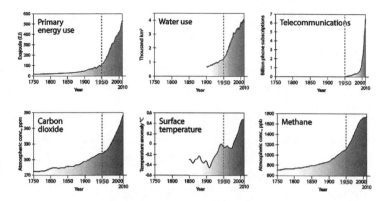

Figure 4.2. Six sample metrics taken from the International Geosphere-Biosphere Programme's (IGBP) report on the global impacts of human activity on social and biophysical systems showing the accelerating growth of each system starting with the European industrial revolution and jumping exponentially in the 1950s (Steffen et al. 2015). The six indices shown here are (a) primary energy use, (b) water use, (c) telecommunications use, (d) atmospheric concentration of CO_2, (e) surface temperature, and (f) atmospheric concentration of methane. The same upward trend is consistent across all 24 indices measured by the IGBP. (Permissions by SAGE Publications.)

4.4b at end of chapter for info-graphic depicting the energy use of data centers in the U.S.).

Fortunately, over the past several years, the IT industries have made great strides in both the efficiency of their operations and in their commitments to use more renewable energy. The big four in particular—Google, Apple, Facebook, and Amazon (GAFA) are leading the way. All four companies are investing heavily in renewable energy sources and they have all made commitments to use a majority of renewable energy to power their data centers within the next decade. While such commitments are necessary and commendable, it also means that the largest data corporations are getting into the energy sector and centralizing more market power in the hands of the IT industries (Mulherkar 2016). In any case, while GAFA is certainly setting the example and the use of renewable energy is on the rise in the industry, as of 2017 some 80 percent of the global archive was still powered by fossil fuels (Cook and Jardim 2017).

Even with GAFA taking the lead in corporate responsibility, the majority of the corporate data complex and device manufacturers from around the world still lag behind GAFA's leadership and there continues to be a culture of secrecy around the number of data centers and how much energy is actually being used around the globe (Moss 2019).

It is important that we support those in the IT industries that are behaving responsibly towards citizen-consumers and the environment, but we should remember that in the context of neoliberal, informational capitalism and very few regulatory controls, the task of getting data corporations to be better stewards of the environment falls on the those who use their products and services. Up until around 2012, being green wasn't much of a thought for GAFA and the rest of the IT industry. These companies didn't go green without the rhetorical and activist work of organizations like Greenpeace and the Electronic Frontier Foundation. Greenpeace has been tenacious in raising public awareness about the growing energy use by the IT industries.[6] Since 2008 they have released environmental report cards for all the major technology companies, putting pressure on them to improve their energy efficiency, develop more earth-friendly products, and invest in renewable energy. Thus, while we should commend GAFA for their environmental consciousness, because they are so central to how energy and information flow around the globe, there is an ongoing need on the part of citizen-consumers to hold them and other technology companies accountable and push for more oversight and regulation in the United States.

THE PARADOX OF ENERGY EFFICIENCY
AND METABOLIC ACCELERATION

In maintaining accountability, we can begin by addressing those aspects of corporate data production that continue to do environmental harm. Perhaps the most baffling is the contradiction that arises in capitalist modes of production between energy efficiency, information production, and human consumption.

Despite great gains in the energy efficiency of computers and electronics over the decades, the IGBP graphs clearly indicate that the world's energy demands continue to grow faster than our efforts at energy efficiency. This contradiction is often referred to as "Jevons paradox"—the socioeconomic phenomenon whereby gains in energy and resource efficiency produce greater rates of consumption as energy becomes cheaper and more accessible (Foster et al. 2010; Cook et al. 2017).[7] As John Bellamy Foster notes of the paradox, "since 1975 the amount of energy expended per dollar of GDP in the United States has decreased by half, marking an increase in energy efficiency by that amount. But at the same time the overall consumption of energy by U.S. society has risen by some 40 percent" (Foster et al. 2010, 43). Such a paradox is the kind of stubborn antagonism that characterizes neoliberal, corporate capitalism and it reminds us where to focus our critical efforts when trying to ameliorate the environmental impacts of corporate activity. Technological efficiency alone cannot create more environmentally sustainable socioeconomic systems, and as Jevons paradox shows, gains in energy efficiency, more often than not, can harm the environment because that very efficiency accelerates consumption.

While I can't unravel the complete workings of Jevons paradox here, one kind of behavior we can address that contributes to it is the corporate practice of *planned obsolescence* used extensively by the IT industries. Planned obsolescence is the practice of making products with short useable lives. To persuade consumers to buy new versions of their devices, manufacturers design products that cannot be repaired easily or that do not allow parts to be replaced when they stop working (for example, smartphone batteries). Designers push out frequent software updates that often do not function as well on older devices, rendering them more and more obsolete with each update. Practices like planned obsolescence harm the environment in two fundamental ways. First, it leads to intensive over-mining of the raw materials used in the manufacture of electronics while simultaneously exploiting cheap labor in China, Taiwan,

India, and other developing countries of the global south. And second, it greatly increases the production of electronic waste, outpacing our abilities as a global community to legislate and handle waste that is complex and toxic when not disposed of properly. All of these practices are cause for concern and they are all expressions of how our digital writing technologies, and the commodified data production they foster, pose serious concerns for the health and sustainability of living systems by the way they accelerate human consumption and waste production.

When we move from the shiny, burnished steel of the data center to the more obscure world of electronics manufacture and electronic waste, we see other metabolic problems arise related to planned obsolescence. The manufacturing of electronics is an energy-intensive process that consumes 70–80 percent of the total environmental footprint of a single computer or smartphone (Cook and Jardim 2017). The manufacture of computers and smartphones, comprising hundreds of parts, depends on a complex global supply chain, from mining the precious metal cobalt in Congo to the production of silicon microchips in northern California. The need for gold, silver, and copper in phones and computers requires extractive open-pit mining that produces enormous amounts of hazardous waste while destroying local habitat and often polluting local water systems for decades (Grossman 2006; Walt and Meyer 2018). According to Greenpeace researchers, "smartphones and other electronic devices are among the most resource intensive by weight on the planet—miners must dig through more than 30 kilos of rock to obtain the 100 or so grams of minerals used in a smartphone" (Cook and Jardim 2017, 6). Some of the basic components used in computers and smartphones, like microchips, also require large amounts of energy and matter to be produced. As Elizabeth Grossman lucidly shows in *High Tech Trash*: "one individual semiconductor fabrication plant may use as many as five hundred to a thousand different chemicals" (Grossman 2006, 45) and the production of a single 30cm wafer of semiconductor can use up to two thousand gallons of water (China Water Risk 2017; Grossman 2006). In Silicon Valley, the birthplace of microchip technology, there are currently seven toxic waste sites from microchip manufacturing that are listed on the federal governments Superfund program,[8] and there are over a dozen more such sites around the country (Grossman 2006, 3). While we rarely think about the incredible amount of energy and labor that is embodied in a computer or smartphone, their complex manufacturing process exacts a huge environmental cost and contributes greatly to the flows of waste that are created by information production and planned obsolescence (see figure 4.4a at end of chapter for visual statistics of device manufacturing).

On the other side of the waste created by manufacturing electronics is the inevitable acceleration of waste that comes with their end-of-life disposal (see figure 4.4c at end of chapter for visual statistics of e-waste). Categories of e-waste include computers, monitors, keyboards, televisions, mobile phones, faxes, and printers, but it also includes any product that has electrical circuitry like light bulbs and refrigerators. According to the United Nations (UN), over 40 million metric tons of electronics have been discarded worldwide every year since 2014. They estimate that this number will grow to fifty million tons a year by 2021—the weight equivalency of more than sixteen million cars (at 3,000 pounds a car) (Jardim 2017; Balde et al. 2017). Discarded electronics are now the fastest-growing part of the waste stream in many countries. With the rise of mobile computing and smartphones, along with the business practice of planned obsolescence, flows of electronic waste are accelerating. It's been estimated that over seven billion smartphones have been manufactured since 2007, with the average US consumer buying a new phone every twenty-six months. In 2020 over six billion people worldwide will own a mobile phone, with over three billion people using smartphones (Jardim 2017). This growth and turnover in phone ownership has also help create the largest flow of e-waste around world.

E-waste is a particularly challenging form of waste too. Unlike simpler waste products like paper or glass, electronics can contain hundreds of individual components, many potentially hazardous to the environment when not recycled properly. Monitors, circuit boards, and batteries often use lead and mercury—heavy metals known to affect human brain development and cause reproductive problems in marine life. Recycling e-waste is expensive, requiring trained labor and proper tools to do it safely. Currently, there is no way to mass recycle e-waste. Wires, circuit boards, monitors, and plastics must be broken down manually. When e-waste recycling is done correctly, no toxins are released at the end of a product's life, and the great majority of precious metals used can be recovered for resale. Because of the high costs associated with proper e-waste disposal, many recyclers in the global North (United States, European Union) ship the waste to developing counties in the global South. Research from the Basel Action Network (BAN) and the United Nations estimates that in the United States, only 20 percent of the e-waste produced is properly recycled by licensed recyclers (United Nations Management Group 2017; BAN 2019). The rest is stockpiled by consumers, dumped in landfills (both legally and illegally), or sent to developing countries for recycling. It is estimated that the United States, one of the largest producers of e-waste in the world (along with the European Union and China), is also the largest exporter, potentially exporting up to 30 percent of its total e-waste production (total e-waste weighing in at just over 10 million tons) to developing countries in 2017 (BAN 2019; Balde et al. 2017).[9]

Such numbers exhibit another enduring corporate practice, that of *externalization*. Externalization is the practice of transferring the more laborious and dangerous aspects of waste management from wealthy countries to poorer countries with large, cheap labor markets: "[T]he developed nations of the global north consume 75 percent of all electronics produced globally, then export anywhere from 15 to 30 percent of these products to developing nations in the south" (Khetriwal et al. 2013). Externalizing waste has long been a primary way that capitalist forms of industrial production exploit both natural and human ecosystems by offloading the burden of waste to poorer, more disadvantaged communities and monopolizing the benefits of

Figure 4.3. Images of e-waste processing in Guiyu, China, circa 2017. (Permissions by Basel Action Network; copyright Basel Action Network, 2016.)

cutting-edge technology. This is undoubtedly a form of Marxian fetishization—the systematic obscuring of electronics manufacturing and the social and natural resources necessary for their production and disposal. The city of Guiyu, China, is a case in point. Guiyu was once considered the largest e-waste processing center in the world (Standaert 2015. See figure 4.3). From 2000 to 2010, 75 percent (1.25 million tons) of the e-waste received at Guiyu came from North America (BAN 2016). The facilities there, like others around the world now, used open-air flames and chemical baths to break down the circuit boards of old electronics and melt the plastics holding them together to get to the precious metals inside. The population of the city has been found to have higher rates of "digestive, neurological, repository, and bone problems" (Wang et al. 2013) than cities of comparable size. Thanks to the ardent activism of groups like Basel Action Network and the StEP Initiative (Solving the E-waste Problem), conditions in Guiyu have improved significantly (Griner 2017; Pinghui 2017). However, thousands of such processing plants around the world still remain obscure and unregulated. Other studies done in Nigeria (Manhart et al. 2011; Olubanjo 2013) and India (Inagaki 2013) show the same harmful effects brought on by the externalization of electronic waste that researchers found in Guiyu.

In 1989, in response to the growing export of hazardous waste going from the global North to the global South, the United Nations adopted the Basel Convention, a treaty designed to halt the illegal transport of hazardous waste across national lines. Electronic waste falls into this category. As of 2020, 186 countries have ratified the treaty. The United States has yet to ratify it in Congress. On the federal level it is still legal in the United States to export used electronics to other countries (United Nations Management Group 2017).[10] Currently in the United States, twenty five states have enacted e-waste regulations of their own (Maps of States with [E-Waste] Legislation 2020).

CONCLUSION

While progress is surely being made, the discordant juxtaposition of data center/e-waste dump is a fitting trope for the asymmetrical relations that persist in Web 3.0 between the global North and South. Because the benefits and risks of electronic production and waste are unevenly shared, corporate practices like planned obsolescence and the externalization of waste make the issue of electronic waste one of environmental and social justice. From an ecological point of view, externalizing waste only conceals where it goes. The environmental impacts of electronics manufacture and disposal don't end in Guiyu or Silicon Valley. The toxins wend their way, via air, water, and soil, into other ecosystems around the globe. Grossman vividly captures this metabolic movement:

> A polar bear settles down to sleep in a den carved out of Arctic ice. A whale cruises the depths of the North Sea and . . . a bottlenose dolphin leaps above the waves . . . A [human] mother in Sweden nurses her baby, as does a mother in Oakland, California. Tissue samples taken from these animals and from these women's breasts contain synthetic chemicals used to make the plastics used in computers, televisions, cell phones, and other electronics [to] resist fire. Americans have the highest levels of these compounds in their blood of any people yet tested, and the same chemicals have been found in food purchased in grocery stores throughout the United States. (Grossman 2006, 2)

This is what it means to be in a metabolic relationship with a multitude of human and nonhuman systems. In theorizing the cultural and material realities of inscription and information production in Web 3.0, we must consider the environmental hazards created by the accelerating production and consumption of electronics. By including the biophysical environment and considering the thermodynamic and metabolic impact of accelerating information production in our new materialist theories of writing, we open up new ways to theorize writing in the broader contexts of Web 3.0 and environmental crisis.

In the next chapter I stay within the third material cumulus of the biophysical world but shift from the impact of accelerating information production on the larger ecosystem of the planet to its impact on the permeable, organic space of the writing body, our memory, and our abilities to read and write.

MATERIALIST ECOLOGY OF WRITING (MEOW)

MEOW is a theoretical framework for studying the ecological, metabolic relations between human literacy practices, information production, digital technology, capital circulation, and the surrounding biophysical environment.

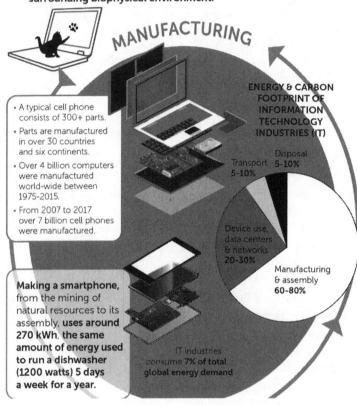

MANUFACTURING

- A typical cell phone consists of 300+ parts.
- Parts are manufactured in over 30 countries and six continents.
- Over 4 billion computers were manufactured world-wide between 1975-2015.
- From 2007 to 2017 over 7 billion cell phones were manufactured.

Making a smartphone, from the mining of natural resources to its assembly, uses around 270 kWh, the same amount of energy used to run a dishwasher (1200 watts) 5 days a week for a year.

ENERGY & CARBON FOOTPRINT OF INFORMATION TECHNOLOGY INDUSTRIES (IT)

Disposal 5-10%

Transport 5-10%

Device use, data centers & networks 20-30%

Manufacturing & assembly 60-80%

IT industries consume 7% of total global energy demand

Figure 4.4a–c. Infographic depicting the three primary stages of energy use by the IT industries—manufacturing, use, and disposal—with basic facts and figures about how much energy is used, at what stage, and some of the social and environmental costs associated with information and data production. Because the numbers for energy use by the IT industries and the amounts of e-waste produced varies widely from study to study, I've tried to choose the most up-to-date resources and cross-reference them with each other to come up with a mean average based on the most reliable studies. (Illustration created by Martha D. Langer, Pear Ink Design.)

Sources: Elkhir, Lotfi, and Ahmed Elmeligi. "Assessing ICT Global Emissions Footprint: Trends to 2040 & recommendations." *Journal of Cleaner Production* 177 (2018): 448–63; Jardim, Elizabeth. From Smart to Senseless: The Global Impact of 10 Years of Smartphones. Report. Washington, DC: Greenpeace, 2017; Cook, Gary, and Elizabeth Jardim. Guide to Greener Electronics. Report. Washington, DC: Greenpeace, 2017; Manhart, Andreas, et al. Resource Efficiency in the ICT Sector. Report by Oeko-Institute for Greenpeace. November 2016.

In the USAGE phase, MEOW highlights the energy consumed by our use of digital electronics, data centers, and the networked infrastructure they are connected through.

- Large data brokers have an average of 1500 pieces of information on 500 million consumers.
- The majority of cookies and other tracking software installed by popular applications and websites are from third-party data brokers.
- Revenue from online advertising has grown at a rate of 10% annually since 2000, surpassing $50B in 2018.

The time we spend online, and the writing we do there, produces the consumer data and metadata that drive our modern information economy.

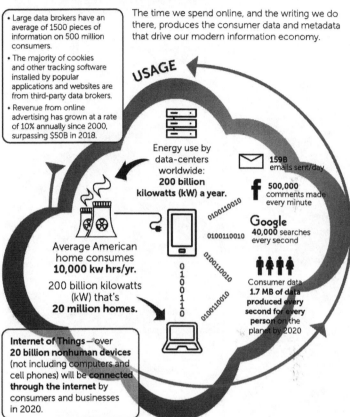

USAGE

Energy use by data-centers worldwide: **200 billion kilowatts (kW) a year.**

159B emails sent/day

500,000 comments made every minute

Google 40,000 searches every second

Average American home consumes **10,000 kw hrs/yr.**

200 billion kilowatts (kW) that's **20 million homes.**

Consumer data 1.7 MB of data produced every second for every person on the planet by 2020

Internet of Things — over 20 billion nonhuman devices (not including computers and cell phones) **will be connected through the internet** by consumers and businesses in 2020.

Figure 4.4b.

Sources: "Gartner Says Worldwide Device Shipments Will Increase 2.1 Percent in 2018." January 29, 2018. Accessed February 05, 2019. https://www.gartner.com; Jardim, Elizabeth. From Smart to Senseless: The Global Impact of 10 Years of Smartphones. Report. Washington, DC: Greenpeace, 2017; Jones, Nicola. "How to Stop Data Centres from Gobbling up the World's Electricity." *Nature News.* September 12, 2018. Accessed February 1, 2019. https://www.nature.com/articles/d41586-018-06610-y; Internet Live Stats. Accessed February 1, 2019. http://www.internetlivestats.com/; Domo, Inc. "Connecting Your Data, Systems & People | Domo." Connecting Your Data, Systems, & People. 2019. Accessed January 13, 2019. https://www.domo.com.

Electronic waste includes phones, refrigerators, sensors, televisions, computers, printers & monitors.

- The United States is the largest producer of e-waste, per capita, in the world.
- 17% of the e-waste created in the U.S. is recycled legally. The other 83% ends up in closets, landfills, or developing countries for recycling and second-hand use.
- On average, Americans buy a new cellphone every 26 months.
- In 2010, Americans disposed of 350,000 cell phones a day —over 120 million for the year.

Billions of computers and phones have been discarded dating back to the 1960s. While recycling efforts are improving, countries in the global north continue to ship e-waste to less developed countries like China, Ghana, and India despite international laws that forbid it. The toxins released from improper electronics recycling can be found in water and food systems throughout the world.

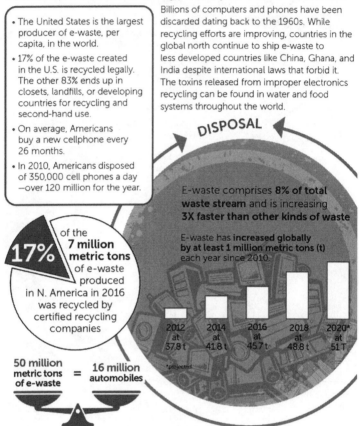

DISPOSAL

E-waste comprises **8% of total waste stream** and is increasing **3X faster than other kinds of waste**

E-waste has **increased globally by at least 1 million metric tons (t)** each year since 2010.

| 2012 at 37.8 t | 2014 at 41.8 t | 2016 at 45.7 t | 2018 at 48.8 t | 2020* at 51 T |

*projected

17% of the **7 million metric tons** of e-waste produced in N. America in 2016 was recycled by certified recycling companies

50 million metric tons of e-waste = **16 million automobiles**

Figure 4.4c.

Sources: Baldé, C.P., Forti, V., Gray, V., Kuehr, R., Stegmann, P.: The Global E-waste Monitor—2017, United Nations University (UNU), International Telecommunication Union (ITU) & International Solid Waste Association (ISWA), Bonn/Geneva/Vienna; "Cleaning Up Electronic Waste (E-Waste)." EPA. December 3, 2018. Accessed january 14, 2019. https://www.epa.gov/international-cooperation/cleaning-electronic-waste-e-waste; Salehabadi, Djahane. Transboundary Movements of Discarded Electrical and Electronic Equipment. Report. United Nations University, 2013.

5

THE EFFECTS OF MANUFACTURED DISTRACTION ON THE BODY

The degree of slowness is directly proportional to the intensity of memory; the degree of speed is directly proportional to the intensity of forgetting. (Kundera 2014)

Staying in the third material cumulus of the biophysical environment, in this chapter I move from how accelerating information production radically impacts the planet's ecosystems to how it radically impacts the permeable space of the writing body. Of the many metabolic effects we are experiencing in Web 3.0, many scholars and popular writers alike have commented on the ways the internet and information overload tamper with our abilities to focus, listen, and solve complex problems (Carr 2010; Andrejevic 2013; Turkle 2017; Aboujaoude 2011). Life online seems to be a persistent state of distraction as we "zip along the surface [of the internet] like a guy on a Jet Ski" (Carr 2008). The rise of persistent distraction, enabled by the spread of the global internet, has other scholars and researchers worried about the simultaneous rise in *internet addiction* that has emerged alongside persistent distraction (Carr 2010; Lustig 2018; Alter 2018; Tweange 2018). This developmental relationship between distraction *and* addiction raises troubling questions about the amount of time we spend online and the material effects it has on us. We don't simply jet-ski across the internet anymore; we deep-dive daily into a constant flow of inscription, data, information, news, social media, apps, videos, feeds, notifications, chirps, and reminders.

DOI: 10.7330/9781607329688.c005

Generally speaking, concerns over distraction and internet addiction haven't been taken very seriously in writing studies. Yet, as we transition into the maturing digital world of Web 3.0, there's a pressing need in our new materialist theories of writing to understand the dialectical relation between manufactured distraction and internet addiction and how this relation impacts our minds, bodies, and abilities to write.

WRITING AND THE SOMATIC MIND

Since the expansion and commercialization of the internet in the mid-1990s, writing studies scholars have urged us to consider the body in our materialist theories of writing and rhetoric (Selzer and Crowley 1999; Fleckenstein 1999; Haas 1996; Reynolds 2007). More recently, new materialist work that draws on *neurorhetorics, embodiment,* and *attunement* is raising challenging questions about our ontological experience of writing and rhetoric and how our bodies entangle with nonhuman writing technologies (Cooper 2011, 2017; Nicotra 2017a; Gries 2015; Gibbons 2018). The intensifying, often antagonistic dynamic between individual human bodies and ubiquitous inscription greatly problematizes our understanding of agency and the ways digital writing technologies radically affect the human agents who use them. By focusing on our *embodied* experience of writing, our goal is to understand the deeper metabolic and ecological antagonisms that arise in Web 3.0 by tapping the full sensorium of our knowing bodies.

In considering the material social effects of Web 3.0 on our bodies then, we are led to the vital process of *embodiment.* Embodiment is a useful concept for theorizing new materialist theories of writing for the ways it shifts our focus from local writing situations and individual writers to the metabolic exchange that occurs between our bodies and the writing tools we use. Kristie Fleckenstein recognized this fluid boundary twenty years ago: "The physical demarcations constituting who we are (and what we are) at any moment must enclose, not cut, the relevant pathways that create a specific context thereby blurring the boundaries of what constitutes flesh and technology, flesh and culture, flesh and other" (Fleckenstein 1999, 287). In place of embodiment to describe the merging of flesh and technology, Fleckenstein uses the concept of the *somatic mind*[1] to empha- size our hypersensitivity to the symbols and technologies that surround us. Somatic mind in this sense is very much like exo- somatic (outside of the body) metabolism; embodied human writers intra-act with their material and semiotic surroundings and "are (re)constituted through the mutual play of discursive and corporeal coding" (Fleckenstein 1999, 282). Though it may appear from the perspective of the human agent that we use a writing technology to write the world, from an embodied, metabolic perspective, those same tools very much inscribe our somatic minds in every act of literacy.

Acknowledging the embodied experience of writing, and, more precisely, learning to attune to it as a metabolic relation, is vital for developing not only new materialist theories of writ- ing, but also the critical pedagogies that will help students grow in embodiment. As Fleckenstein argues, "without bodies . . . no resistance or systemic transformation can be effected" and "it is only *through* the body that competing (con)textualities mate- rialize" (Fleckenstein 1999, 284). Without considering our felt experience of ubiquitous inscription and accelerating infor- mation production, we won't be able to draw on the wealth of intuitive knowledge the full sensorium of our body provides. This is all the more true today in the commodified, datafied spaces of Web 3.0 where the corporate data complex is target- ing our somatic minds in new and powerful ways by manufactur- ing distraction and promoting internet addiction in the users of their products. Such tactics have become primary drivers of commodified information production and they are having pro- found effects on our bodies and our lived experience of writing and rhetoric.

Manufactured distraction and internet addiction are mani- festing in several ways in American culture. Current research in these areas suggests that the rise in distraction and addictive behaviors that is emerging in Web 3.0 are contributing to rises in stress, depression, and anxiety levels in the United States (Weissman 2016; Lustig 2018; Twenge 2018; ADAA 2020; Lin et al. 2014; Carli et al. 2013; Rumpf et al. 2015). All of these concerns have important implications for our embodied experience of writing in Web 3.0, but in this chapter I focus specifically on how the relationship between manufactured distraction and internet addiction negatively affect our ability to write by the way they hinder our ability to encode and remember information. Because such corporate tactics bear directly on questions of attention and memory, they also bear directly on questions of writing and learning. By better understanding the ways manufactured distraction and internet addiction disrupt the focus necessary for becoming a skilled reader and writer, we can help students develop the critical, embodied awareness they'll need to grapple with the accelerating world of Web 3.0, informational capitalism, and environmental crises.

DISTRACTION AND INTERNET ADDICTION

The terms "distraction" and "addiction" have become popular tropes for describing our felt experience of the last 20 years and the rise of the commercial internet. Scholars and journalists have written extensively about how our growing use of the internet fosters a media environment of distraction and multitasking rather than one of deep, reflective thinking (Turkle 2005; Greenfield 2015; Aagaard 2014; Junco 2012, 2013; Junco and Cotton 2012; Carr 2010). Others have argued that the rise of distraction is directly associated with the intentional manufacturing of behavioral addictions by corporate data platforms and device designers in their drive to collect data on users (Alter 2018; Lustig 2018; Bogost 2017, 2018).

In contrast to popular claims about distraction and addiction, writing scholars Kelly Blewett, Janine Morris, Hannah J. Rule (2016), and Jenae Cohn (2016) have argued that, while our concerns about distraction and internet addiction are certainly warranted by current research, we need to be careful when invoking these terms as blanket critiques of how the internet affects writers and writing practices. As Blewett, Morris, and Rule argue, "as the primary concept writers have had for understanding non-writing activities, distraction has created a wholly unrealistic expectation for what a focused, environmentally-engaged, and intentional writer does. To have focus is not to stare, immoveable, engaged with only fingers typing. The detours are a part of it, not something necessarily to avoid" (Blewett et al. 2016, 36). In theorizing the more diffuse and automated writing environments of Web 3.0, the authors remind us not to oversimplify the diverse ways in which writers actually engage with digital, networked writing technologies.

Cohn echoes a similar concern with the use of the "addiction" trope by students to describe their relationship with the internet and mobile phones. She notes in her study of seventy-five student literacy narratives that, for those students who preferred face-to-face ("embodied") over online communication, both "distraction" and "addiction" were two of the most commonly used words to describe their online literacies. Cohn emphasizes that we need to be aware of how such tropes can "pathologize" our relationship to technology and hinder our ability to act rhetorically (Cohn 2016). In helping students refine their thinking about how they use digital writing tools, Cohn argues that we can use the "distraction" and "addiction" tropes as critical spaces for reflecting on our embodied experience of writing. By raising their awareness of how networked technologies transform their writing environments in both positive and negative ways, students become more attuned to the nonhuman writing agents we spend so much of our lives interacting with (Cohn 2016, 93).

I find these arguments from Blewitt et al. and Cohn cogent and necessary, and they surely will help students become more aware of their embodied experience of writing. At the same time, in light of Web 3.0 and the intensification of data collection on citizen-consumers, we have to be careful not to fall into the same habit of undertheorizing the economic motivations at play when we write online. In the studies by Blewett et al. and Cohn, the smartphone and the computer are each seen as just another object in the students' local writing environment. Yet, when working from a distributed model of agency, such local spaces are teeming with a mixture of agencies, along with the cumulative agency of the writing tools being used and the larger networks of inscription those tools are connected to. Internet-connected devices are different from more traditional writing tools (pen/paper, word processors) by nature of their bi-directionality. Their pervasive reach provide constant access to the local space of writing, accessible not just by friends and family, but also the corporate data platforms that depend on citizen-consumers to produce the data needed to circulate capital in Web 3.0.

One of the primary ways corporate data platforms keep data flowing is by designing devices, apps, and products that encourage habit formation in users, or what psychologists call *behavioral addictions*. While we have historically thought of addiction as related to substance abuse, behavioral addictions refer to other behaviors outside of substance abuse that become compulsive for an individual and detrimental to other aspects of their lives like work, personal relationships, and physical health. Common examples include excessive gambling, compulsive shopping, and problematic internet use. In 2013, the American Psychiatric Association's authoritative *Diagnostic and Statistical Manual of Mental Disorders, 5th Edition (DSM-5)* (American Psychiatric Association 2017) renamed problematic gambling behaviors from "pathological gambling" to "gambling disorder" and moved them to a new category called "Substance-Related and Addictive Disorders." The move is significant because it is the first time the *DSM* has grouped a behavioral addiction like gambling with substance abuse disorders like alcoholism (Petry 2015; Grant and Chamberlain 2016).

Though our understanding of behavioral addictions is still young, the *DSM*'s inclusion of excessive gambling as an addictive disorder is a sign that our understanding of addiction is evolving. A growing amount of research is finding that many of the problematic behaviors typically associated with substance abuse—tolerance to the substance, inability to stop using it, relapse, withdrawal, and damage to personal and professional life—often emerge in behavioral addictions associated with the internet and excessive time spent on social media, gaming, shopping, and pornography (Lin et al. 2014; Carli et al. 2013; Rumpf et al. 2015; Lustig 2018). To be sure, the term "internet addiction" (IA) is a contested term in the medical and psychiatric fields, and scholars and professionals disagree on the use of "addiction" to describe excessive internet use (Grant and Chamberlain 2016; Rumpf et al. 2015; Starcevic and Khazaal 2017). I'll be using the term throughout this chapter based on its use in the medical and psychiatric research I draw on here, with the caveat that the term's meaning and application are currently under debate. One thing is for certain, though we are just starting to understand the kinds of behavioral issues and patterns that are emerging, research on, and public concern over, internet addiction clearly points to the radical ways our bodies and minds entangle with ubiquitous inscription and accelerating data collection.

In terms of brain chemistry and the body, behavioral addictions are associated with the brains release of the neurotransmitter *dopamine*. This neurotransmitter is part of what neuroscientists call the *dopamine reward pathway*. Dopamine is released in the brain as a signaling agent to motivate an organism to act based on the expectation of the pleasure they will receive by engaging in that activity. As psychologist Adam Alter explains, "just as drugs trigger dopamine production, so do behavioral cues" (Alter 2018, 89). Behavioral cues constantly beckon from the world around us, triggering our dopamine reward pathway to motivate our behavior, from the smell of coffee in the morning, to the twinge we feel when our phone vibrates in our pocket. As Alter notes about these external cues, "when a gaming addict fires up his laptop, his dopamine levels spike; when an exercise addict laces her running shoes, her dopamine levels spike. From there, these behavioral addicts look a lot like drug addicts" (Alter 2018, 89). Research into excessive social media and video game use[2] shows compelling evidence that high-frequency internet users experience similar rushes of dopamine and pleasure more commonly associated with traditional drug use (Lustig 2018; Alter 2018). Alter's research echoes what other research into behavioral addictions is showing—that "addiction" has more to do with brain chemistry and our need to "soothe psychological distress" (Alter 2018, 79) than it has to do with any particular substance and the individual's "will power" to resist that substance (Petry 2015).

With the expansion of the internet and mobile computing, behavioral addictions are becoming more prevalent as our interactions with automated, digital technologies increase (Sussman et al. 2010; Lin et al. 2014; Carli et al. 2013; Rumpf et al. 2015). While clearly differences exist between substance and behavioral addictions, research suggests that "moderate behavioral addictions are far more common" (Alter 2018, 24) than acute substance addictions and they can have similar negative effects in the long term on personal relationships, work performance, and financial stability (Lustig 2018; Alter 2018; Sussman et al. 2010; Rumpf et al. 2015). As Alter notes, "the environment and circumstance of the digital age are far more conducive to addiction than anything humans have experienced in our history" (Alter 2018, 4).

DATA AS RHETORICAL WEAPON

Of course, corporate data platforms and device designers are very aware of these emerging behavioral trends because they actively encourage them. Drawing extensively on research in psychology, neuroscience, and human behavior, corporate platforms and designers build products that are as habit-forming as possible by specifically targeting users' dopamine reward pathway. The intent, of course, is to bypass conscious rhetorical awareness and communicate directly through our natural vulnerabilities to environmental rewards and behavioral cues. This sensitivity to environmental stimuli is a constituent part of how our bodies experience embodied knowing and attunement. However, without critical awareness, the permeability of our somatic minds make us susceptible to interactive platforms, devices, and software designed to hyper-stimulate our reward and pleasure centers.

While online data collection began with corporate data platforms like Google and Facebook, as data's value has grown, data brokers, marketers, and product developers have all intensified their efforts to stimulate and collect more data on citizen-consumers. Whereas Google and Facebook tend to downplay the vast reach of their data collection[3] efforts, the other players in the corporate data complex are unabashedly clear about their intentions and methods. A glance at recent books on "neuromarketing" confirms this:

> *The Neuro Design: Neuromarketing to Boost Engagement and Profitability* (Bridger 2017)
>
> *Persuasion Code: How Neuromarketing Can Help You Persuade Anyone, Anywhere, Anytime* (Morin and Renvoise 2018)
>
> *Neuromarketing: Exploring the Brain of the Customer* (Zurawicki 2010)

"Neuromarketing" is a clear testament to the ways the corporate data complex uses research on brain chemistry and human behavior to exploit the dopamine reward pathway and our deep, often unconscious decision-making processes. While it's easy to dismiss this as just another advertising tactic to sell products, we mustn't underestimate the predatory nature of nueromarketing as a rhetorical tool. The use of devices and applications designed specifically to influence behavior, stimulate consumption, and accelerate data production *at the level of our brain chemistry* is an expression of the aggressive nature of corporate data collection in Web 3.0.

It's no coincidence that the discourse of neuromarketing sounds very similar to the kinds of terms usually associated with illicit drug dealing: consumers are "users" that companies want to "get hooked" on their platforms and products. In their book *Hooked: How to Build Habit Forming Products* (2014), authors Nir Eyal and Ryan Hoover draw on work from behavioral scientist B. J. Fogg to outline what they call the *hook cycle*, the process that successful online companies use to attract and keep users using their products. The hook cycle consists of four basic steps: (1) the product must *trigger* something that compels users to use the technology and take steps to (2) *engage* with the technology, which is then (3) backed up by changing *rewards* that provide new stimuli to keep users in a state of constant anticipation. If these three steps are fulfilled, platforms and devices can complete the final step in the hook cycle by (4) establishing themselves as *normalized* parts of the daily lives of their users. In completing the cycle, users now provide consistent flows of valuable data about themselves and their behavior.

A simple example of the hook cycle in action is Facebook and its subsidiary, Instagram. These popular data platforms hook users by offering "free" services designed to trigger our need to connect and communicate with each other (stage 1). Like all useful platforms, they're designed for ease of use so there are, for the most part, few technical or economic barriers to their use (stage 2). The ubiquitous "Like" button and posting functions provide the ultimate mechanism for keeping users hooked by giving users the ability to give and receive constant feedback, rewards, and new stiumuli as they engage in social interaction and bonding (stage 3). With over 2 billion active users, Facebook's and Instagram's innovations and well-designed hook cycle has given them a massive monopoly over other social media platforms and, thus, immense access to greater flows of citizen-consumer data.

Although Eyal and Hoover don't talk much about dopamine as a part of the hook cycle, when corporations say they are trying to hook us, they are describing the persistent effort to activate our dopamine reward pathway. When we look closely at the language of neuromarketing, we see a new level of exploitation in which corporate data platforms prey on our body's automatic propensity for environmental stimuli:

> If our programmed behaviors are so influential in guiding our everyday actions, surely harnessing the same power of habits can be a boon for industry. Indeed, for those able to shape them in an effective way, habits can be very good for the bottom line. Habit-forming products change user behavior and create

unprompted user engagement. The aim is to influence customers to use your product on their own, again and again, without
relying on overt calls to action such as ads or promotions. Once
a habit is formed, the user is automatically triggered to use the
product during routine events such as wanting to kill time while
waiting in line. (Eyal and Hoover 2014, 17)

In this instance, Eyal and Hoover's language sounds less like
illicit drug dealing and more like the ways psychologists talk
about behavioral addictions: products are designed to create
"unprompted user engagement" using "triggers" to stimulate
unconscious activity. They go on to say that "instead of relying
on expensive marketing, habit-forming companies link their
services to the users' daily routines and emotions" (Eyal and
Hoover 2014, 3), and they do so by exploiting basic human
needs for information (especially new information), social
support, and positive feedback. As the authors note, "How do
[online platforms] create habits? The answer: They manufacture them" (Ayal and Hoover 2014, 3).

While surely designers and developers are building habit-
forming technologies that improve our lives, these tactics
should give us pause. When inscription technologies are developed with the stated intent of manipulating brain chemistry
and exploiting our basic human social needs, we've entered a
new rhetorical realm of information asymmetry. By intentionally targeting our natural brain chemistry, the corporate data
complex turns our bodies, desires, needs, fears, and socialness
against us in order to accelerate capital circulation. The persuasion and influence that is developed by the use of widespread
surveillance and data collection on citizen-consumers greatly
challenges our understanding of the available means of persuasion and the extent of individual human agency.

Though the correlation between manufactured distraction
and behavioral internet addiction is just starting to come into
focus in Web 3.0, there appears to be a developmental, dialectical relation between the two phenomena. Distraction is both a
byproduct of our compulsive use of the internet *and* a basic corporate tactic to collect more data on citizen-consumers. In our

daily lives this combination of distraction and internet addiction manifests in the lived experience of constant interruption—the nudging and notifying that our phones and computers transmit, triggering our attention from one platform, app, interaction, post, and engagement to the next. While not all of this is nefarious, the normalization of persistent distraction is having profound effects on our somatic minds, curtailing our abilities to focus and reflect, and replacing these habits of mind with more frenetic behavior and consumption. The implications for how and what we write are cause for concern and something our new materialist theories of writing can and should address.

TEACHING WRITING AND READING IN WEB 3.0

Naturally, I can't address all of the concerns associated with manufactured distraction and internet addiction here, but MEOW is designed to help guide such questions. For the rest of this chapter, I'd like to explore how manufactured distraction and habit-forming technologies impact our ability to write by interrupting the delicate process of building a *working memory* capable of writing longer, more complex texts. Research on how memory works and the central role that working memory plays in the process of memory formation has long shown that distraction, via the common practice of media multitasking, diminishes our performance on both tasks, as well as the amount of information we are able to encode and remember (Greenfield 2015; Aagaard 2014; Junco 2012; Mark 2015; Adler and Benbunan-Fich 2012, 2014). We've thus known for a long time that human brains cannot dual process like computers, nor can we remember like computers do. One outcome of manufactured distraction, then, is the profound ways it affects our ability to remember what we read. As a result, constant distractions can curtail the critical process of thinking required to write about complex problems and issues.

An interesting lens for exploring how distractions affect our ability to write can be glimpsed in a study on the teaching of writing done by the Pew Research Internet Project, "The Impact of Digital Tools on Student Writing and How Writing is Taught in Schools" (Purcell et al. 2013). Researchers surveyed over twenty-four hundred advanced placement (AP) and National Writing Project (NWP) teachers from around the country to understand their perceptions of how the internet and digital technology impact student writing in high school. The overall tenor of the study is one of optimism and technological progress: "[T]eachers see the internet and digital technologies such as social networking sites, cell phones and texting, generally facilitating teens' personal expression and creativity, broadening the audience for their written material, and encouraging teens to write more often in more formats than may have been the case in prior generations" (Purcell et al. 2013). On the surface, the teachers response seems to confirm what Web 2.0 writing theory has been telling us all along: digital, networked writing technologies allow for a richer rhetorical experience for students and for writing instruction in general.

On closer inspection, though, interesting tensions appear in the study. When contrasting the benefits of digital writing tools with their more "undesirable effects," the teachers' responses reveal a surprisingly superficial list of concerns: the use of informal language in formal writing assignments; "truncated forms of expression," as seen in texting (acronyms, emojis); a sense of digital tools as "toys" that students learned as children; and unequal access to digital tools amongst students (Purcell et al. 2013).

While I think all of us can sympathize with these teacherly concerns, they lean towards more traditional ideas about writing instruction. Certainly the access question raises real concerns, but even then, it has become less of an issue as internet access and mobile phones have proliferated globally. The other three concerns seem rather trite in the face of the larger cultural implications of digital literacy and the socioeconomic impacts of a global internet. Though these highlighted "undesirable effects" tell us little, directly, about the embodied impact of digital tools on student writing and memory, they do provide us with two key insights about current writing instruction in American secondary schools as articulated by professional teachers:

- The "undesirable effects" of digital writing are based on more traditional assumptions about writing pedagogy—belief in a tamed and standardized tongue, the poverty of abbreviated forms of expression, and the principle that writing is "serious" business and not child's play.
- In line with Web 2.0 writing theory, the teachers in the Pew study see the use value of digital writing for students, in terms of personal expression and sharing, as an intrinsic benefit of *more writing*. Thus, there is a productivist logic of *more writing is better*, where more writing, more texts, and more participation translates into more engaged individuals and a more democratic public sphere.

I find the juxtaposition fascinating—the conflicting desire on the part of writing teachers to embrace the wildness of Web 3.0 writing while trying to contain its influence on the writing that takes place in the classroom. These two traditions, social-constructionism and current-traditionalism alike, have been absorbed into our understanding of writing today. They are useful and important ways to think about writing, but alone they are not sufficient for theorizing the dynamic materiality of writing in the datafied age of Web 3.0. An excessive focus on the social or mechanical aspects of writing limits our critical materialist understanding of writing as a fully embodied, ecological, and metabolic experience.

While the study doesn't look explicitly at how digital writing technologies may affect memory, some of the less-emphasized statistics from the study show some interesting patterns:

- 69 percent of students were rated as "fair" or "poor" at "reading and digesting long or complicated texts."
- 68 percent of teachers said that digital writing tools encourage students to "take shortcuts" and "not put effort into their writing."
- 46 percent of teachers noted that digital writing tools encourage students to "write too fast and be careless."
- No more than 3 percent of students were rated as "excellent" on any of the core writing abilities.

Figure 5.1 is the chart from the study that shows how teachers responded to the survey. Though not explicitly noted, the

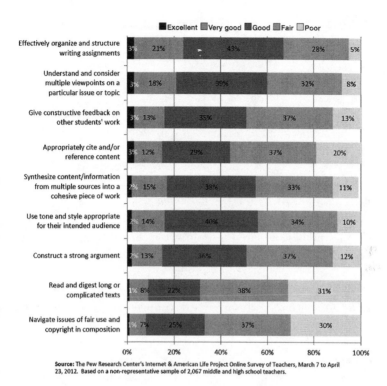

Source: The Pew Research Center's Internet & American Life Project Online Survey of Teachers, March 7 to April 23, 2012. Based on a non-representative sample of 2,067 middle and high school teachers.

Figure 5.1. Teacher ratings of high school students' writing and reading abilities, from a survey conducted by the Pew Research Center. (Purcell et al. 2013; permissions by Pew Research Center.)

patterns that emerge in the chart seem to point towards many of the embodied effects of ubiquitous inscription we see emerging in Web 3.0. These are not surface-level questions about grammar or whether or not students are composing more texts; these are concerns about the writing process, the careful, thoughtful work of composition, and a critical breakdown of this metabolic process. I'm baffled by the fact that no more than 3 percent of students were rated "excellent" on any of the writing competencies. That means that, out of the twenty-four hundred teachers that took the survey, only seventy-two teachers rated their students as excellent in any of the categories. Perhaps we could explain the 3 percent ceiling as a product of poorer school districts with fewer resources. Unfortunately, the majority of respondents were "leading edge" AP instructors teaching high-achieving students in resource-rich schools. Maybe the problem is that writing teachers have become more stringent in their assessment of writing, or maybe our most privileged students are getting complacent. Whatever the reasons are, the chart tells us something more radical is happening to students' abilities to think and write in the hyper-mediated spaces of Web 3.0.

My purpose here is not to dismiss the undeniable conveniences that digital writing tools have brought us and the ways they have improved the teaching and learning of writing. But concerns over shortcut taking, careless writing, and poor reading comprehension are profoundly concerns about the writing body and memory, learning and intellectual development, and how these processes change in digital environments. What we recognize in the study's results are young, beleaguered somatic minds interfacing with the nonhuman agents and information flows of Web 3.0—and struggling. As we adapt to conditions of persistent distraction and behavioral addiction, there is growing evidence of a simultaneous erosion of our abilities to remember, focus, and sustain attention—habits of mind necessary for intuitive, embodied thinking and writing well.

REINTEGRATING COGNITIVE RESEARCH WITH WRITING STUDIES

To think of writing as an embodied, somatic experience is to see our whole bodies as sites of meaning-making where the metabolic relations between corporeal and discursive flows of information merge. And while it's not always easy to see how digital environments and accelerating flows of information directly affect our bodies, one way to do so is to study how persistent distraction tampers with cognition and memory. My use of *cognition* may not sit well with some in writing studies. We're all aware of the tradition of "cognitivism" that dominated the study of writing during the late 1970s and early 1980s and the field's sound rejection of it for more social models of writing—what many have called the "social turn" in the field (Trimbur 1994; Faigley 1986). However, in light of Web 3.0 and the profound effects of the corporate assault on our somatic minds, there's a need to reintegrate contemporary cognitive studies of writing into our materialist theories to more clearly articulate how accelerating information production affects how we think and write today.

In making this move to reintegrate cognitive science, we can begin by revisiting the rift that occurred in the 1980s between cognitive and social-constructionist models of writing. James Berlin's definitive taxonomy of writing "ideologies" in *Rhetoric and Reality* (1987) firmly framed the cognitive tradition, as represented by the work of Janet Emig, Nancy Sommers, and Linda Flower and John Hayes, as losing relevance in the field's social turn. Berlin argued that cognitive rhetoric was a kind of transition phase into the critically imbued *social-epistemic* model of writing. His main critique was directed at the cognitivists' lack of engagement with the ideological and cultural aspects of writing: "The rhetoric of cognitive psychology refuses the ideological question altogether, claiming for itself the transcendent neutrality of science" (Berlin 1987, 178). Berlin argued that if we want to understand writing in culture we need to study it as a socially situated activity, one rife with questions of rhetoric and power. Because cognitive models of writing didn't acknowledge the ideological aspects of situated writing, they were thus limited in what they could tell us about writing as inherently a social and political activity.

While writing studies has moved on from Berlin's taxonomy, its impact on our materialist and embodied theories of writing cannot be overstated. In fact, his critique was so influential that it helped create a major schism in writing studies. As the majority of writing scholars were making the social turn in the 1980s, the cognitive researchers broke away and created their own branch of writing research within the cloisters of cognitive psychology and education. This schism, and Berlin's taxonomy, have been unfortunate for the field's materialist theories of writing in one main way. By dismissing cognition as a site for studying writing, we essentially erased the body as a source of meaning-making (Fleckenstein 1999, 286). While there were certainly theoretical limitations to early cognitivist models of writing, their focus on the somatic mind of the writer was an acknowledgement of the embodied experience of writing. In fact, the cognitivists had recognized the importance of the somatic mind as a material site for understanding embodied writing five decades ago.

A quick return to the seminal "A Cognitive Process Theory of Writing" (Flower and Hayes 1981) will help make my point. It's important to keep its publication in context. Flower and Hayes were responding to the limited "stage model" of the writing process, the basic prewrite-write-revise model that was then popular in writing textbooks. Their response was to develop a more empirical study of the writing process by studying actual writers (novice and advanced) in the act of writing.[4] Using out-loud protocols, Flower and Hayes recorded writers talking out-loud as they described what they were thinking during the act of composing a text. Berlin critiqued Flower and Hayes for the apolitical nature of their research, but the value of their research lies less in ideological critique and more in their effort to define a generalizable writing process that could be applied across writing situations and could be taught through direct instruction. Nothing more, nothing less. Some of our most lucid descriptions of the "writing process," the one we all teach in our classrooms, are found in this essay:

> A [writing] process that is hierarchical and admits many embedded sub-processes is powerful because it is flexible: it lets a writer do a great deal with only a few relatively simple processes—the basic ones being plan, translate, and review. This means, for instance, that we do not need to define "revision" as a unique stage in composing, but as a thinking process that can occur at any time a writer chooses to evaluate or revise his text or his plans. As an important part of writing, it constantly leads to new planning or a "re-vision" of what one wanted to say. (Flower and Hayes 1981, 285)

Their use of the term "hierarchical" describes the basic, recursive structure of the writing process. Steps in the process

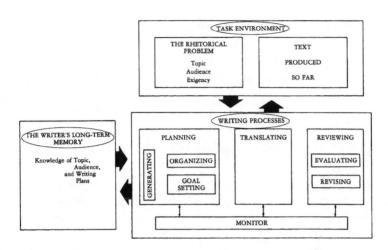

Figure 5.2. Flower and Hayes's cognitive writing process, with its three major components: the task environment, the writing process, and the writer's long-term memory. (Flower and Hayes 1981, figure 1.5); permissions by Lawrence Erlbaum Associates Incorporated.

move fluidly through a hierarchical structure that is an ever-changing, dialectical process *between* writing processes. Berlin interprets this "hierarchy" as a rigid framework, but, as Flower and Hayes continually stress, a hierarchical system does not necessitate that the hierarchy stays the same—it means that, at any one point in the writing process, experienced writers usually prioritize one composing task over the next.

Figure 5.2 is Flower and Hayes's model of the cognitive writing process. I still find this diagram an instructive, albeit limited, representation of the writing process. It essentially captures the basic pedagogical framework of first-year composition. Any act of writing entails these basic components and their interactions: the *task environment* includes the rhetorical situation and the broader cultural context of the writing; the *writing process* includes the recursive work that writing requires; and the *writer's long-term memory* includes the writer's working understanding of a particular topic and audience. As the bidirectional arrows suggest, in the cognitive writing process, the body of the writer, as represented by *working memory*, is an integral component of the model. That is to say, it's the working memory of the writer that actively initiates and manages the iterative process of moving amongst these three components when composing a text.

The inclusion of working memory in our understanding of the writing process is particularly relevant for my discussion of persistent distraction and how it negatively affects the writing body. Memory, as one of the rhetorical canons of ancient Greece, had once been a skill on par with *invention, arrangement, style,* and *delivery.* But with the rise of writing and print, memory receded into the background behind the other canons and those more germane to print literacy. With the emergence of Web 3.0 and the manufacture of micro-distractions, the canon of memory once again takes on relevance.

For cognitivist approaches to writing, memory has always been at the center of the writing process. In fact, to understand how we are able to write at all depends on the central role memory plays in, first, acquiring basic writing skills, and second, in developing the discursive structures to write more advanced texts (Flower and Hayes 1981, 276). While Berlin had felt it necessary to dichotomize the "cognitive" and the "social," the cognitivists would never make this distinction. Later work by Hayes (2012) would strike a better balance between the cognitive and the social by adding the concept of *domain knowledge* to Flower and Hayes's original cognitive process model. Domain knowledge includes audience and genre awareness, and discourse competence. As cognitive writing theorists Ronald T. Kellogg and Alison P. Whiteford argue, "in cognitive science today it is taken as axiomatic that both general strategies and domain-specific knowledge are required for expertise" in writing (Kellogg and Whiteford 2012, 266–267). Along with new advances in neuro- and cognitive science and the growth in research on the role memory plays in writing, contemporary cognitive models of writing offer a valuable resource for developing our embodied, ecological, and materialist theories of writing in Web 3.0.[5]

MEMORY AS SYSTEM

In understanding how persistent distraction affects memory, it helps to have a clear sense of how cognitive science explains memory formation. In his work on memory, neuropsychologist Jonathan K. Foster has shown that our current models of human memory have been greatly influenced by the rise of computers in the second half of the twentieth century (Foster 2009, 604–607). What emerges in cognitive psychology post-WW2 is a three-stage "memory system," a basic framework for understanding memory, in computer and human alike, that is still accepted today. All memory systems must be able to *encode*, *store*, and *retrieve* information in an ongoing way to function as a *working* memory system. Foster calls this basic system the "fundamental logic of memory" (Foster 2009, 26).

In addition to this basic process of memory, it is now well understood after decades of cognitive research on healthy individuals and people with brain injuries that the process of memory consists of two general components: *short-term* and *long-term memory*. Short-term memory is the thoughts we hold in conscious attention, while long-term memory stores memories over time, many becoming automatic like remembering how to walk or drive (Foster 2009, 33–34).[6] Today, the concept of short-term memory has evolved into the more dynamic "working-memory" model developed by Alan Baddeley and G. J. Hitch (Baddeley and Hitch 1974; Baddeley 2010). In their research on learning and memory, Baddeley and Hitch noticed that, when given two learning tasks at the same time, a primary and secondary one (e.g., remember a set of words *while* listening to a lecture), performance on the primary task always decreased when compared to participants doing the primary task alone. They reasoned that this decrease in performance implied that short-term memory is only capable of holding in conscious attention a limited amount of incoming information. Over time, they realized that "short" didn't capture the complex processes of active memory, so they turned short-term memory into "working memory" with three components (Figure 5.3): the visuospatial sketchpad (VSSP), the phonological loop (PL), and a central executive (CE).

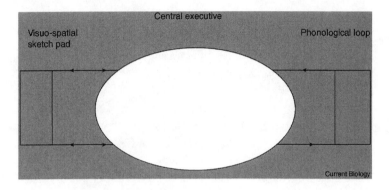

Figure 5.3. Baddeley and Hitch's (1974) working-memory model, with three components: the visuospatial sketch pad (VSSP), which encodes visual and spatial experience; the phonological loop (PL), which encodes sound and language; and the central executive (CE), which processes both memory channels in real time. (Permissions by Elsevier.)

The VSSP and PL are temporary storage systems that encode our immediate experience. The VSSP encodes visual and spatial experience while the PL encodes sound and language (Baddeley 2010). While both the VSSP and the PL work together in the writing process, the PL takes a primary role in the process of composing a written text. Managing and making sense of this stream of information is the CE, the attentional center of our conscious awareness that actively processes incoming stimuli from the world in real time (see Baddeley 2010; Foster 2009; Raulerson et al. 2010; McCutchen et al. 2008).

Figure 5.4 is the most recent iteration of working memory. In this version we see the accumulation of over forty years of cognitive study on memory. The three-part structure of the VSSP, PL, and CE are now embedded in a more detailed memory system. *Long-term memory* is described as a "crystallized system," the more fixed, steady part of memory that interacts with the more ephemeral systems of working memory (in the row above the shaded long-term memory). The *episodic buffer* is the point where consciousness emerges as our working memory actively reconstructs our lived experience by integrating our current temporal moment with the more stable language and visual

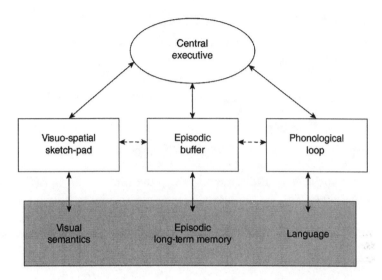

Figure 5.4. A recent model of working memory (Baddeley 2010), showing the dynamic interchange between episodic long-term memory (shaded) and working memory, whose central executive (CE) actively produces consciousness as it draws from long-term memory and synthesizes it with the current moment via the episodic buffer. (Permissions by Elsevier)

structures of long-term memory ("episodic long-term memory") (Baddeley 2010). Directing in the background is the central executive (CE), the component of cognition and memory that, ideally, directs our conscious attention to that which needs our attention most.

I've provided this overview for a two reasons. First, this cumulative model of working memory has helped cognitive research on writing articulate more sophisticated understandings of the writing process and the vital role memory plays in writing. And second, it gives us a discursive bridge, however imperfect, to reintegrate cognitive theory into our new materialist theories of writing as we grapple with the effects of manufactured distraction and behavioral addictions on our somatic minds, our memories, and our abilities to write.

WORKING MEMORY AND WRITING

With this more developed understanding of working memory, cognitive research on writing has considerably revised Flower and Hayes's model of writing. Cognitive studies through the 1990s and into the new millennium have drawn on Baddeley and Hitch's model of working memory to explore memory's critical role in writing and the kinds of problems that arise when we can't sustain the focused attention necessary for more advanced writing tasks. The longer, more involved a writing task is, the more involved working memory is in the process (McCutchen et al. 2008; Kellogg et al. 2016). For writing even to begin, we must be able to hold a mix of knowledge and understanding in our conscious attention long enough to actually write something, even something as simple as a text message. Once the writing process begins, working memory kicks in and begins to coordinate our awareness of the rhetorical situation with understandings retrieved from long-term memory—everything from semantic meaning to genre awareness to orthographic and lexical knowledge. This is the process of meaning-making, one that requires the conscious attention of the writer to unfold (Olive 2012; Kellogg and Whiteford 2012; Rider 1995).

Cognitive research on writing tells us that more experienced writers exhibit a long-term and working memory trained to handle longer, more sophisticated writing tasks than do novice writers (McCutchen et al. 2008; Kellogg and Whiteford 2012; Torrance and Galbraith 2006). This fact has nothing to do with inherent differences in the brains of experienced writers versus those of novices. Rather, it has to do with the amount of time and intensity a writer spends within a discourse. More familiarity with a discourse, as well as mastery of the techniques for advanced composition, help writers become more conversant in a discourse through more concentrated and intense encoding, storing, and retrieving of information from long-term memory (McCutchen et al. 2008, 462). In addition, experienced writers consistently draw on standard writing strategies—rereading, prewriting, outlining, revising, note-taking—to extend their working memory and manage the cognitive demands of writing longer texts (McCutchen et al. 2008; Young and Williams 1984; Ransdell et al. 2002). Thus, not only have experienced writers built a richer discursive storehouse in long-term memory, they have also learned strategies to manage information more effectively and free up space in working memory to extend the writing process. The same is true in reverse: a *novice* simply means a somatic mind that is just beginning to build the "cognitive architecture" of a memory conversant in a discourse (McCutchen et al. 2008, 453). The teaching of writing is the process we use to help students learn a discourse by preparing their long-term and working memories to absorb and learn the shape of the discourses and genres they are writing in.

The implications for embodied, new materialist theories of writing seem clear. As writers build up stores of discursive knowledge, they are at the same time conditioning their long-term and working memories to handle progressively more sophisticated and expansive writing projects (Bereiter and Scardamalia 1987; Foster 2009). When we write, we often intuit this. We know that writing longer texts is challenging, and we know the kinds of intellectual growth that occur in this process: associative thinking, perspective-taking, abstract and critical thinking, synthesis of ideas, and reflective thought. These are the kinds of literacies that emerge when students have the opportunity to write progressively longer, more challenging texts. Writing teachers also intimately know the struggles and joys of mastering a discourse, the time and patience it takes, and the need to engage with it in diverse ways. If the writing practices of experienced writers tell us anything, they tell us that successfully engaging in academic or research-oriented writing critically depends on the practiced integration of working memory, discourse, and advanced literacy skills.

Critical to this endeavor is having the time and space to develop the habits of mind and sustained attention typical of advanced writing (Kellogg and Whiteford 2012). Without sustained attention, working-memory cannot transfer meaning into long-term memory, a process called *memory consolidation* (Kandel 2006). In order for us to remember and learn, information that we discern as important and worth remembering must go through a delicate consolidation process in long-term memory where "any disruption, whether a jab to the head or a simple distraction, can sweep the nascent memories from the mind" (Carr 2010, 184). This is precisely why manufactured distraction is such a problem. Building and consolidating long-term memory requires long stretches of concentration. Frequent interruptions in this process make it difficult for the working memory of a writer to compose any text, let alone longer, more advanced texts. Micro-distractions, often triggered by manufactured behavioral addictions, impede the process of building long-term memory by interrupting the consolidating process of working memory. What the teachers in the Pew study noticed about their students' struggles to concentrate and read longer texts is, in part, an outcome of persistent micro-distractions and their effects on working memory.

Research on media-multitasking reflects these same concerns. In the popular mind, "multitasking" is often seen as something we do "naturally" as a matter of course as we juggle our lives. But multitasking online is different in the sense that we are asking our limited working memory to handle the hypermediated spaces of Web 3.0. While most humans are able to handle information flowing into working memory via the linguistic and visual channels at the same time, we begin to overtax memory formation when we overload either channel, or both channels together, as when we try to listen simultaneously to music, send a text message, and read an email. One of the most misleading claims in Web 3.0 has been labeling contemporary students as "digital natives." We often assume that, because young people came of age with social media and smartphones, they have somehow outwitted their brain's evolution and are able to manage distraction and media-multitasking more effectively than the print generations that preceded them. The problem with this stereotype is that it isn't true. As psychologist Jesper Aagaard candidly puts it, "we simply do not have any evidence of young people's superior technological abilities and multitasking skills" (Aagaard 2014, 2). Research on multitasking in cognitive psychology and neuroscience has known for decades that the human mind does not perform well at "parallel-processing"— that is, at engaging with two or more activities or tasks simultaneously (Sana et al. 2013; Wood et al. 2012; Junco 2015; Bellur et al. 2015). The American Psychology Association stresses that even quick switches between tasks distract and interrupt memory encoding, what they call "switch costs." As these little shifts and distractions accumulate throughout the day, people tend to get less overall work done and make more errors in the process ("Multitasking: Switching Costs" 2019).

The effects of manufactured distraction on memory are even more pronounced when writers try more advanced writing tasks that demand the full capacity of both long-term and working memory. Because writing uses both the VSSP and PL in working memory, *most* concurrent verbal, visual, or spatial tasks have been shown to adversely affect a writing task by slowing the writing process down and producing more grammatical errors and less-sophisticated syntax (Ransdell et al. 2002; Levy et al. 2012; Olive 2012). Skilled writers build a global understanding of their writing situation through sustained time and focus in a discourse. This time spent dwelling in a discourse, via the reflexive process of retrieving and encoding meaning with working memory, helps build the necessary long-term memory structures necessary for writing well in a discourse. Thus, neither emerging practices like media-multitasking nor the manufacturing of persistent micro-distractions are conducive to the patient, engaged process of consolidating memory and learning to write proficiently in a discourse.

CONCLUSION

The rise of manufactured distraction and behavioral addictions in Web 3.0 are expressions of a commercialized internet and the intensifying production of data and information. The once disconnected space of writing before the Web, whether it was pen and paper or word processing, is now ensconced in a networked, global archive that relentlessly seeks the attention and engagement of citizen-consumers. Today, the global archive gives corporations direct and intimate access to each of us through personalized mobile devices and the internet-of-things. In the commodified, accelerating writing environments of Web 3.0, such easy access can negatively affect our abilities to think and write, and it's leading to other harmful effects on our minds and bodies that we are just beginning to understand.

Thus, in the third material cumulus, the acceleration of commodified information production is manifesting in several antagonistic and unsustainable ways with the biophysical environment, from the macrosystem of the planet to the microsystem of our somatic minds. Such ecological problems are educational ones, and how we teach writing and rhetoric in the twenty-first century will play a vital role in helping us build more sustainable ways of life. In light of manufactured distraction and the behavioral addictions associated with internet use, we must stay vigilant to the powerful fetishizing effects of informational capitalism, especially in this time of environmental crisis. We need to be aware of how persistent micro-distractions conceal our metabolic relations with the biophysical environment and weaken those embodied thinking and writing skills necessary for critical, intuitive, and ecological awareness. In the next and final chapter, I look at ways we can integrate MEOW at the level of university curricula and writing pedagogy and continue to revamp higher education to cope with our corporatized digital environments and the metabolic acceleration of energy, matter, information, and capital they underwrite.

6

DEVELOPING CRITICAL, ECOLOGICAL LITERACIES

This theoretical connection of body with place allows us to see more precisely how eco-rhetoric departs from techno-rhetoric. If techno-rhetoric resents the demands of the body and seeks to remake it in the image of the machine . . . eco-rhetoric celebrates the body's connection to the earth and strives to accept the limits of the body as part of the perpetual struggle against the human hubris and overreaching that deplete resources and erode the Earth. (Killingsworth 2010)

In the preceding chapters, I've laid out some ways to extend our materialist, ecological theories of writing in Web 3.0. The intensification of data collection and the accelerating flows of information it feeds are contributing to many of the ecological problems we are grappling with today. As informational flows speed up, so too do our metabolic relations with energy, matter, and capital in ways that are becoming problematic for the health and sustainability of ecosystems at every scale.

Accelerating information production, the energy it consumes and the waste it produces, are global concerns that impact us all. Due to their scope, solving them will require concerted effort at all levels of culture and from all fields, especially education. As environmental scientist and educator David W. Orr argues, "the ecological crisis is in every way a crisis of education" (Orr 2005, xi). At all levels of education in the United States there is growing emphasis on environmental awareness and stewardship. Environmental science and sustainability programs are growing, and many universities are making great

DOI: 10.7330/9781607329688.c006

strides in becoming more sustainable. But, as will always be the case in an insatiable neoliberal, informational capitalism, protecting the environment and developing more environmentally sustainable ways of life are an ongoing struggle.

In light of big data, e-waste, and manufactured distraction by the corporate data complex, we must be on guard against the powerful fetishizing effects of informational capitalism, especially in this time of environmental crisis. While the literacies that are emerging online are essential skills today, we need to be aware of how they often conceal our metabolic relations with the biophysical environment and potentially weaken the literacies necessary for critical ecological awareness. Web 3.0 is a more aggressive semiotic environment than the print world that preceded it, and it often encourages behaviors that run counter to the habits of mind—creative, critical, and reflective—we are trying to develop in our classrooms. With literacy and writing instruction at the center of education around the world, the field of writing studies has a role to play in ameliorating environmental problems by helping students cultivate embodied, ecological literacies in our writing courses.

In this final chapter I look at ways to integrate MEOW in the classroom and university curricula more broadly. The chapter begins with an outline of four basic competencies for critical, ecological awareness and ends with a unit on *defetishization* in which students engage in a sequence of phenomenological and exploratory writing assignments intended to help them cultivate the ecological thinking they'll need to envision and enact a more sustainable world.

FOUR BASIC COMPETENCIES OF CRITICAL, ECOLOGICAL LITERACY

Towards this end, I have pulled together an initial framework for teaching critical ecological literacies that could be used to guide curricular development at both the university and departmental levels. It's a work in progress and it overlaps with many of the environmental and sustainability programs that are emerging around the country. Drawing on Robert Diamond's widely used model for curriculum development, I begin by articulating some of the possible learning outcomes of such a curriculum. Diamond notes that curricular development is an ongoing process of practice, data collection, and reflection on the kinds of competencies programs want students to develop. The framework I present here is not intended to be a one-size-fits-all approach—it's more of a starting point. Diamond argues that, not only should the curriculum teach the core competencies of a program, it should also take into account the basic survival competencies students will need to live meaningful lives in the future. He emphasizes that "there is far more agreement about basic competencies than one might first expect" across disciplines. Typically, shared competencies include *communication skills, interpersonal skills, problem-solving skills,* and *participatory citizenship* (Diamond 2008, 87). These are vital and necessary skills that all teachers want their students to develop, but in light of the environmental problems we are experiencing, we need to start including in these shared competencies a basic ecological understanding of metabolism and how ecosystems function.

If we are interested in having students learn the basic skills to survive in informational capitalism, they will need to be equipped with the critical acumen to understand and help solve the social and environmental problems we are facing in Web 3.0. The basic skills to survive in a time of ecological crisis *must* include critical, *ecological literacy.* Tackling global, systemic concerns like accelerating information production, climate change, and e-waste will require that we include ecological literacy as a core competency at all levels of education.

I present here four broad competencies that form the basic learning outcomes of a critical, ecological curriculum that could be integrated across various levels of schooling. Generally, such outcomes emerge organically from a school or department, so the competencies I present here are intended to be broad and adaptable. They are based on a synthesis of my own thinking about writing and ecology, and work in cognitive psychology, neurobiology, ecoliteracy (Orr 2004; Goleman et al. 2012;

Capra 1997; Louv 2012), ecopedagogy (Kahn 2010; Bowers 2003, 2010), composition (Owens 2001; Yagelski 2011; Patrick 2011), rhetoric (Killingsworth 2007, 2010), and phenomenology (Van Manen 2014).

1. Use Eco-Logic to Understand the Metabolic Nature of Actor Networks

The first competency is a guiding heuristic. Students will develop a deep understanding of systems and how to reason ecologically. Cultivating this kind of intelligence includes a basic understanding of the interdependent relations between information production, the biophysical environment, and the receptive space of the body. The Center for Ecoliteracy (CEL) emphasizes that the core of ecological literacy is understanding that "nature sustains life by creating and nurturing communities" (Stone and Barlow 2005, 3). This foundational competency provides students with the ability to explore ecological processes, apply the basic physical and thermodynamic laws that govern them, and articulate their own intra-relations with the ongoing metabolism of the natural and social systems they are a part of.

In developing eco-logic, they will learn to understand the vital ways energy, matter, information, and capital metabolize through ecosystems via the following characteristics and structures: networks, nested systems, interdependence, diversity, cycles, flows (energy, matter, information, and capital feedback loops), co-development, and dynamic balance (Capra 2005).[1] The idea of interdependence tells us that, while humans as a species have come to dominate the planet, we cannot survive, let alone live well, without acknowledging our metabolic interdependence with the biophysical systems we are a part of and the living, nonhuman agents we share them with. As the Center for Ecological Literacy emphasizes, we have much to learn from nonhuman systems and other animals about how to live sustainably in the world. Physicist Fritjof Capra puts it succinctly: "economics emphasizes competition, expansion, and domination;

ecology emphasizes cooperation, conservation, and partnership" (Capra 1997, 301). In this way, critical, ecological literacy should serve as a counterbalance to intensifying data collection, manufactured distraction, and acceleration in Web 3.0 and foster the kinds of thoughtful, reflective thinking necessary for living more sustainably in the world.

Both e-waste and big data are useful starting points for developing ecological thinking and for understanding the environmental impacts of information production and inscription. When seen through the basic attributes of a living system, a problem like e-waste quickly expands well beyond an individual user throwing away an old desktop. When embedded in intra-dependent networks and nested systems, the desktop computer becomes the cumulative embodiment of global supply chains of natural resources, labor, energy, and data. Through studying and writing about the metabolic relations between the production, use, and disposal of electronics, students can begin to make connections between their use of digital writing tools and the flows of energy, matter, information, and capital they entangle with. What we are trying to seed with this outcome is greater attunement to the embodied experience of literacy and cultivate students' abilities to understand how accelerating information production dangerously accelerates other basic flows in ways that can potentially harm other living systems, including our bodies.

2. Attunement to Nonhuman Things

Students will be competent in fostering techniques and strategies for attuning to their body's experience of the world beyond simply that which we consciously understand. They will learn to draw from both logical and emotional meanings, and they will learn to think of their lived experience as the dynamic, metabolic exchange between our somatic minds and the living and nonliving things with which we share the biophysical environment.

This competency corresponds with the first material cumulus in MEOW: writing technologies and their embodied, cumulative

history of use. Understanding the social and historical development of a technology is vital for understanding how nonhuman
technologies, including writing tools, take on agency. Students
will learn the historical conditions that give rise to informational
capitalism and sharpen their embodied sense of the technological imperative at the heart of neoliberal capitalism. They will
learn to understand the socioeconomic roots behind technological development and how technologies become the living
byproducts of centuries of human use and enhancement. In the
hypermediated world of Web 3.0, such understandings should
include a thorough understanding of the socioeconomic motivations behind wide-scale data collection and the ideologies behind
the design of hardware and software, algorithms, and artificial
intelligence. Ultimately, in understanding the cumulative history of any technology, students become more discerning of the
agency in things and the potential harm technology can facilitate.

In developing this kind of discerning attunement to the world,
the activity of writing presents for us a potent vehicle for activat-
ing embodied knowing. Robert Yagelski writes that "in the act of
writing, our consciousness and the world . . . become one; thus,
our experience of our self as a being-in-the-world is intensified
as we make meaning through the act of writing" (Yagelski 2011,
115). As Yagelski stresses, the *intensity* of writing makes it qualitatively different from other forms of human activity (e.g., watch-
ing a movie or listening to music) in the unique ways it pushes
our subjectivity to the edge of meaning and back. This intensity
has been observed in cognitive studies on writing that show differences between novice and advanced writers. In the process of
grappling with a discourse, advanced writers have undergone a
more intense process of memory building that will help them
write effectivity in that discourse. That is to say, the experience
of writing is always more than its textual and rhetorical purposes.
To say writing is an embodied experience is to say that we live
writing through the full sensorium of our bodies. Writing thus
is a powerful tool and practice for learning to attune to the
biophysical environment and our metabolic relations with the
human and nonhuman agents with which we intra-act.

A useful starting point for developing attunement and embodiment in students is to have them explore their lived experience *through* writing using the five "existentials" of phenomenological inquiry: *relationality, corporeality, spatiality, temporality,* and *materiality* (van Manen 2014). I say more about these existentials when I describe the first writing activity in the unit on defetishization. Such writing exercises are intended to sharpen students' sensitivity to nonhuman things and metabolic processes, and help them apply their embodied learning in ways that help them build healthier, more sustainable ways of living in the world.

3. Cultivate Practices of Strong Sustainability

Developing more sustainable ways of living is a fundamental goal of critical, ecological literacy. As ecological in nature, our literacy practices play a central role in building healthy ecosystems that are sustainable both socially and environmentally. By *sustainable* I am referring to the "strong" version that includes the *intergenerational requirement:* the idea that those of us living today have a responsibility to use earth's natural resources in ways that "meet the needs of the present without compromising the ability of future generations to meet their own needs" (Owens 2001, 22; Secretary-General of the United Nations 2013). Like ecology, sustainability is often co-opted by corporations as a way to talk about economic growth and development. This is the "weak" version of sustainability (Nobbs 2013, 144), an anthropocentric model that measures sustainability by how well human ecosystems (businesses, corporations, cities, nations) can maintain economic growth in the short-term. It is weak because it erroneously separates human ecosystems from the natural systems in which they are embedded. The "strong" version of sustainability shifts the focus on economic growth to a more holistic, long-range, and ecological understanding of sustainable development. A healthy ecosystem, whether it be a pond, a cell, or a city, must be able to metabolize the energy for life to exist and handle the inevitable waste produced by the system. Weak versions of sustainability ignore the intrinsic waste produced by all systems, as well as the finite limits of the planet's raw materials.

Prioritizing the health of future generations also injects a social justice component into the concept of sustainability and sets the ethical foundation for developing practices that will sustain both economic and environmental health for generations to come. Thus, teaching writing and rhetoric in Web 3.0 cannot simply be about teaching individuals to become stronger readers and writers; it must also help them develop the abilities to collaborate and work with others in sustainable ways. As Capra notes, "the tendency to associate, establish links, live inside one another, and cooperate—is one of the hallmarks of life" (Capra 2004, 301). Sustainable literacies include practices like involved listening, invitational rhetorics, perspective-taking, empathy-building, and collaboration—that is, rhetorical practices that are "a collaborative process of growth and transformation, a continual communal effort of truth-seeking" (Couture 1998, 6).

4. Imaginative, Utopian Thinking

Among other things, this competency is about averting the poison of cynicism. Although dystopian films and TV shows are popular these days, solving environmental problems requires, first, a belief that the global community can work together to solve these problems and, second, a vision of a future that can be better, more humane, more patient, more utopian. "Imagination" and "utopian thinking" come out of my synthesis of work by compositionist Ann E. Berthoff and philosopher Ernst Bloch. Berthoff's *Reclaiming the Imagination* (Berthoff 1984) gives an impassioned defense of the imagination and its centrality in making meaning. It integrates well with Ernst Bloch's three-volume opus, *The Principle of Hope* (1995). In an oft-cited passage, Bloch writes that, "expectation, hope and intention, directed towards the possibility which has not yet arrived, constitute not only a fundamental property of the human consciousness but also, provided they are rectified and grasped in their concrete aspect, a fundamental determination at the heart of objective reality itself" (Bloch 1995). Bloch's massive treatise was in response to the horrific amount of killing that occurred in WW2 and a steadfast defense of the necessity of utopian thinking and the nurturing of hope. As he notes, when we grasp the concrete aspects of hope historically and the significant role it has played as each generation struggles for a better life, it reminds us of the role that hope plays as a force for good and for creating sustainable living practices that consider those generations that will come after us. Developing imaginative, utopian thinking is central to MEOW and critical, ecological literacy because it is a way for students to put their ecological intelligence into practice and work towards a more sustainable, just, and ecological world.

Together, these four competencies are intended to provide a broad framework for guiding the development of critical, ecological literacies at all levels of education.

WRITING UNIT ON DEFETISHIZATION

In this final section I present a sequence of writing activities designed to foster critical, ecological literacy. Using a combination of phenomenological inquiry and critical genre analysis, I present a unit on *defetishization*—a sequence of writing and reading activities intended to develop ecological literacies and attune the senses of the somatic mind. We can think of defetishization as the critical practice of *reconnection*—of articulating the metabolic relations between literacy, writing technologies, capital circulation, and the biophysical environment. This process fundamentally depends on how we conceptualize and teach the activity of writing.

As Yagelski argues, to begin this process of reconnection, "we will need to understand writing in ontological terms; we will need to understand the experience of writing and of learning to write in order to understand the implications of that experience on students' sense of self. We will need, that is, a theory of writing as a way of being" (Yagelski 2011, 12). Understanding writing as a way of being means shifting our pedagogical focus from the production of texts (both "process" and "product") to the *phenomenological experience* of writing. As the study of lived experience, phenomenology assumes that the "truth" of human experience is best captured through direct, preverbal contact with the phenomenal world.[2] Phenomenologists seek to capture the experience of being *drawn into relation* with objects and people before ideology and convention can adulterate the encounter (Abram 1997, 56).[3] In thinking about writing in these terms, we are still thinking about "process," but not the standard understanding of process as the steps we go through in drafting and revising a text. Rather, we are thinking about the process of transformation and self-discovery we go through when we attune to the ontological and embodied experience of writing.

When we understand writing as a means to engage in phenomenological inquiry, as a way of being, we can see how to use it as a vehicle for exploring our metabolic experience of the world and, ideally, discover more meaningful ways to live in it. It is *through* the writing process that we are "attempting to recover and express the ways we experience our life as we live it—and ultimately to be able to act practically in our lives with greater thoughtfulness and tact" (van Manen 2014, 20). The sequence of writing assignments that follow are suggested activities for developing the four ecological competencies I've outlined above. The activities aren't groundbreaking; they build from standard writing pedagogies (journaling and genre analysis) and adapt them to specifically encourage the development of critical, ecological literacies in the context of Web 3.0.

Activity 1: Writing Phenomenologically

Phenomenological writing is a kind of mental gymnastics. The goal is to *suspend* our knee-jerk interpretations of the world—the ideologies, judgments, and biases—and try to grasp "that raw moment . . . of existence that we lift up and bring into focus with language" (van Manen 2014, 53). Writing sits at the heart of this process. Phenomenological questions tend to eschew analytical practices like generalization, theory formation, opinions, and moral judgments. A phenomenologist might ask, "how do we experience sickness?" or, "how do we experience time," or "what is my experience with *X* [object, person]." Writing teachers will notice how similar these questions are to more personal, journal-like writing. In phenomenological writing the explicit goal is conscious, directed attention on the thoughts and sensations of any particular embodied experience *before* the strictures of discourse and culture intervene to make sense of it on their terms—a state similar to what Buddhists refer to as "being present."

As van Manen notes, while we will never be able to completely access some raw, unmediated experience of the world, we can certainly learn practices and literacies that help us clarify our lived experience and act in better accordance with the planet, our bodies, and the other human and nonhuman agents we intra-act with. In this way, writing phenomenologically is a practice of writing that is intentionally exploratory, experiential, and generative—a practice of writing that is more than a just means for communicating or assessing students' knowledge, but a somatic practice intended to help them act in "a more reflective, self-aware, and . . . altruistic way" (Yagelski 2011, 159).

Here's an example of phenomenological inquiry by J. H. Van Den Berg on his lived experience of time:

> Compared with the toad, the frog is fast, even when it doesn't stir and, on the basis of its particular speed, the frog leaps, while the toad crawls by virtue of the time that is its own. Even people have a time of their own; each one, I suspect, has one for himself. The botanist is marked by a different time than the geologist. The zoologist who specializes in diptera is by virtue of his time, his tempo and duration, a different man than his colleague who prefers to limit himself to bumble bees. Compare the gracefully and rapidly alighting dragonfly with the busy, ungainly, searching bumbling bee: they represent two tempos, two forms of time, and the zoologist has to make a choice if he wishes to have the specific interest which he professes to have. (van den Berg 1970, 123)

In addition to the journal-like qualities of the passage, there's a certain contemplative tone that uses vivid details, concrete images, attention to pattern, associative thinking, and metaphor.

These are the impressions phenomenological inquiry is trying to capture *via writing*—listening to our senses and thoughts, and noting relations, feeling, movement, and concrete details as they metabolize through the permeable boundary of our body all while attempting to withhold judgment of our experience so that novel, embodied understandings can emerge.

What are we hoping to achieve with such experiential writing? First, to begin cultivating critical, ecological literacies, writing phenomenologically is an intentional literacy practice for exploring the dynamic reciprocity between our bodies and the other human and nonhuman agents we intra-act with. We can hardly expect students to develop ecological literacies without writing activities that practice this kind of "intensive meaning-making" (Yagelski 2011, 115). A second goal is to shift our ultimate emphasis from the production of a finished, polished text to the transformative power of writing in which "the text serves the purpose of writing, rather than writing having only the purpose of producing a certain kind of text" (Yagelski 2011, 147).

The Phenomenological Journal

There are many ways to approach phenomenological inquiry, but it is essential that teachers provide phenomenologically appropriate writing assignments. The topic or theme students will examine must be "experientially recognizable and experientially accessible," and provide students with a fertile space for exploring their metabolic experience with the world around them (van Manen 2014, 297).

A text I've used in class and one that works well for opening up phenomenological inquiry is to ask students to participate in Jake Reilly's "Amish Project." As an undergraduate at the Chicago Portfolio School, Reilly began to notice how his online life dominated his life offline: "It was pretty bad. I was reading every single tweet and I follow 250 people. Then, I would waste a good hour and a half on Facebook. I was sending more than 1,500 texts a month" (Sylvester 2012, interview). He also noticed how it was changing his relationships, and how he and his friends talked more online than actually face-to-face. In response to this felt discomfort, Jake decided to take a break from social media for three months. He deactivated his Facebook and Twitter accounts and put away his smartphone (and installed a landline). As Jake explained in an interview after the experiment, while it was difficult at first, he discovered he had more free-time and he learned to be more "present" when hanging out with his friends in person (Sylvester 2012, interview).

Jake's experiment echoes many of the same experiences other young people have expressed in similar studies conducted on college campuses. The University of Maryland's "Unplugged" study (2012) surveyed close to a thousand students from around the world after asking them to go "24 hours without media."[4] Researchers concluded that "going without media made students dramatically more cognizant of their own media" (Moeller et al. 2012, 45). Students self-reported that they felt addicted to social media and struggled without it, and they expressed how essential it was in helping them manage their relationships and work lives. In either case, both of these understandings are exactly the kinds of meanings phenomenological inquiry is hoping to evoke, as well as give students the chance to discover, through the embodied experience of limiting their use of social media, a deeper understanding of their relationship to nonhuman technologies. As the researchers note, "a clear majority in every country admitted outright failure of their efforts to go unplugged" (Moeller et al. 2012, 48), though many of the respondents expressed a sense of relief from unplugging and how it helped them feel more connected with the people around them (Moeller at al. 2012).

Jake's experience and the "Unplugged" study both exemplify the embodied and metabolic relations we carry on with our digital writing tools. While we can't ask students to abstain from social media for 90 days, we can ask them to try a day, or a week, and to keep a phenomenological journal of the experience. Unplugging works well as an initial phenomenological inquiry because of the potential for strong visceral responses that can denaturalize students' relations with their writing technologies.

Other activities could ask students to observe their time online: how they feel after a long stint on social media or a video game, and what they actually remember. Another assignment could have students write about a special place or an awkward situation; or sitting in a park; or by a lake. A final entry in this sequence could have students write about a place where technology clashes with the environment.[5] Both technology and the biophysical world offer an infinite number of opportunities to practice phenomenological inquiry, and unplugging can be the first step in helping students do that.

Using the Existentials

To help students explore their experience of unplugging, teachers can draw on what van Manen calls "experiential" or "universal themes of life" (van Manen 2014, 7487–7492): relationality (lived relations), corporeality (lived body), spatiality (lived space), temporality (lived time), and materiality (lived things). These existentials are conceptual tools used throughout several works on phenomenology by key phenomenological philosophers like Martin Heidegger, Jean-Paul Sarte, Maurice Merleau-Ponty. For phenomenologists, "we all experience our world and our reality through these existentials" (van Manen 2014, 302). Such a framework provides the conceptual architecture for engaging in phenomenological inquiry. To help guide students in attuning to their lived experience of unplugging, the existentials can help them pursue the kinds of questions that lead to more embodied understandings. Their separation is only for creating ways into phenomenological inquiry.

Relationality (lived relations). The shape and experience of our lived relations, especially with our closest intimates, comes sharply to life when we do not have access to easy communication. As Jake noted in his three-month experiment, those relations that were the strongest continued (and grew) with more face-to-face interaction, and those that were more media based tended to fade away easier. Exploring the relational qualities of unplugging, students might ask questions like:

- What role do social media play in my relationships?
- How do social media affect my relations both online and off?
- How much time do I actually spend in face-to-face contact with friends?
- What is the quality of my interactions online versus offline? (Consider actions like touching, smiling, winking, banter, dialogue, innuendo, etc.)
- What is my relationship with my technology?
- What is my relationship with nature and other living, non-human agents?

One of the vital things we are trying develop in thinking relationally is *empathic thinking*—that is, helping students grow their innate abilities to take on others' perspectives, to show compassion and concern (Goleman and Senge 2014). As Daniel Goleman and Peter Senge emphasize, though, empathic intelligence will only emerge when given the right conditions to do so (Goleman and Senge 2014, 29-31). This is something the phenomenological journal is intended to do.

Corporeality (lived body). Corporeality entails a focus on embodiment—the sensual experience of the somatic mind in the act of making meaning. Van Manen provides the quintessential question for pursuing this existential: "How is the phenomena we study perceived, sensed, touched by the body?" (van Manen 2014, 304). In Web 3.0 we could ask more specific questions like, how does accelerating information production and ubiquitous inscription affect my body and mind? What kinds of impulses do I experience online? What kind of emotional world do I experience online? Does it cause anxiety? Joy? Depression? What is my lived experience of interfacing with media—my hands, back, eyes? How do I feel about wearable technology? Having students explore this existential through writing is intended to help them tap the full sensorium of their body as meaning makers.

Spatiality (lived space). As I argued throughout the previous chapters, one of the defining features of informational capitalism is how intensifying flows of data and information radically change our experience of time and space while accelerating capital circulation in the process. By unplugging, students create a space to step back from their hypermediated lives and reflect on how social and mental spaces change when we leave our mobile phones at home. We can ask them to explore the experience of having to find their way around an unfamiliar area without GPS, the sense of disorientation they might feel, or a sense of physical liberation like the one Jake experienced. Exploring spatial questions inevitably intersects with relationality and can tell us a lot about our dependency on technology and how it changes our lived experience of time and space.[6]

Temporality (lived time). In thinking about the temporality of unplugging, we are asking students to reflect on how their experience of time changes. Jake notes several times in his experiment how much free time he seemed to have once he unplugged. When asked if this free time translated into being a better student, Jake responded:

> Yeah, a hundred times over. Like I said, there wasn't really much to do at the house, so I stayed at school most nights until 10 when everyone else leaves around 6, without a doubt. I think what's so hard for people and so distracting for people is that where they work, there are social media distractions on the same machine that they are supposed to be using to do their work . . . when you can't distract yourself, all you can do is work. (Silfer 2012).

Anyone who has played a multiplayer online game has had the experience of compressed time when twelve hours of game play are experienced unconsciously by the gamer as less than five minutes. Having students inquire into their sense of time when unplugged is ideal because of the cognitive dissonance that can be generated. If students express anxiety, or feel disoriented, or, like Jake, experience the sensation of creating time, students are drawing on their lived experience of temporality in Web 3.0.

Materiality (lived things). Materiality was defined in the first chapter as the ceaseless intra-action of human and nonhuman agents in the larger natural world of physical, metabolic, and thermodynamic laws. Asking questions about the phenomenology of materiality means inquiring into our lived experience of both internal and external metabolism. This fundamentally includes understanding how accelerating information production accelerates how energy and matter flow in ways that are, in the long run, environmentally unsustainable. The goal with this existential is to provide students with a space to write about their meta experience of metabolizing with the bio-physical world and how information production fundamentally changes this experience. What are the material implications of citizen-consumer data collection on our digital writing practices? What linguistic and written forms emerge as information production accelerates? How do algorithms and automation change our lived experience of writing and materiality? What does a vibrant, healthy public sphere look like in Web 3.0?

Exploring the existentials is just one way to approach a phenomenological journal with students. The idea is to create some dissonance in their normalized experience of living online and have them explore this embodied (and disembodied) experience through writing. As van Manen emphasizes, phenomenological writing "does not just aim for the clarification of meaning, it aims for meaning to become experienced as meaningful. Meaningfulness happens when meaning speaks to our existence in such a way that it makes 'contact' and touches us" (van Manen 2014, 373). The basic idea in phenomenological writing is to heighten student awareness of their metabolic relations with the world in ways that help them attune to the innate wisdom of their sensing bodies.

The phenomenological journal begins the unit because it helps ground students in the practice of phenomenological inquiry and how to use writing as a tool for developing embodied, ecological understandings of their lived experience. Stepping away from the internet to do this kind of contemplative, exploratory work gives students a creative space removed from online distractions, a space to give full attention to an experience through writing.

Activity 2: Slavery Footprint

With the phenomenological journal at the heart of the unit, instructors have some flexibility in how they pursue other

Figure 6.1. Entry page for slaveryfootprint.org. (Permissions by Made in a Free World.)

reading and writing activities. A text I have found to be useful for helping students defetishize Web 3.0. is slaveryfootprint.org (SFP) (figure 6.1). SFP was developed by the nonprofit organization Made In A Free World (MIFW) to help raise awareness about the pervasive use of slave labor in global chains of production. MIFW estimates that there are over twenty-nine million slaves worldwide—men, women, and children forced into labor through coercion and violence. Roughly 10 percent of this population will be sold into the illegal sex trade, while the rest work, in one way or another, within the global flows of state and corporate capital (MIFW 2019). Like e-waste, slave labor is another example of how neoliberal capitalism externalizes the environmental and human costs of maintaining capital circulation, shifting the most dangerous, monotonous, and labor-intensive work to developing countries while accumulating large profits in American and European markets.

SFP is an interactive online survey that collects user data about our day-to-day consumption patterns, asking basic questions about what you consume (food, commodities, energy) and how much. Typical questions include things like "How many times a week do you eat meat?" and "How often do you

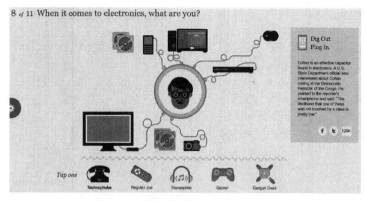

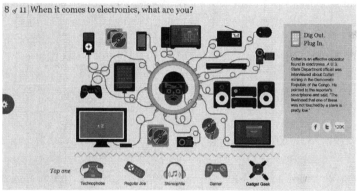

Figure 6.2. Two ends of the spectrum in levels of electronics ownership at slaveryfootprint.org: the "technophobe" (top) owns at least five devices, and the "gadget geek" (bottom) owns 15 or more devices. (Permissions by Made in a Free World.)

wash clothes?" The survey takes about fifteen minutes to complete. Through a very simple, user-friendly interface, SFP turns our consumption practices into a game composed of colorful, visual imagery. Figure 6.2 shows how SFP uses a rhetoric of play to sweet-talk users into providing honest information about how much they consume.

In one example, SFP asks respondents to answer the following question about their use of electronic technology: "When it comes to electronics, what are you?" Respondents can choose from five categories: *Technophobe, Regular Joe, Stereophile, Gamer,* and *Gadget Geek*. With each change in identity comes more electronics. Even the technophobe, according to SFP, owns a minimum of five electronic devices. As you move up the chain, the Gadget Geek comes in owning at least fifteen devices including two televisions, a desktop, laptop, phone, and tablet. To keep survey respondents grounded in reality, SFP includes a sobering figure about the global slave trade in coltan, a metallic ore used to make the capacitors in electronic circuits. The Democratic Republic of Congo is home to one of the largest coltan mines in the world. Western demand for it has fueled internal strife in Congo and helped create inequitable labor relations and dangerous working conditions (Jardim 2017; Balde et al. 2017).

SFP is a counterexample to the more commodified data collection of the corporate data complex. Rather than commodifying consumer data, SFP uses consumer data to inform the public and connect consumers to the class and labor relations behind the commodities we purchase. In this way, SFP performs two defetishizing moves. First, it is a model of digital data collection that is more communitarian, helping us understand the cumulative impacts of our consumption and the ripple effects it causes across the globe. Second, SFP directly confronts Marx's classic understanding of commodity fetishism as our inability to see the commodity form for what it really is, "a material form of a fundamental social relation" (Marx 1990). SFP uses modern writing and inscription technologies to demystify the social and global chain of power relations that support Western levels of consumption.

I find the site to be quite useful in the writing classroom for several reasons. One, it's a good example of the layered nature of a Web 3.0 text: the server and database layer; the algorithmic, programming layer; the coding and design layer; and the semiotic, rhetorical layer of the interface. This kind of example serves well as a model for a range of writing assignments and new media composition, such as writing for the web, visual rhetorics, web design, programming, and database design. As a critical text, it helps writers imagine a different paradigm for big data and new media writing, one that actively undercuts our current model of data collection that dominates Web 3.0. By actively revealing the social relations behind commodities and the complex actor networks that make them possible, SFP effectively models how to use big data ethically and how to think ecologically with it.

Activity 3: Life-Cycle Assessment (LCA) as Critical Research
Cultivating ecological literacies is a gradual process of helping students defetishize Web 3.0 and develop the critical faculties for complex, systems thinking. In the hypermediated environment of Web 3.0, we must help students develop ecological kinds of research that are a nuanced, deliberate process of understanding the social and ecological systems that commodities emerge from. An ideal genre for fostering this kind of ecological thinking is the *life-cycle assessment (LCA)*. LCAs came out of the environmentalism of the 1960s as a method for studying the effects of energy use on the environment. Now an established genre, LCAs quantify the total amount of energy and emissions produced in the manufacture, use, and disposal of a product (Curan 2006). Figure 6.3 shows some of the basic stages in an LCA.

LCAs can be long, technical documents, written by a team of scientists or researchers. They can also be shorter documents that look at a particular part of a larger process, or that zoom out to look at the basic stages of manufacturing, distribution, consumption, and disposal. They are used by governments and corporations to assess both energy and disposal needs associated with manufacturing and releasing a product for public consumption.

Students new to the genre could begin by using the basic stages of a products life cycle—manufacture, use, and disposal—to develop a sense of the sheer amount of energy and materials used from the initial manufacture of the product to its eventual end-of-life disposal. This object may have been something they discovered in their phenomenological inquiries. Take, for

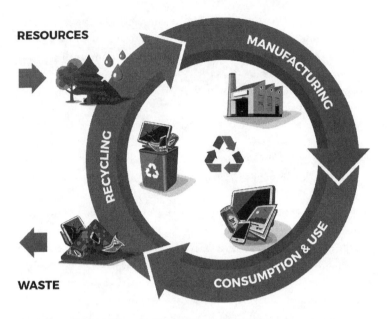

RESOURCES

MANUFACTURING

RECYCLING

CONSUMPTION & USE

WASTE

Figure 6.3. Simplified diagram of the basic stages of a life-cycle assessment (LCA). LCAs are documents that study the total amount of resources and energy used in creating a product, from mining natural resources, to manufacturing, distribution, consumption and use, disposal and recycling. (Image owned by author. Permissions by petovarga/Shutterstock.com.)

example, headphones. Students could research what materials are used in manufacturing headphones (the plastic, rubber, and wire), the kinds of labor that go into the product, and where they go when they no longer work.[7] Depending on the teacher's goals, the LCA might take a more narrative, phenomenological tone that explores other social and cultural aspects of commodity use and circulation. For example, students could research where their food comes from, how a fresh tomato ends up in New England in mid-January, and the different human and nonhuman agents who play a part in this process. Because LCAs are primarily concerned with processes and relationships, they are well suited for visual presentation,[8] thus making them also useful for courses on visual rhetorics and design. Because they tend to be longer, researched texts, LCAs present the kinds of writing challenges that help students cultivate their working memories and grow as critical, ecological thinkers.

CONCLUSION

The efficacy of the unit can be assessed by how well it succeeds in teaching the four competencies of critical ecological literacy. Because literacy instruction sits at the heart of the educational system, we need to be teaching the kinds of literacies that will prepare students to build a more just and sustainable world. It will take our concerted effort to continually confront the productivist tendencies of informational capitalism and develop strong sustainable practices that bring the writing body into closer alignment with the rhythms of the biophysical environment. As we learn more about the material social effects of Web 3.0 and corporate data collection, we must be wary of how these practices change our experience of literacy and how they potentially erode our abilities to focus, think critically and reflectively, and grow as writers. It's not simply that our minds are in the balance; our minds, and the ecosystems they depend on, both hang in the balance as we figure out how to cope with the ecological challenges of Web 3.0.

CODA

As I've explored it here as a critical, ecological framework for theorizing writing, MEOW is a work in progress. My hope is that it will help further our materialist understandings in a world of ubiquitous inscription and accelerating information production.

As a working theory, MEOW is open-ended and meant to serve as a heuristic for ecological and systems thinking. This openness brings with it both strengths and weaknesses. On one hand, the strength of ecological frameworks rests in their scalability and how they support multilevel analyses of individuals and the local and global systems they are a part of. On the other hand, this strength highlights a limitation. In MEOW, like other ecological frameworks, it can be hard to know where to set a boundary in analysis. If human and nonhuman actors are in metabolic intra-action with each other and the systems they are a part of, where does the actor network or human ecosystem begin or end? Where does the analysis of writing begin and end? The sheer richness of human rhetorical activity and the abundance of nonhuman writing technologies to consider in an ecological analysis raises questions about the practicality of ecological research for studying human semiotic systems. As such, it's important to keep in mind that the strength of ecological frameworks lies not only in their use as a guide for developing more robust materialist theories, but also for building more specific models that can be applied to local research sites.

Another notable strength of ecological frameworks is their emphasis on movement and emergence. Ecological thinking is uniquely fit for articulating how texts and technologies are always on the move, and, more specifically, understanding that movement as a product of the basic metabolic relations

DOI: 10.7330/9781607329688.c007

between flows of writing, information, capital, energy, and matter. Of course, trying to capture the motion of material social metabolism in real time has always been a challenge, and one that grows more challenging with the ongoing expansion of the global archive and accelerating data collection.

As we continue to develop our new materialist theories of writing, more interdisciplinary work with the natural sciences is necessary, in particular ecology, biology, physics, and thermodynamics. As I've argued throughout this work, the concept of *information* is an obvious contact zone between writing studies and the natural sciences. With greater synthesis of these knowledge domains, we can push our theories of writing and rhetoric in new ways and deepen our critical insight into the social and environmental effects of accelerating information production. This vitally includes grappling with the two most challenging metabolic rifts we are facing today as a global community: climate change and growing wealth inquality around the world.

As far as climate change goes, as atmospheric CO_2 levels continue to rise globally, climate scientists argue that we need to be prepared for more unpredictable weather patterns, fiercer hurricanes, and more drought (Baker et al. 2018; "Climate Science" 2020). For writing studies, by developing our new materialist, ecological theories of writing we can help develop responsive solutions to climate change by articulating the role that accelerating information production plays in speeding up energy consumption and CO_2 emissions.

As far as widening wealth inequity goes, climate change only exacerbates the already extreme discrepancies we see across the globe (Diffenbaugh and Burke 2019; Shorrocks et al. 2018). Despite the awareness raised by the Occupy Wall Street protests in 2011–2012, the gap between the top 1 percent and the rest of the world has only increased. In 2018, it was estimated that near 50 percent of total global wealth was owned by less than 1 percent of the world's population ("Global Inequality" 2020). At current rates, that 50 percent could potentially reach two-thirds of total wealth by 2030 (Savage 2018). It's vital we continue to address these persistent antagonisms in order to build more environmentally sustainable ways of living with each other and the planet. It will be impossible to do so without understanding the metabolic relationship between writing, information, capital, matter, and energy. MEOW has been designed with this specific goal in mind.

Throughout the time I've been writing this book, I've become keenly aware of the urgent need to develop more diverse solutions to the social and environmental problems emerging in Web 3.0. When theorizing, it's important we don't stop at the critique: it must lead to ideas and solutions. As we continue to point out how information production can lead to social and economic problems, we must also acknowledge those practices that are progressive and sustainable. Throughout the text, I've tried to point out examples of more environmentally aware practices as they relate to information production, such as the use of more renewable energy by the IT industries, the clean-up of illegal e-waste plants, and the implementation of recent data privacy laws passed in the European Union. These are all good signs that we are starting to take more seriously the social, economic, and environmental issues raised by acceleration and commodified data collection on citizen-consumers. However, as long as we live within a predatory, neoliberal informational capitalism, we must always struggle to hold corporations accountable and fight for more just and sustainable ways of living.

Looking backward and projecting forward, here's a list of some of the questions I have covered in this book, as well as possible future ones that others may want to explore:

- How does information flow, who owns it, where is it stored, and how is it used?
- How does capital drive information production in ways that harm the environment?
- What is the relationship between writing and different kinds of information production?
- How does ubiquitous inscription and data collection affect our bodies and the ecosystems we are a part of?
- How does information acceleration affect our somatic minds and, as a result, our writing and rhetorical practices?

- How does ubiquitous inscription and information acceleration enable the spread of misinformation/disinformation?
- How is nonhuman, artificial intelligence radically changing
  the nature of rhetoric and who or what can write?
- How does the concept of information act as a bridge concept between the natural sciences and the study of writing
  and rhetoric?
- How is writing and information production both a physical
  and a thermodynamic phenomenon?
- What are the relationships among writing, information, and
  entropy?
- What are the environmental effects of accelerating informational production at different ecological scales (micro,
  medial, macro)?
- How can we use data collection on citizen-consumers to
  promote environmentally sustainable ways of living?
- How does the manufacture, use, and disposal of electronics
  contribute to growing wealth inequality and class conflict?

While there's a lot more work to do in understanding these
questions, they point us towards some of the issues now emerging in Web 3.0. In response to acceleration and new digital phenomena like the internet-of-things, algorithms and automation,
and advancements in machine learning and artificial intelligence, we will continually need to refine and sharpen our materialist ecological theories of writing. By doing so, we can do our
part to develop literacies and social practices that work towards
a more sustainable future for ourselves, our children, and the
countless living organisms that will inherit the Earth after us.[1]

NOTES

INTRODUCTION: TOWARDS A MATERIALIST ECOLOGY OF WRITING

1. I use the term *writing studies* throughout this work as a catchall phrase to describe the larger field of rhetoric, composition, and literacy studies. I realize the term is up for debate, but I think its emergence is a reflection of the field's desire to deepen our materialist analyses of writing.

2. My use of the term *materiality* throughout this work is very much in line with Anis Bawarshi's fine explanation in *Key Words for Writing Studies* (2015): "Materiality is used to signify that which surrounds us: the places we inhabit; the climate (political, geographical, ambient) that affects how we encounter one another, what we do, and how we do it; the tools that mediate our social activities and relations; and the institutions, resources and socio-economic conditions that shape the means of textual production, distribution, and assessment. *Materiality* is also used to describe our bodies; our embodied experiences and expressions of emotion; our movements and gestures; the ways we negotiate space, objects, technologies, and time as we enact our daily routines and improvisations" (Bawarshi 2015, 108). To focus on the materiality of writing in this sense is to foreground how our rhetorical practices and writing technologies deeply affect and intertwine with both natural and built environments, including our bodies.

3. I'll be using the term *citizen-consumer* throughout this work. I realize it's cumbersome, but it's meant to highlight our roles as citizens in a democratic state over the vaguely parasitic and crude way humans are generally understood through the logic of capitalism as "consumers."

4. One *zettabyte* is equivalent to one billion gigabytes, or 90 years of HD video (Khoso 2016).

5. By *information technology industries* I am referring to what is more commonly called the *technology sector* in the North American Industry Classification System (NAICS). They define this industry as "computer and electronic product manufacturing, data processing, hosting, and related services, other information services, and computer systems design and related services" (Srnicek 2017). I prefer the term *information technology industries* for how it foregrounds information as the vital commodity that flows through much of this technology.

6. My use of the word *archive* comes out of the work of Jacques Derrida and Michel Foucault, using *archive* as a metonym for ubiquitous inscription and textuality, what Derrida called *arch-writing*. As Christopher Johnson explains, in theorizing *writing* as a material social force that actually precedes speech, Derrida sought "to move beyond the everyday

understanding of writing in order to postulate a 'writing' more fundamental to signifying practices in general, a 'writing' that is the condition of all forms of expression, whether scriptural, vocal, or otherwise" (Johnson 1993). By *global archive*, then, I mean the material, networked infrastructure of ubiquitous inscription technologies that we spend a good deal of our lives interacting with and the datafied textuality those relations foster.

7. One of the best examples of the giddy excitement provoked by Web 2.0 is captured in Time Magazine's iconic "Person of the Year" in 2006 as "You," with the tagline, "You control the information age. Welcome to your world."

8. LinkedIn founder Reid Hoffman explains Web 3.0 in these terms: "Clearly what's happening is that there's going to be this massive substructure of data . . . data is a platform . . . [and] it's not just one data set in Facebook, or one data set in LinkedIn, or one data set in Twitter, but it's actually these sets indexed by people, indexed by location, and across the multiple data sets on a kind of grass-roots basis that's going to create really amazing applications" (Hoffman and O'Reilly 2012).

9. What's important to note about the debate over writing and technological determinism that continues to linger in the field is that, in the field's genuine effort to resist deterministic thinking, we developed an exaggerated sense of individual human agency in the process. While the critique of technological determinism may have been appropriate for the study of writing and literacy in the print-dominated world of the 1980s and 1990s, we have moved into a qualitatively new sociotechnological phase with the emergence of digital textuality. While we must continue to value local literacy practices, we cannot be so naïve as to think those literacy practices are immune to the larger agentive forces of the global archive and capital circulation.

10. My definition of rhetoric here as the "deliberate use (and misuse) complex, symbolic, and semantic information . . ." is drawing on Kenneth Burke's well known definition of man as the "symbol using, symbol abusing, animal" (Burke 2013).

11. While circulation studies acknowledges the influence of neoliberal capitalism (Trimbur 2000; Chaput 2010; Dingo 2018), it is less explicit in articulating how processes of capital circulation actually entangle with the circulation of writing.

12. One concern I have with the term *circulation studies* is that we are just trying to get our head around *writing studies*. I think we can make *circulation* a threshold concept without making it a branch of study and preserve the robustness of a term like writing *studies*.

13. The basal metabolic rate of the average human being is about 90 watts, or around 2,000 calories a day (that is, every second of the day we use 90 watts of energy). Today in the United States, each individual uses around 11,000 watts per day (West 2018).

14. The simplest example of this can be seen in the way metabolic processes consistently scale from smaller to larger organisms. Research on energy use and body mass shows that as organisms grow bigger in size, their

metabolic rates scale *sublinearly* at a 3:4 ratio. That is to say, as animals double in size the amount of energy they need daily decreases by 1:4 ratio (West 2017). This metabolic ratio, and the way it uniformly scales, has important consequences for how we study and think about writing, inscription, and information production, and how such flows impact human energy and material needs, and, how that activity, and the waste it creates, seriously strain the planet's ecosystems.

15.   This ridiculous acronym, much to my chagrin, finally dawned on me after a year of typing out "materialist ecology of writing." It has provided great comic relief for me while writing this book, and it has helped me to not take myself too seriously. Thankfully Bruno Latour's actor network theory (ANT) has already cleared the way for more species-based acronyms. :) It also serves as homage to arguably the most significant rhetorical phenomenon to emerge in digital culture: cat videos (see cat video festival, catfestmn.com).

16.   An excellent of example of this kind of scaled ecological approach in writing studies can be seen in the article "Globalization and Agency: Designing and Redesigning the Literacies of Cyberspace" (Hawisher et al. 2006). Using a nested, ecological model, the authors study the literacy narratives of two graduates to how show the various micro, medial, and macro forces helped shape their students journeys from growing up in the school systems of China and Taiwan to attending graduate school in the United States. MEOW is similar in the way it imagines nested cumuli, but rather than focusing on individual writers in context, it looks at the material, ecological development of networked writing technologies and the textuality they foster over longer stretches of history.

CHAPTER 1. THE THEORETICAL ROOTS OF MEOW

1.   The formal study of metabolism can be traced back to Aristotle's observations on how food moved through human and animal bodies and how it transformed from food into bodily waste. The origins of the modern study of metabolism are often traced back to Venetian physician Santorio Santorio (1561–1636). For thirty years, Santorio weighed himself before and after eating, as well as everything he ate, drank, and excreted, and he found that there was a noticeable difference in weight between what he put in his body and the waste his body excreted. Santorio believed that this difference in weight could be attributed to another bodily process of "insensible perspiration." (Brunner 2012).

2.   The concept of *self-augmentation* comes out of the work of philosopher Jacques Ellul. Self-augmentation occurs when the drive to technologize all aspects of life becomes the dominant ethos of a culture. It isn't a particular technology that becomes self-augmenting, but rather the technical impulse itself as individual technologies begin to qualitatively affect a culture (Ellul 1964, 64–133). Once writing is unleashed in the world, textuality ensues, giving rise to more textuality as more texts are

created, saved, and circulated. Thus, writing, textuality, and the archive are, together, the quintessential self-augmenting technologies in culture.

3. IGBP is a nongovernmental organization composed of scientists from all disciplines and nationalities.

CHAPTER 2. WRITING TECHNOLOGIES AND THEIR EMBODIED HISTORY OF USE

1. For a field so deeply invested in the study and teaching of writing, I find odd our noticeable lack of engagement with ancient writing systems. I realize there are several good reasons for this, but I believe we have a lot to gain in exploring the history of ancient writing systems. Fields that specialize in ancient cultures like archaeology, history, and Near East studies (among but a few) provide a wealth of historical and archaeological knowledge that writing studies could tap, especially in our effort to develop more critical materialist and ecological theories of writing. The analysis of both rhetoric and literacy, while present in this scholarship, could, in turn, be enriched by some of the expertise we bring to the study of writing as a socially situated practice.

2. I have done my best here to stay true to the current research and knowledge about Mesopotamian life and to stay humble in the face of the overwhelming amount of scholarship on cuneiform. As someone fairly new to the scholarship, my goal is to provide a general, but detailed engagement with the development of cuneiform for the field and to encourage more research in the area of ancient writing and communication systems.

3. "We do not deny that there are important differences between industrial capitalism and the ancient systems. It is clear that the modern system in which industrial capitals compete for survival by direct investment in the productive forces implies a kind of dynamic unknown in the past. The accumulation of capital as a form of abstract wealth, however, is a truly ancient phenomenon. To say that this ancient 'capital' played a fundamental economic role is not to say that it functioned directly in the production process, but that its accumulation and control were dominant features of those economies" (Ekholm and Friedman 1982, 88).

4. Affordance is a long-discussed topic in writing studies, as well as other disciplines like communications, media studies, and psychology. For more discussion about medial affordances, see work by Kress and Bezemer 2008; Van Leeuwen 2004; Jewitt 2016.

5. *Uruk* itself means "the city" in ancient Sumerian (Yoffee 1995, 292).

CHAPTER 3. WEB 3.0 AND INFORMATIONAL CAPITALISM

1. See note 3, chapter 1 for explanation of my use of *citizen-consumer*.

2. See note 5, introduction for explanation of my use of information technology industries.

3. Although the term *Web 2.0* was originally coined in the late 1990s, it is web evangelist and media publisher Tim O'Reilly's article "What is Web 2.0?" (2005) that stands as the earliest and most thorough discussion of the concept. O'Reilly invoked the term to describe the state of the Web after the dot.com crash of the late 1990s. He argued that the companies that had survived the crash—Google, Napster, Amazon, Yahoo—possessed certain traits that distinguished them from those that failed. These companies were built on a more flexible "web-as-platform" model that was data-driven and favored a more social and interactive Web over the static homepages and link indexes of Web 1.0. What emerges in Web 2.0 (circa 2005), according to O'Reilly, was a slicker Web, built on a more transparent and cooperative ethos, propelled by digital platforms that supported collaboration, participation, and sharing.

4. Lightbeam was originally called "Collusion"—a name I find more fitting to describe the actual level of surveillance and data collection that is occurring in Web 3.0 by governments and corporations. In 2019, Lightbeam was integrated into the Firefox browser as Enhanced Tracking Protection and is no longer a stand-alone application.

5. *Cookies* are small lines of text that get downloaded by your browser when you visit a site online. Their purpose is to collect information about how you interact with a particular website. Cookies are used for basic site functions like saving username and password information, but they are also used by third-party data brokers to track you as you move through the internet, recording where you go and what you click (likes, ads, products, links). *Beacons* are small, invisible objects hidden on a webpage you visit. When you visit a webpage with a beacon, the beacon sends a message to the server of the webpage that the page has been opened. Companies use beacons to know whether or not a customer opens their emails and advertisers use beacons to know how often their ads appear and where.

6. In 2018, in response to Russian meddling in the 2016 U.S presidential election, the United States Congress summoned Facebook's CEO Mark Zuckerberg and COO Sheryl Sandburg (COO), and Twitter's CEO Jack Dorsey, to question them about their data collection practices. While the United States still lacks federal regulations for corporate data collection and consumer privacy, it appears we are moving in the right direction and towards federal legislation hopefully by 2020.

7. While many corporations that make up the corporate data complex give consumers full access to the data that has been collected about them, the majority of companies do not allow this, and many make it very difficult to find out. Moreover, this data is now held by thousands of companies, so the task of tracking down one's data is practically impossible. And, finally, knowing this data doesn't tell us how proprietary algorithms categorize and automate this data. As a form of intellectual property, such technical expertise is usually kept secret from the public.

8. One argument that the data collection industry uses to justify widescale data collection on citizen-consumers is their claim that the data they collect is "anonymized"—meaning, users' personal names or other

identifying categories are not associated with their data. However, research on Facebook and Netflix has shown how easy it is, with just a few data points, to de-anonymize someone's data (Espinoza 2017; Andrejevic 2013; Chester et al. 2014).

9.   The IAB's annual report describes the organization in this way: "The IAB sponsors the IAB Internet Advertising Revenue Report, which is conducted independently by the New Media Group of PwC. The results are considered the most accurate measurement of interactive advertising revenues because the data is compiled directly from information supplied by companies selling advertising on the internet. The survey includes data concerning online advertising revenues from web sites, commercial online services, free e-mail providers, and all other companies selling online advertising" (IAB 2018).

CHAPTER 4. INFORMATION PRODUCTION, ACCELERATION, AND THE BIOPHYSICAL WORLD

1.   My treatment of thermodynamics is based on a very general, basic definition of it as the study of the relationship between heat and temperature, and the conversion of energy from one form to another. I'm certainly not an expert in the field, so my goal here is to introduce the basic idea behind thermodynamics as it relates to everyday life and the materiality of writing.

2.   There are four thermodynamic laws that define the properties of energy and its transformation from one form into another.

> ZEROTH LAW: Relates to the properties of temperature. If system A is in thermal equilibrium [same temperature] with system B, and system B is in thermal equilibrium with system C, then system C and system A will be in thermal equilibrium.
>
> FIRST: The law of the conservation of energy—energy is neither created nor destroyed.
>
> SECOND: Entropy and the arrow of time. When energy does work or is transferred from one form to another, some energy, in the form of heat, is *always* lost in the process, a process that is irreversible in time (see footnote 4 for longer explanation).
>
> THIRD: As matter approaches absolute 0 degrees in temperature (-273 degrees Celsius, 0 degrees Kelvin), its measure of entropy also drops to 0 (Adapted and summarized from Atkins 2010; Drake 2020).

3.   Albert Einstein famously said of thermodynamics that "it is the only physical theory of universal content that, within the framework of applicability of its basic concepts, will never be overthrown" (Grossman 2014).

4.   Entropy, in its simplest definition as the second law of thermodynamics, is the measure of disorder in a system. A common example is putting an ice cube (system one) into a glass of water at room temperature (system

two). Eventually the ice will melt and the potential energy of the once frozen ice cube will dissipate into the surrounding system, affecting the temperature of the water for awhile, until reaching the equilibrium of the ambient environment the glass is sitting in. The law of entropy tells us that we cannot reverse this process—that is, we cannot recapture the energy that is lost from the ice cube. We can, of course, freeze the water again, but that would require a new input of energy. The energy that was earlier transferred from the ice to the water cannot, retroactively, be put back into the ice cube.

Entropy is also used in information theory as the measure of *uncertainty*. In this book I am mainly drawing on classical thermodynamics, but information production is related to both uses of the term. While entropy has several meanings and applications, the concept describes the basic irreversibility and one-directionality of how energy, matter, and information cycle through all systems. There's a lot more theoretical work to do in thinking through entropy's relation to writing and information. My purpose here is to introduce the idea and, hopefully, start a conversation with other interested scholars in writing studies. The Wikipedia entry for *entropy* is excellent.

5. The 24 total metrics consist of 12 socioeconomic trends (population, real GDP, foreign direct investment, urban population, primary energy use, fertilizer consumption, large dams, water use, paper production, transportation, telecommunications, and international tourism) and 12 earth system trends (carbon dioxide, nitrous oxide, methane, stratospheric ozone, surface temperature, ocean acidification, marine fish capture, shrimp aquaculture, nitrogen coastal zone, tropical forest loss, domesticated land, AND terrestrial biosphere degradation) (Steffen et al. 2015).

6. I just want to give a shout out to Greenpeace and all the environmental organizations out there working to protect the environment in the face of a neoliberal capitalism that often hinders our ability to be environmentally conscious. This work is desperately needed and it is in our interests as global citizens to support it. While we should commend data platforms like Google and Amazon for demonstrating corporate responsibility to the public, protecting our shared environment will always be a struggle against predatory, extractive, corporate capitalism.

7. The Jevons paradox is named after the work of English economist William Stanly Jevons who observed in 1865 that technological improvements in the efficient use of coal didn't promote less energy use but actually led to greater use of and demand for cheaper energy. See Wikipedia entry on "Jevons paradox."

8. Established in 1980, the EPA's Superfund program was created to help identify and clean up significant cases of hazardous-waste sites throughout the country.

9. The Chinese government banned all importation of electronic waste in 2000, but e-waste continues to flow into China from the West while its growing domestic disposal of electronics is now the largest in the world (Balde et al. 2017).

10.   Growing awareness of e-waste has helped stem the flow of electronics into China. The crackdown on exports has created problems in the flow of domestic e-waste with recycling companies often transporting e-waste across state lines. ("California's E-Waste Ending Up in Toxic Mountain in Arizona" 2014).

CHAPTER 5. THE EFFECTS OF MANUFACTURED DISTRACTION ON THE BODY

1.   "Using the work of cultural anthropologist Greg Bateson, I define the somatic mind as a 'being-in-a-material-place' whose fluid and permeable boundaries are (re)constituted through the mutual play of discursive and corporeal coding" (Fleckenstein 1999, 282).

2.   In the latest edition of the *Diagnostic and Statistical Manual of Mental Disorders (DSM-5)* "internet gaming disorder" is mentioned in the appendix as an area in need of more research (American Psychiatric Association 2017).

3.   While Facebook, Google, and other players in the corporate data complex have been more transparent in recent years with the data they are collecting, they are still very secretive about how much they collect, what they do with it, and how exactly their algorithms work.

4.   The standard research method used in these earlier cognitive studies of writing was out-loud protocols that record writers talking out loud about what they are consciously thinking about when writing—how they are planning, organizing, synthesizing, and so on.

5.   An interesting outlier in the social/cognitive split is Richard Young and Patricia Williams's article "Why Write? A Reconsideration" (1984). Written contemporaneously with much of the cognitivists' work, "Why Write" is arguably a more nuanced discussion of memory and writing than Flower and Hayes's. Young and Williams make the simple argument that, because writing depends on the limited capacity of a writer's short-term memory, the more taxed that memory becomes, the more difficult it becomes to write. Therefore, writers can learn specific writing strategies [the writing process] to extend the capacity of short-term memory.

6.   Baddeley explains that the original distinction between short-term memory and long-term memory came out of work by pioneering neuropsychologist Donald Hebb. Hebb proposed a distinction between STM (temporary electrical activation held in conscious awareness) and LTM (physical growth of neurons through "rehearsal") (Baddeley 2003, 830).

CHAPTER 6. DEVELOPING CRITICAL, ECOLOGICAL LITERACIES

1.   This is very similar to Goleman and Senge's (2014) framework for *ecological intelligence.*

2. Philosopher David Abram explains phenomenological experience in this way: "Our most immediate experience of things . . . is necessarily an experience of reciprocal encounter—of tension, communication and commingling. From within the depths of this encounter, we know the thing or phenomenon only as our interlocutor—as a dynamic presence that confronts us and draws us into relation" (Abram 1996, 56).

3. The irony of trying to capture preverbal experience through the verbal activity of writing didn't seem to deter phenomenologists like Maurice Merleau Ponty and Martin Heidegger from writing profusely.

4. This included no cellphones and no email.

5. See Derek Owens's superb chapter on writing about place in *Composition and Sustainability* (2001).

6. I realize this may sound a little too binary—clearly in Web 3.0 our online and offline worlds are completely intertwined. I use the distinction here only to explore the different embodied experiences of chatting on the phone, sending a text, or sitting across the table from someone we are talking to.

7. Many of the LCA activities here were adapted from the excellent Carnegie Melon's Center for Climate and Energy Decision Making.

8. There's an excellent example of an LCA infographic of a CD at epa.gov /students ("The Life Cycle of a CD or DVD" 2003).

CODA

1. Image created by author with images purchased from Shutterstock.

REFERENCES

Aagaard, Jesper. "Media Multitasking, Attention, and Distraction: A Critical Discussion." *Phenomenology and the Cognitive Sciences* 14, no. 4 (2014): 885–96. https://doi.org/10.1007/s11097-014-9375-x.

Aboujaoude, Elias. 2012. *Virtually You: The Dangerous Powers of the e-Personality*. New York: W. W. Norton.

Abram, David. 1997. *The Spell of the Sensuous*. New York: Vintage.

Acxiom. Accessed January 16, 2019.

ADAA. Anxiety and Depression Association of America. Accessed January 10, 2020. https://adaa.org/.

Adler, Rachel F., and Raquel Benbunan-Fich. 2012. "Juggling on a High Wire: Multitasking Effects on Performance." *International Journal of Human-Computer Studies* 70, no. 2: 156–68.

Adler, Rachel F., and Raquel Benbunan-Fich. 2014. "The Effects of Task Difficulty and Multitasking on Performance." *Interacting with Computers* 27, no. 4: 430–39. https://doi.org/10.1093/iwc/iwu005.

Allen, Mitchell. 1992. "The Mechanisms of Underdevelopment: An Ancient Mesopotamian Example." *Review* 15, no. 3: 453–76.

Alter, Adam L. 2018. *Irresistible: The Rise of Addictive Technology and the Business of Keeping Us Hooked*. New York: Penguin Books.

American Psychiatric Association. 2017. *Diagnostic and Statistical Manual of Mental Disorders: DSM-5*. Arlington, VA: American Psychiatric Association.

Andrejevic, Mark. 2013. *Infoglut: How Too Much Information Is Changing the Way We Think and Know*. New York: Routledge.

Angwin, Julia. 2016. "Facebook Doesn't Tell Users Everything It Really Knows About Them." ProPublica. https://www.propublica.org/.

Atkins, Peter William. 2010. *The Laws of Thermodynamics: A Very Short Introduction*. Oxford: Oxford University Press.

Aubet, María Eugenia. 2013. *Commerce and Colonization in the Ancient Near East*. Cambridge: Cambridge University Press.

Baddeley, Alan D., and Graham Hitch. 1974. "Working Memory." In *The Psychology of Learning and Motivation: Advances in Research and Theory*, edited by Gordon H. Bower, 47–90. New York: Academic Press.

Baddeley, Alan D. 2003. "Working Memory: Looking Back and Looking Forward." *Nature Reviews Neuroscience* 4, no. 10: 829–39.

Baddeley, Alan D. 2010. "Working Memory." *Current Biology* 20, no. 4: R136–R140.

Baker, Hugh S., Richard J. Millar, David J. Karoly, Urs Beyerle, Benoit P. Guillod, Dann Mitchell, Hideo Shiogama, Sarah Sparrow, Tim Woollings, and Myles R. Allen. 2018. "Higher CO2 Concentrations Increase Extreme Event Risk in a 1.5°C World." *Nature Climate Change* 8, no. 7: 604–8. https://doi.org/10.1038/s41558-018-0190-1.

DOI: 10.7330/9781607329688.c008

Balde, C. P, V. Forti, R. Kuehr, and P. Stegmann. 2017. "The Global E-Waste Monitor 2017." *The Global E-Waste Monitor 2017.* Bonn/Geneva/Vienna: United Nations University.

Barad, Karen Michelle. 2007. *Meeting the Universe Halfway: Quantum Physics and the Entanglement of Matter and Meaning.* Durham, NC: Duke University Press.

Barnett, Scot, and Casey Boyle. 2017. *Rhetoric, Through Everyday Things.* Tuscaloosa: The University of Alabama Press.

BAN. "More Energy Needed in Battle Against E-Waste." Report. Basel Action Network, July 23, 2019. https://www.ban.org/news/2019/7/23/more-energy -needed-in-battle-against-e-waste.

BAN. "Scam Recycling: e-Dumping on Asia by US Recyclers." Report, Basel Action Network, September 15, 2016. www.ban.org.

Bawarshi, Anis. 2015. "Materiality." In *Keywords in Writing Studies,* edited by Paul Heilker and Peter Vandenberg, 108–13. Logan: Utah State University Press.

Bazerman, Charles. 2006. "The Writing of Social Organization and the Literate Situating of Cognition: Extending Goody's Social Implications of Writing." In *Technology, Literacy and the Evolution of Society: Implications of the Work of Jack Goody,* edited by David R. Olson and Michael Cole, 215–39. Mahwah, NJ: Lawrence Erlbaum.

Bazerman, Charles, Joseph Little, and Teri Chavkin. 2003. "The Production of Information for Genred Activity Spaces." *Written Communication* 20, no. 4: 455–77. https://doi.org/10.1177/0741088303260375.

Beck, Estee N. "Writing Educator Responsibilities for Discussing the History and Practice of Surveillance & Privacy in Writing Classrooms." *Kairos* 20, no. 2 (2015). http://kairos.technorhetoric.net/20.2/topoi/beck-et-al/beck.html.

Beckerman, Michael. "Americans Will Pay a Price for State Privacy Laws." *New York Times,* October 14, 2019. https://www.nytimes.com/2019/10/14/opinion /state-privacy-laws.html.

Bellur, Saraswathi, Kristine L. Nowak, and Kyle S. Hull. 2015. "Make It Our Time: In Class Multitaskers Have Lower Academic Performance." *Computers in Human Behavior* 53: 63–70. https://doi.org/10.1016/j.chb.2015.06.027.

Beniger, James R. 1986. *The Control Revolution: Technological and Economic Origins of the Information Society.* Cambridge, MA: Harvard University Press.

Bennett, Jane. 2010. *Vibrant Matter: A Political Ecology of Things.* Durham, NC: Duke University Press.

Berlin, James A. 1987. *Rhetoric and Reality Writing Instruction in American Colleges, 1900–1985. Studies in Writing and Rhetoric.* Carbondale: Southern Illinois Press.

Bereiter, Carl, and Marlene Scardamalia. 1987. *The Psychology of Written Composition.* Hillsdale, NJ: Lawrence Erlbaum.

Berthoff, Ann E. 1984. *Reclaiming the Imagination: Philosophical Perspectives for Writers and Teachers of Writing.* Upper Montclair, NJ: Boynton/Cook Publishers.

Blewett, Kelly, Janine Morris, and Hannah J. Rule. 2016. "Composing Environments: The Materiality of Reading and Writing." *CEA Critic* 78, no. 1: 24–44. https://doi.org/10.1353/cea.2016.0007.

Bloch, Ernst. 1995. *The Principle of Hope.* Cambridge, MA: MIT Press.

Bogost, Ian. 2017. "You Are Already Living Inside a Computer." *The Atlantic*, September 14, 2017. https://www.theatlantic.com/.

Bogost, Ian. 2018. "Why Is There a 'Gaming Disorder' But No 'Smartphone Disorder'?" *The Atlantic*, June 28, 2018. https://www.theatlantic.com/tech nology/archive/2018/06/whos-afraid-of-virginia-wolfenstein/563843/.

Bolter, J. David. 1991. *Writing Space: The Computer, Hypertext, and the History of Writing*. Hillsdale, NJ: Lawrence Erlbaum.

Bolter, J. David. 2001. *Writing Space: Computers, Hypertext, and the Remediation of Print*. Mahwah, NJ: Lawrence Erlbaum.

Bowers, C. A. 2003. "Can Critical Pedagogy Be Greened?" *Educational Studies* Spring. 1–14.

Bowers, C. A. 2010. "Educational Reforms That Foster Ecological Intelligence." *Teacher Education Quarterly* 37, no. 4, Education and the Environment: 9–31. http://www.jstor.org/stable/10.2307/23479456?ref=no-x-route:e3e0c5058f a65d65aa01b35893df7916.

Boyd, Danah, and Kate Crawford. 2012. "Critical Questions for Big Data." *Information, Communication and Society* 15, no. 5: 662–79.

Boyle, Casey, and Nathaniel Rivers. 2018. "Augmented Publics." In *Circulation, Writing, and Rhetoric*, edited by Laurie E. Gries and Colin Gifford Brooke, 83–101. Logan: Utah State University Press.

Brandt, Deborah. 2005. "Writing for a Living." *Written Communication* 22, no. 2: 166–97. https://doi.org/10.1177/0741088305275218.

Bridger, Darren. 2017. *Neuro Design: Neuromarketing Insights to Boost Engagement and Profitability*. London: Kogan Page.

Brown, James H., Richard M. Sibly, and Astrid Kodric-Brown. 2012. "Introduction: Metaboism as the Basis for a Theoretical Unification of Ecology." In *Metabolic Ecology: A Scaling Approach*, edited by Richard M. Sibly et al., 1–7. West Sussex, UK: Wiley-Blackwell.

Brunner, Paul H., and Helmut Rechberger. 2016. *Practical Handbook of Material Flow Analysis*. CRC Press.

Capra, Fritjof. 1997. *The Web of Life: A New Scientific Understanding of Living Systems*. New York: Anchor Books.

Capra, Fritjof, and Zenobia Barlow. 2005. "Preface." In *Ecological Literacy: Educating Our Children for a Sustainable World*, edited by Michael K Stone, xiii–xvi. San Francisco: Sierra Club Books.

Carli, V., T. Durkee, D. Wasserman, G. Hadlaczky, R. Despalins, E. Kramarz, et al. 2013. "The Association between Pathological Internet Use and Comorbid Psychopathology: A Systematic Review." *Psychopathology* 46: 1–13.

Carr, Nicholas. 2008. "Is Google Making Us Stupid?" *The Atlantic*, 89–94. https://doi.org/10.1111/j.1744–7984.2008.00172.x.

Carr, Nicholas G. 2010. *The Shallows: What the Internet Is Doing to Our Brains*. New York: W. W. Norton.

Castells, Manuel. 2009. *The Rise of the Network Society*. 2nd ed. Oxford: Blackwell.

Castor, Alexis Q. 2013. "Between the Rivers: The History of Ancient Meso- potamia." *The Great Courses* (audiobook). Chantilly, VA: The Teaching Company.

Chaput, Catherine. 2010. "Rhetorical Circulation in Late Capitalism:" *Philosophy and Rhetoric* 43, no. 1: https://doi.org/10.5325/philrhet.43.1.0001.

Charpin, Dominique. 2010. *Reading and Writing in Babylon*. Cambridge, MA: Harvard University Press.

Chester, Sean, Bruce M. Kapron, Gautam Srivastava, Venkatesh Srinivasan, and Alex Thomo. 2014. "Anonymization and De-Anonymization of Social Network Data." *Encyclopedia of Social Network Analysis and Mining*, 48–56. https://doi.org/10.1007/978-1-4614-6170-8_22.

China Water Risk. 2017. Accessed February 10, 2019. http://www.chinawaterrisk .org/.

Clark, J. Elizabeth. 2010. "The Digital Imperative: Making the Case for a 21st-Century Pedagogy." *Computers and Composition* 27, no. 1: 27–35.

"Cleaning Up Electronic Waste (E-Waste)." 2018. EPA, December 3, 2018. https://www.epa.gov/international-cooperation/cleaning-electronic-waste -e-waste.

"Climate Science." Union of Concerned Scientists, 2020. https://www.ucsusa .org/climate/science.

Cohn, Jenae. 2016. "'Devilish Smartphones' and the 'Stone-Cold' Internet: Implications of the Technology Addiction Trope in College Student Digital Literacy Narratives." *Computers and Composition* 42: 80–94. https://doi.org/10 .1016/j.compcom.2016.08.008.

"Consumer View." Experian Information Solutions, 2018. https://www.experian .com/.

Cook, Gary. 2012. *How Clean Is Your Cloud?* Greenpeace. http://www.greenpeace .org/.

Cook, Gary, and Elizabeth Jardim. 2017. *Guide to Greener Electronics*. Washington, DC: Greenpeace.

Cook, Gary, Jude Lee, Tamina Tsai, Ada Kong, John Deans, Brian Johnson, and Elizabeth Jardim. 2017. *Clicking Clean: Who Is Winning the Race to Build a Green Internet?* Washington, DC: Greenpeace.

Coole, Diana H, and Samantha Frost. 2010. *New Materialisms Ontology, Agency, and Politics*. Durham, NC: Duke University Press.

Cooper, Marilyn M. 1986. "The Ecology of Writing." *College English* 48, no. 4: 364–75. https://doi.org/10.2307/377264.

Cooper, Marilyn M. 2011. "Rhetorical Agency as Emergent and Enacted." *College Composition and Communication* 62, no. 3: 420–49.

Cooper, Marilyn M. 2017. "Listening to Strange Strangers, Modifying Dreams." In *Rhetoric, Through Everyday Things*, edited by Scot Barnett and Casey Boyle, 17–29. Tuscaloosa: University of Alabama Press.

Couture, Barbara. 1998. *Toward a Phenomenological Rhetoric: Writing, Profession, and Altruism*. Carbondale: Southern Illinois University Press.

Diffenbaugh, Noah S., and Marshall Burke. 2019. "Global Warming Has Increased Global Economic Inequality." *Proceedings of the National Academy of Sciences* 116, no. 20: 9808–13. https://doi.org/10.1073/pnas.1816020116.

Dilger, Bradley. 2010. "Beyond Star Flashes: The Elements of Web 2.0 Style." *Computers and Composition* 27, no. 1: 15–26.

Dingo, Rebecca. 2018. "Reevaluating a Transnational Feminist Literacy." *Circulation, Writing, and Rhetoric*, edited by Laurie E. Gries and Collin Gifford Brooke, 135–51. Logan: Utah State University Press.

Dobrin, Sidney I., and Christian R. Weisser. 2002. *Natural Discourse: Toward Ecocomposition.* Albany: State University of New York Press.

Dobrin, Sidney I. 2011. *Postcomposition.* Carbondale: Southern Illinois University Press.

Dobrin, Sidney I., ed. 2012. *Ecology, Writing Theory, and New Media: Writing Ecology.* New York: Taylor and Francis.

Dobrin, Sidney I., and Kyle Jensen, eds. 2017. *Abducting Writing Studies.* Carbondale: Southern Illinois University Press.

Dokoupil, Tony. 2012. "Is the Internet Making Us Crazy? What the Research Says." *Newsweek,* September 7, 2012.

Domo. 2019. "Data Never Sleeps 7.0" Accessed January 3, 2020. https://www.domo.com/learn/data-never-sleeps-7.

Domo, Inc. 2018. "Connecting Your Data, Systems and People | Domo." Connecting Your Data, Systems and People. https://www.domo.com/.

Drake, Gordon W.F. "Thermodynamics." In *Encyclopedia Britannica,* January 13, 2020. https://www.britannica.com/science/thermodynamics.

Drucker, Peter F. 2017. *The Age of Discontinuity: Guidelines to Our Changing Society.* New York; London: Routledge.

Edbauer, Jenny. 2005. "Unframing Models of Public Distribution: From Rhetorical Situation to Rhetorical Ecologies." *Rhetoric Society Quarterly* 35, no. 4: 5–24. https://doi.org/10.1080/02773940509391320.

Ekholm, Kajsa, and Jonathan Friedman. 1982. "'Capital' Imperialism and Exploitation in Ancient World-Systems." *Review* (Fernand Braudel Center) 6, no. 1: 87–109. Accessed January 16, 2020. www.jstor.org/stable/40240928.

Ellul, Jacques. 1964. *The Technological Society.* New York: Knopf.

Emig, Janet A. 1971. *The Composing Processes of Twelfth Graders.* Urbana, IL: National Council of Teachers of English.

Englehardt, Steven, and Arvind Narayanan. 2016. "Online Tracking: A 1-Million-Site Measurement and Analysis." Princeton Web Transparency and Accountabiligy Project. https://webtransparency.cs.princeton.edu/webcensus/#.

Espinoza, Nicholas. 2017. "Research: Deanonymizing Browser Data Made Easy." Authentic8 Blog. https://authentic8.blog/.

Eyal, Nir, and Ryan Hoover. 2014. *Hooked: How to Build Habit-Forming Products.* New York: Penguin.

Fabos, Bettina. 2008. "The Price of Information: Critical Literacy, Education, and Today's Internet." *Handbook of Research on New Literacies,* edited by Julie Coiro, Michele Knobel, Colin Lankshear, and Donald J. Leu, 839–70. New York: Routledge.

Faigley, Lester. 1986. "Competing Theories of Process: A Critique and a Proposal." *College English* 48, no. 6: 527. https://doi.org/10.2307/376707.

Faigley, Lester. 1999. "Material Literacy and Visual Design." In *Rhetorical Bodies,* edited by Jack Seltzer and Sharon Crowley. 171–201. Madison: University of Wisconsin Press.

Fleckenstein, Kristie. 1999. "Writing Bodies: Somatic Mind in Composition Studies." *College English* 61, no. 3: 281–306.

"Facebook Market Cap 2009–2019: FB." 2020. Macrotrends. https://www.macrotrends.net/stocks/charts/FB/facebook/market-cap.

Floridi, Luciano. 2010. *Information: A Very Short Introduction*. Oxford: Oxford University Press.

Flower, Linda, and John R. Hayes. 1981. "A Cognitive Process Theory of Writing." *College Composition and Communication* 32, no. 4: 365–87.

Foster, John Bellamy. 2000. *Marx's Ecology: Materialism and Nature*. New York: Monthly Review Press.

Foster, John Bellamy. 2009. *The Ecological Revolution: Making Peace with the Planet*. New York: Monthly Review Press.

Foster, John Bellamy, Brett Clark, and Richard York. 2011. *The Ecological Rift: Capitalism's War on the Earth*. New York: Monthly Review Press.

Foster, Jonathan K. 2009. *Memory: A Very Short Introduction*. Oxford: Oxford University Press.

Foucault, Michel. 2011. *The Archaeology of Knowledge*. London: Routledge.

"4.5 Billion Likes A Day (Info-Graphic)." 2013. Facebook.com, May 13, 2013. https://www.facebook.com/photo.php?fbid=10151908376831729.

Fraud.org. Accessed January 16, 2019. http://www.fraud.org/.

FTC. 2014. *Data Brokers: A Call for Transparency and Accountability: A Report of the Federal Trade Commission*. Washington, DC: Federal Trade Commission.

Fuchs, Christian. 2012. *Foundations of Critical Media and Information Studies*. London: Routledge.

Gabriel, Brian. 2008. "History of Writing Technologies." In *Handbook of Research on Writing: History, Society, School, Individual, Text*, edited by Charles Bazerman, 23–34. London: Routledge.

Gallagher, John R. 2017. "Writing for Algorithmic Audiences." *Computers and Composition* 45: 25–35. https://doi.org/10.1016/j.compcom.2017.06.002.

Galloway, Scott. 2018. *The Four: The Hidden DNA of Amazon, Apple, Facebook, and Google*. New York: Portfolio/Penguin.

Genco, Stephen J., Peter Steidl, and Andrew P. Pohlmann. 2013. *Neuromarketing For Dummies*. Mississauga, Canada: John Wiley & Sons Canada.

Georgescu-Roegen, Nicholas. 1981. *The Entropy Law and the Economic Process*. Cambridge, MA: Harvard University Press.

Giampietro, Mario, Kozo Mayumi, and Alevgül H. Sorman. 2012. *The Metabolic Pattern of Societies: Where Economists Fall Short*. London: Routledge.

Gibbons, Michelle. 2018. "A Neurorhetoric of Incongruity." *Poroi* 13, no. 2. https://doi.org/10.13008/2151-2957.1248.

Giddens, Anthony. 1994. *Beyond Left and Right: The Future of Radical Politics*. Stanford, CA: Stanford University Press.

Giles, Martin. 2018. "Rein in the Data Barons." *MIT Technology Review* 121, no. 4: 28–37. https://doi.org/10.1119/1.3246486.

Glanz, James. 2012. "Power, Pollution and the Internet." *New York Times*, September 22, 2012. http://www.nytimes.com/2012/09/23/technology/data-centers-waste-vast-amounts-of-energy-belying-industry-image.html?_r=0.

"Global Inequality." 2020. Inequality.org. Accessed January 19, 2020. https://inequality.org/facts/global-inequality/.

Goleman, Daniel, Lisa Bennett, and Zenobia Barlow. 2012. *Ecoliterate: How Educators Are Cultivating Emotional, Social, and Ecological Intelligence*. San Francisco: Jossey-Bass.

Goleman, Daniel, and Peter M. Senge. 2014. *The Triple Focus: A New Approach to Education.* Florence, MA: More Than Sound.

Gonzalez de Molina, Manuel, and Victor M. Toledo. 2014. *Social Metabolism: A Socio-Ecological Theory of Historical Change.* Sevilla: Springer.

Goody, Jack. 1986. *The Logic of Writing and the Organization of Society.* Cambridge: Cambridge University Press.

Gotter, Ana. 2019. "The 43 Instagram Statistics You Need to Know in 2019." AdEspresso, August 7, 2019. https://adespresso.com/blog/instagram -statistics/.

Grant, Jon E, and Samuel R Chamberlain. "Expanding the definition of addiction: DSM-5 vs. ICD-11." *CNS spectrums* 21, no. 4 (2016): 300–303. doi:10 .1017/S1092852916000183.

Green, Dennis, and Mary Hanbury. 2018. "If You Shopped at These 16 Stores in the Last Year, Your Data Might Have Been Stolen." *Business Insider,* August 22, 2018. https://www.businessinsider.com/data-breaches-2018-4.

Greenfield, Susan. 2015. *Mind Change: How Digital Technologies Are Leaving Their Mark on Our Brains.* New York: Random House.

Gries, Laurie E. 2015. *Still Life with Rhetoric: A New Materialist Approach for Visual Rhetorics.* Logan: Utah State University Press.

Gries, Laurie E., and Collin Gifford Brooke. 2018. *Circulation, Writing, and Rhetoric.* Logan: Utah State University Press.

Griner, Allison. 2017. "Looks Are Deceiving in Chinese Town That Was US e-Waste Dumping Site." Reveal: The Center for Investigative Reporting, January 6, 2017. https://www.revealnews.org/article/looks-are-deceiving-in -chinese-town-that-was-us-e-waste-dumping-site/.

Grossman, Elizabeth. 2006. *High Tech Trash: Digital Devices, Hidden Toxics, and Human Health.* Washington, DC: Island Press.

Grossman, Jeffrey C. 2014. "Thermodynamics: Four Laws That Move the Universe." Lecture. *The Great Courses Plus.* Chantilly, VI.

Haas, Christina. 1996. *Writing Technology: Studies on the Materiality of Literacy.* Mahwah, NJ: Lawrence Erlbaum.

Harvey, David. 2000. *The Condition of Postmodernity.* Cambridge, MA: Blackwell.

Harvey, David. 2015. *Seventeen Contradictions and the End of Capitalism.* London: Profile Books.

Harvey, David. 2019. "Reading Marx's Capital Volume 1 with David Harvey." Lectures. http://davidharvey.org/reading-capital/#capital-v1–2019.

Hawisher, Gail E., Cynthia L. Selfe, Yi-Huey Guo, and Lu Liu. 2006. "Globalization and Agency: Designing and Redesigning the Literacies of Cyberspace." *College English* 68, no. 6: 619. https://doi.org/10.2307/25472179.

Hess, Aaron, and Amber L. Davisson. 2018. *Theorizing Digital Rhetoric.* New York: Routledge Taylor & Francis Group.

Hicks, Troy, and Kristen Hawley Turner. 2013. "No Longer a Luxury: Digital Literacy Can't Wait." *English Journal* 102, no. 6: 58–65.

Hidalgo, Cesar A. 2016. *Why Information Grows: The Evolution of Order, from Atoms to Economies.* London: Penguin Books.

Hilbert, Martin. 2012. "How Much Information Is There in the 'Information Society'?" *Significance* 9, no. 4: 8–12.

Hilbert, Martin. 2016. "The Data Revolution." In *World Development Report 2016: Digital Dividends*, 244–47. Washington, DC: World Bank.

Hirsu, Lavinia. 2018. "Clicks, Tweets, Links, and Other Global Actions." In *Thinking Globally, Composing Locally: Rethinking Online Writing in the Age of the Global Internet*, edited by Rich Rice and Kirk St.Amant, Loc: 6352–6819. Logan: Utah State University Press.

Hoffman, Reid, and Tim O'Reilly. 2012. Web 3.0 Revolution Part 3. *Tech Crunch*, February 16, 2012. https://youtu.be/VJPiGgh-hjI.

Horowitz, Juliana Menasce, and Nikki Graf. 2019. "Most U.S. Teens See Anxiety and Depression as a Major Problem among Their Peers." *Most U.S. Teens See Anxiety and Depression as a Major Problem Among Their Peers*. Pew Research Center.

Inagaki, Hiromi. 2013. "E-Waste Management: Sustainable Economic Growth or Inequitable Distribution of Environmental Health Risks?" In *Solving the E-Waste Problem: An Interdisciplinary Compilation of International E-Waste Research*, 35–51. New York: United Nations University Press.

"Internet Live Stats—Internet Usage & Social Media Statistics." 2019. Internet Live Stats. Accessed February 1, 2019. http://www.internetlivestats.com/.

Jardim, Elizabeth. 2017. *From Smart to Senseless: The Global Impact of 10 Years of Smartphones*. Washington, DC: Greenpeace.

Jenkins, Tiffany. 2020. "Why an Ancient Mesopotamian Tablet Is Key to Our Future Learning." *Tedx Square Mile*. Accessed January 2, 2020. https://www.youtube.com/watch?v=2VWS_F_UeQI&t=3s.

Jewitt, Carey, ed. 2016. *The Routledge Handbook of Multimodal Analysis*, 2nd. London: Routledge.

Johnson, Christopher. 1993. *System and Writing in the Philosophy of Jacques Derrida*. Cambridge: Cambridge University Press XV.

Jowit, Juliette. 2016. "Work-Life Balance: Flexible Working Can Make You Ill, Experts Say." *The Guardian*. https://www.theguardian.com/.

Junco, Reynol. 2012. "In-Class Multitasking and Academic Performance." *Computers in Human Behavior* 28, no. 6: 2236–43.

Junco, Reynol. 2013. "ISpy: Seeing What Students Really Do Online." *Learning, Media and Technology* 39, no. 1: 75–89. https://doi.org/10.1080/17439884.2013.771782.

Junco, Reynol. 2015. "Student Class Standing, Facebook Use, and Academic Performance." *Journal of Applied Developmental Psychology* 36: 18–29.

Junco, Reynol, and Shelia R. Cotten. 2012. "No A 4 U: The Relationship between Multitasking and Academic Performance." *Computers and Education* 59, no. 2: 505–14.

Kahn, Richard V. 2010. *Critical Pedagogy, Ecoliteracy, and Planetary Crisis: The Ecopedagogy Movement*. New York: Peter Lang.

Kandel, Eric R. 2006. *In Search of Memory: The Emergence of a New Science of Mind*. New York: W.W. Norton.

Kaspari, Michael. 2012. "Stoichiometry." *Metabolic Ecology: A Scaling Approach*, edited by R. M. Sibly, James H. Brown, and Astrid Kodric-Brown, 34–47. Chichester, West Sussex: Wiley-Blackwell.

Keller, Daniel. 2014. *Chasing Literacy: Reading and Writing in an Age of Acceleration*. Logan: Utah State University Press.

Kellogg, Ronald T., and Alison P. Whiteford. 2012. "The Development of Writing Expertise." In *Writing: A Mosaic of New Perspectives*, edited by Elena L. Grigorenko, Elisa Mambrino, and David D. Preiss, 109–25. New York: Psychology Press.

Kellogg, R. T., C. E. Turner, A. P. Whiteford, and A. Mertens. 2016. "The Role of Working Memory in Planning and Generating Written Sentences." *Journal of Writing Research* 7, no. 3 (February): 397–416. https://doi.org/10.17239 /jowr-2016.07.03.04.

Khetriwal, Deepali Sinha, Claudia Luepschen, and Ruediger Kuehr, eds. 2013. *Solving the E-Waste Problem: An Interdisciplinary Compilation of International E-Waste Research*. New York: United Nations University Press.

Killingsworth, M. Jimmie. 2010. "Appeals to the Body in Eco-Rhetoric and Techno-Rhetoric." In *Rhetorics and Technologies: New Directions in Writing and Communication*, edited by Stuart A. Selber, 77–93. Columbia: University of South Carolina Press.

Killingsworth, M. Jimmie, Christian Weisser, and Sidney Dobrin. 2001. "Ecology, Alienation, and Literacy: Contraints and Possibilities in Ecocomposition." In *Ecocomposition: Theoretical and Pedagogical Approaches*, edited by Christian R. Weisser and Sidney I. Dobrin. Albany: State University of New York Press.

Kornberg, Hans. 2019. "Metabolism." *Encyclopediabritannica.com*. https://www .britannica.com/science/metabolism/The-carrier-of-chemical-energy.

Kreft, S., D. Eckstein, L. Junghans, and C. Kerestan. 2015. "Global Climate Risk Index 2015." *Global Climate Risk Index 2015*. Berlin: German Watch.

Kress, Gunther, and Jeff Bezemer. 2008. "Writing in Multimodal Texts: A Social Semiotic Account of Designs for Learning." *Written Communication* 25, no. 166: 166–95.

Kundera, Milan. 2014. *Slowness*. New York: Harper Perennial.

Lanham, Richard A. 2007. *The Economics of Attention: Style and Substance in the Age of Information*. Chicago: University of Chicago Press.

Lanier, Jaron. 2014. *Who Owns the Future?* London: Penguin Books.

Law, Danny, Wang Haicheng, Hans J. Nissen, and Gary Urton. 2017. "Writing and Record-Keeping in Early Cities." In *Early Cities in Comparative Perspective, 4000 BCE–1200 CE*, edited by Norman Yoffee, 208–25. Cambridge: Cambridge University Press.

Levermore, Kirsten. 2017. "A Brief History of the Microchip." *Dialogue Review*, November 15, 2017. http://dialoguereview.com/brief-history-microchip/.

Levy, David M, Jacob O. Wobbrock, Alfred W Kasizniak, and Marilyn Ostergren. 2012. "The Effects of Mindfulness Mediation Training on Multitasking in a High-Stress Information Environment." In *Proceedings: Graphics Interface 2012, Toronto, Ontario, Canada, 28–30 May 2012*. Mississauga, Ontario: Canadian Information Processing Society.

Lin, I. H., C. H. Ko, Y. P. Chang, T. L. Liu, P. W. Wang, H. C. Lin, et al. 2014. "The Association between Suicidality and Internet Addiction and Activities in Taiwanese Adolescents." *Comp Psychiatry* 55: 504–10.

Logan, Robert K. 2004. *The Alphabet Effect: A Media Ecology Understanding of the Making of Western Civilization*. Cresskill, NJ: Hampton Press.

Louv, Richard. 2012. *The Nature Principle: Reconnecting with Life in a Virtual Age*. Chapel Hill, NC: Algonquin Books of Chapel Hill.

Lunsford, Andrea and team. 2019. "Stanford Study of Writing." Home. Accessed January 17, 2019. https://ssw.stanford.edu/.

Lunsford, Andrea, and Paul Prior. 2008. "History of Reflection, Theory, and Research on Writing." In *Handbook of Research on Writing: History, Society, School, Individual, Text*, edited by Charles Bazerman, 81–96. New York: Lawrence Erlbaum Assoc.

Lustig, Robert H. 2018. *Hacking of the American Mind: The Science behind the Corporate Takeover of Our Bodies and Brains*. New York: Avery Publishing, Penguin.

Lynch, Paul, and Nathaniel Rivers, eds. 2015. *Thinking with Bruno Latour in Rhetoric and Composition*. Carbondale: Southern Illinois University Press.

Made in a Free World. Accessed January 17, 2020. https://madeinafreeworld.org/.

Madrigal, Alexis C. 2017. "The Weird Thing About Today's Internet." *The Atlantic*, May 16,

2017. theatlantic.com.

Manhart, Andreas, Oladele Osibanjo, Adeyinka Aderinto, and Siddharth Prakash. 2011. "Informal e-Waste Management in Lagos Nigeria: Socio-Economic Impacts and Feasibility of International Recycling Co-Operations." Oko Institute: Institute for Applied Ecology. Frieberg, Germany.

Map of States with [E-Waste] Legislation. 2020. ERCC: Electronics Recycling Coordination Clearinghouse. https://www.ecycleclearinghouse.org/content page.aspx?pageid=10.

Maranto, Gina, and Matt Barton. 2010. "Paradox and Promise: MySpace, Facebook, and the Sociopolitics of Social Networking in the Writing Classroom." *Computers and Composition* 27, no. 1: 36–47.

Mark, Gloria. 2015. *Multitasking in the Digital Age*. San Rafael, CA: Morgan and Claypool.

Marx, Karl. 1973. *Grundrisse. Foundations of the Critique of Political Economy*. Translated by Martin Nicolaus. New York: Random House.

Marx, Karl. 1988. *Economic and Philosophic Manuscripts of 1844 / and the Communist Manifesto*; Karl Marx and Frederick Engels. Translated by Martin Milligan. Buffalo, NY: Prometheus Books.

Marx, Karl. 1990. *Capital: A Critique of Political Economy*. Edited by Ernest Mandel. Translated by Ben Fowkes. London: Penguin Books in association with New Left Review.

Mayer-Schönberger Viktor, and Kenneth Cukier. 2013. *Big Data: A Revolution That Will Transform How We Live, Work and Think*. London: John Murray.

McCutchen, Deborah, Paul Teske, and Catherine Bankston. 2008. "Writing and Cognition: Implications of the Cognitive Architecture for Learning to Write and Writing to Learn." In *Handbook of Research on Writing: History, Society, School, Individual, Text*, edited by Charles Bazerman, 451–71. New York: Lawrence Erlbaum.

Moeller, Susan, Elia Powers, and Jessica Roberts. 2012. "'The World Unplugged' and '24 Hours without Media': Media Literacy to Develop Self-Awareness Regarding Media." *Comunicar* 20, no. 39: 45–52. https://doi.org/10.3916/c39-2012-02-04.

Montasell, Gerard. 2019. "Global Top Online Store Sales 2018." Statista, December 9, 2019. https://www.statista.com/statistics/860716/top-online-stores-global-ecommercedb/.

Moran, Charles. 1999a. "Access: The 'A' Word in Technology Studies." In *Passions, Pedagogies, and 21st Century Technologies*, edited by Gail E. Hawisher and Cynthia L. Selfe, 205–20. Logan: Utah State University Press.

Moran, Charles. 1999b. "Teaching English across the Technology/Wealth Gap." *The English Journal* 88, no. 6: 48–55. http://www.jstor.org/stable/10.2307/822187?ref=no-x-route:3c92263383e93bae7f33022dba8ee1cf.

Moran, Charles. 2005. "Powerful Medicine with Long-Term Side Effects." *Computers and Composition* 22, no. 1: 63–68.

Morin, Christopher, and Patrick Renvoise. 2018. *The Persuasion Code: How Neuromarketing Can Help You Persuade Anyone, Anywhere, Anytime*. Hoboken, NJ: Wiley.

Moss, Sebastian. 2019. "Data Center and Cloud Companies Need to Be More Transparent about Energy Usage." datacenterdynamics.com, July 13, 2019. https://www.datacenterdynamics.com/analysis/data-center-and-cloud-companies-need-be-more-transparent-about-energy-usage/.

Mulherkar, Andrew. 2016. "Google, Amazon and Apple Are Forging the Future of Corporate Energy Management." Greentech Media, July 8, 2016. https://www.greentechmedia.com/articles/read/what-google-amazon-and-apples-recent-moves-reveal-about-the-future-of-cor.

"Multitasking: Switching Costs." 2019. American Psychology Association. Accessed January 17, 2019. http://www.apa.org/research/action/multitask.aspx.

Nicotra, Jodie. 2017a. "Assemblage Rhetorics: Creating New Frameworks for Rhetorical Action." In *Rhetoric, Through Everyday Things*, edited by Scot Barnett and Casey Boyle, 185–97. Tuscaloosa: University of Alabama Press.

Nicotra, Jodie 2017b. "Metaphors for the Future: How to Train the Riparian Subjects of 'Writing' Studies." In *Abducting Writing Studies*, edited by Sidney Dobrin and Kyle Jensen, 203–17. Carbondale: Southern Illinois University Press.

Nobbs, Christopher L. 2013. *Economics, Sustainability and Democracy: Economics in the Era of Climate Change*. New York: Routledge.

Olive, Thierry. 2012. "Writing and Working Memory: A Summary of Theories and Findings." In *Writing: A Mosaic of New Perspectives*, edited by Elena L. Grigorenko, Elisa Mambrino, and David D. Preiss, 125–41. New York: Psychology Press.

Olubanjo, Kehinde. 2013. "Comparison of Lead and Copper Concentrations in Different Parts of Electronic Computer Waste Imported into Nigeria." In *Solving the E-Waste Problem: An Interdisciplinary Compilation of International E-Waste Research*, edited by Deepali Sinha Khetriwal, 87–99. New York: United Nations University Press.

O'Reilly, Tim. 2005. "What Is Web 2.0?" O'Reilly Media, September 30, 2005.

Orr, David W. 2005. "Foreword." In *Ecological Literacy: Educating Our Children for a Sustainable World*, edited by Michael K. Stone and Zenobia Barlow, ix–xiii. San Francisco: Sierra Club Books.

Orr, David W. 2004. *Earth in Mind: on Education, Environment, and the Human Prospect.* Washington, DC: Island Press.

Owen, Clive. 2009. "Clive Thompson on the New Literacy." Wired.com, September 24, 2009.

Owens, Derek. 2001. *Composition and Sustainability: Teaching for a Threatened Generation.* Urbana, IL: National Council of Teachers of English.

Patrick, Amy. 2011. "Sustaining Writing Theory." *Composition Forum* 21 (February 2010). In *The Best of the Independent Rhetoric and Composition Journals: 2010*, edited by Steve Parks and Brian Bailie. Anderson, SC: Parlor Press.

Perelman, Les. 2008. "Information Illiteracy and Mass Market Writing Assessments." *College Composition and Communication* 60, no. 1: 128–41. www.jstor.org/stable/20457047.

Petry, Nancy M., ed. 2015. *Behavioral Addictions: DSM-5® and Beyond.* Oxford: Oxford University Press.

Pfister, Damien Smith. 2018. "The Terms of Technoliberalism." In *Theorizing Digital Rhetoric*, edited by Aaron Hess and Amber L. Davisson, 32–43. New York: Routledge.

Pflugfelder, Ehren Helmut. 2015. "Is No One at the Wheel? Nonhuman Agency and Agentive Movement." In *Thinking with Bruno Latour in Rhetoric and Composition*, 115–30. Southern Illinois University Press.

Pinghui, Zhuang. 2017. "China's Notorious e-Waste Dumping Ground Cleaner but Poorer." *South China Morning Post*, September 22, 2017. https://www.scmp.com/news/china/society/article/2112226/chinas-most-notorious-e-waste-dumping-ground-now-cleaner-poorer.

Porter, James E. 2010. "Rhetoric in (as) a Digital Economy." In *Rhetorics and Technologies: New Directions in Writing and Communication*, edited by Stuart A. Selber, 173–97. Columbia: University of South Carolina Press.

Powell, Marvin A. 1996. "Money in Mesopotamia." *Journal of the Economic and Social History of the Orient* 39, no. 3: 224–42.

Purcell, Kristen, Judy Buchanan, and Linda Friedrich. 2013. "The Impact of Digital Tools on Student Writing and How Writing Is Taught in Schools." Pew Research Center. Accessed January 10, 2020. https://www.pewresearch.org/internet/2013/07/16/the-impact-of-digital-tools-on-student-writing-and-how-writing-is-taught-in-schools/.

Ransdell, Sarah, C. Michael Levy, and Ronald T. Kellogg. 2002. "The Structure of Writing Processes as Revealed by Secondary Task Demands." *Educational Studies in Language and Literature* 2: 141–1.

Raulerson, Bascom A., Michael J. Donovan, Alison P. Whiteford, and Ronald T. Kellogg. 2010. "Differential Verbal, Visual, and Spatial Working Memory in Written Language Production." *Perceptual and Motor Skills* 110, no. 1: 229–44. https://doi.org/10.2466/pms.110.1.229-44.

Reisman, David. 2012. *The Social Economics of Thorstein Veblen.* Cheltenham: E. Elgar.

Reyman, Jessica. 2018. "The Rhetorical Agency of Algorithms." In *Theorizing Digital Rhetoric*, edited by Aaron Hess and Amber Davisson 112–25. New York: Routledge.

Reynolds, Nedra. 2007. *Geographies of Writing.* Carbondale: Southern Illinois University Press.

Rice, Rich, and Kirk St.Amant. 2018. *Thinking Globally, Composing Locally: Rethinking Online Writing in the Age of the Global Internet.* Logan: Utah State University Press.

Rickert, Thomas. 2013. *Ambient Rhetoric: The Attunements of Rhetorical Being.* Pittsburgh, PA: University of Pittsburgh Press.

Rickert, Thomas. 2015. "The Whole of the Moon: Latour, Context, and the Problem of Holism." In *Thinking with Bruno Latour in Rhetoric and Composition,* edited by Paul Lynch and Nathaniel Rivers, 135–50. Carbondale: Southern Illinois University Press.

Rider, Janine. 1995. *The Writer's Book of Memory: An Interdisciplinary Study for Writing Teachers.* Mahwah, NJ: Lawrence Erlbaum.

Roaf, Michael. 1990. *Cultural Atlas of Mesopotamia and the Ancient Near East.* New York: Facts on File.

Robinson, Andrew. 2009. *The Story of Writing: Alphabets, Hieroglyphs and Pictograms.* London: Thames & Hudson.

Rumpf, Hans-Jurgen, Rant Tao, Florian Rehbein, and Nancy M. Petry. 2015. "Internet Addiction: A Future Addictive Disorder?" *Behavioral Addictions: DSM-5® and Beyond,* edited by Nancy M. Petry, 71–99. Oxford: Oxford University Press.

Saltz, Andre. 2017. "The Web Began Dying in 2014, Here's How." Web log. *Andre Stalz: Open Source Freelancer* (blog). https://staltz.com/the-web-began-dying-in-2014-heres-how.html.

Sana, Faria, Tina Weston, and Nicholas J. Cepeda. 2013. "Laptop Multitasking Hinders Classroom Learning for Both Users and Nearby Peers." *Computers and Education* 62: 24–31.

Savage, Michael. 2018. "Richest 1% on Target to Own Two-Thirds of All Wealth by 2030." The Guardian, April 7, 2018. https://www.theguardian.com/business/2018/apr/07/global-inequality-tipping-point-2030.

Schmandt-Besserat, Denise. 1996. *How Writing Came About.* Austin: University of Texas Press.

Schmandt-Besserat, Denise, and Michael Erard. 2008. "Origins and Forms of Writing." In *Handbook of Research on Writing: History, Society, School, Individual, Text,* edited by Charles Bazerman, 7–22. New York: Lawrence Erlbaum.

Schneier, Bruce. 2016. *Data and Goliath: The Hidden Battles to Collect Your Data and Control Your World.* New York: W. W. Norton.

Secretary-General of the United Nations. 2013. "Intergenerational Solidarity and the Needs of Future Generations." Report. United Nations General Assembly.

Selber, Stuart A. 2004. *Multiliteracies for a Digital Age.* Carbondale: Southern Illinois University Press.

Selfe, Cynthia L. 1999. "Technology and Literacy: A Story about the Perils of Not Paying Attention." *College Composition and Communication* 50, no. 3: 411. https://doi.org/10.2307/358859.

Selzer, Jack, and Sharon Crowley. 1999. *Rhetorical Bodies.* Madison: University of Wisconsin Press.

Sheridan, David M., Jim Ridolfo, and Anthony J. Michel. 2012. *The Available Means of Persuasion: Mapping a Theory and Pedagogy of Multimodal Public Rhetoric.* Anderson, SC: Parlor Press.

Shorrocks, Anthony, Jim Davies, and Rodrigo Lluberas. 2018. "Global Wealth Report 201." Rep. *Global Wealth Report 201.* Zurich: Credit Suisse.

Sibly, Richard M., James H. Brown, and Astrid Kodric Brown. 2012. *Metabolic Ecology: A Scaling Approach.* Chichester: Wiley-Blackwell.

Siegel, Eric. 2013. *Predictive Analytics: The Power to Predict Who Will Click, Buy, Lie, or Die.* Hoboken, NJ: Wiley.

Singer, Natasha. 2019. "The Government Protects Our Food and Cars. Why Not Our Data?" *New York Times,* November 2, 2019. https://www.nytimes.com/2019/11/02/sunday-review/data-protection-privacy.html.

Slack, Jon, John Morton, and Graham Hitch. 1977. *Introduction: The Human Memory System / Perception to Memory / John Morton. Working Memory / Graham Hitch and Alan Baddeley.* Milton Keynes: Open University Press.

Slaveryfootprint.org. 2019. Accessed January 17, 2019. http://slaveryfootprint.org/.

Smith, Chris. 2014. "Brits Spend More Time on Media than Sleep—Digiday." August 7, 2014. http://digiday.com/uk/brits-spend-time-media-technology-sleep/.

Socolof, Maria Leet, Jonathon G. Overly, Lori E. Kincaid, and Jack R. Geibig. 2001. "Desktop Computer Displays: A Life Cycle Assessment." Report. Vol. 1. EPA.

Sorapure, Madeleine. 2010. "Information Visualization, Web 2.0, and the Teaching of Writing." *Computers and Composition* 27, no. 1: 59–70.

Spinuzzi, Clay. 2003. *Tracing Genres through Organizations: A Sociocultural Approach to Information Design.* Cambridge, MA: MIT Press.

Srnicek, Nick. 2017. *Platform Capitalism.* Cambridge: Polity Press.

Staltz, Andre. 2017. "The Web Began Dying in 2014, Here's How." Staltz.com, October 2017. https://staltz.com/the-web-began-dying-in-2014-heres-how.html.

Standaert, Michael. 2015. "China's Notorious E-Waste Village Disappears Almost Overnight." Basel Action Network, December 17, 2015. https://www.ban.org/news/2015/12/17/chinas-notorious-e-waste-village-disappears-almost-overnight.

Starcevic, Vladan, and Yasser Khazaal. "Relationships between Behavioural Addictions and Psychiatric Disorders: What Is Known and What Is Yet to Be Learned?." *Frontiers in psychiatry* vol. 8 53. 7 Apr. 2017, doi:10.3389/fpsyt.2017.00053.

Statista. "Google, Apple, Facebook, and Amazon (GAFA)—Statistics and Facts." 2017. Statista. statista.com.

Steffen, Will, Wendy Broadgate, Lisa Deutsch, Owen Gaffney, and Cornelia Ludwig. 2015.

"The Trajectory of the Anthropocene: The Great Acceleration." *The Anthropocene Review* 2: 81–98.

"StEP Annual Report." 2016. "*StEP Annual Report (Solving the E-waste Problem).*" http://www.step-initiative.org/.

Stephens-Davidowitz, Seth. 2018. *Everybody Lies: What the Internet Can Tell Us about Who We Really Are.* New York: Bloomsbury Publishing.

Stone, Michael K., and Zenobia Barlow, eds. 2005. *Ecological Literacy: Educating Our Children for a Sustainable World.* San Francisco: Sierra Club Books.

Street, Brian V. 1984. *Literacy in Theory and Practice*. Cambridge: Cambridge University Press.

Sussman, Steve, Nadra Lisha, and Mark Griffiths. 2010. "Prevalence of the Addictions: A Problem of the Majority or the Minority?" *Evaluation and the Health Professions* 34, no. 1: 3–56. https://doi.org/10.1177/016327871 0380124.

Sylvester, Brad. 2012. "Jake Reilly's 'Amish Project': 90 Days Without a Cell Phone, Email and Social Media." Interview. Yahoo News, January 30, 2012. https://news.tfionline.com/post/16860880068/jake-reillys-amish-project -90-days-without-a.

Syverson, Margaret A. 1999. *The Wealth of Reality: An Ecology of Composition*. Carbondale: Southern Illinois University Press.

The Economist. "The World's Most Valuable Resource Is No Longer Oil, but Data." The Economist Newspaper, 2017. https://www.economist.com /leaders/2017/05/06/the-worlds-most-valuable-resource-is-no-longer-oil -but-data.

"The Life Cycle of a CD or DVD." 2003. Environmental Protection Agency. https://www.epa.gov/students.

"The Top 500 Sites on the Web." 2020. Alexa.com. https://www.alexa.com /topsites.

Thompson, Clive. 2009. "Clive Thompson on the New Literacy." *Wired*, August 24, 2009.

Trimbur, John. 2000. "Composition and the Circulation of Writing." *College Composition and Communication* 52, no. 2: 188. https://doi.org/10.2307/35 8493.

Trimbur, John. 1994. "Taking the Social Turn: Teaching Writing Post-Process." *College Composition and Communication* 45, no. 1: 108. https://doi.org/10.23 07/358592.

Torrance, Mark, and David Galbraith. 2006. "The Processing Demands of Writing." *Handbook of Writing Research*, edited by Charles A. MacArthur, Steve Graham, and Jill Fitzgerald, 67–82. New York: The Guilford Press.

Turkle, Sherry. 2005. *The Second Self: Computers and the Human Spirit*. Cambridge, MA: MIT Press.

Turkle, Sherry. 2017. *Alone Together: Why We Expect More from Technology and Less from Each Other*. New York: Basic Books.

Turow, Joseph. 2013. *The Daily You: How the New Advertising Industry Is Defining Your Identity and Your World*. New Haven, CT: Yale University Press.

Twenge, Jean M. 2018. *IGEN: Why Today's Super-Connected Kids Are Growing up Less Rebellious, More Tolerant, Less Less Happy—and Completely Unprepared for Adulthood—and What That Means for the Rest of Us*. New York: Atria Books.

United Nations Management Group. 2017. "United Nations System-Wide Response to Tackling E-Waste." *United Nations System-Wide Response to Tackling E-Waste*. United Nations Management Group.

Urbanski, Heather. 2010. *Writing and the Digital Generation: Essays on New Media Rhetoric*. Jefferson, NC: McFarland.

Van De Mieroop, Marc. 1999. *Cuneiform Texts and the Writing of History*. London: Routledge.

Van De Mieroop, Marc. 2007. *A History of the Ancient Near East: Ca. 3000–323 BC.* Malden, MA: Blackwell.

Van De Mieroop, Marc. 2014. "Silver as a Financial Tool in Mesopotamia." In *Explaining Monetary and Financial Innovation: A Historical Analysis,* edited by P. Bernholz and R. Vaubel, 17–29. Cham, Switzerland: Springer International Publishing.

van den Berg, J. H. 1970. *Things: Four Metabletic Reflections.* Pittsburgh, PA: Duquesne University Press.

van Leeuwen, Theo. 2004. "Ten Reasons Why Linguists Should Pay Attention to Visual Communication." *Discourse and Technology Multimodal Discourse Analysis,* edited by Ronald Scollon and Philip LeVine, 7–19. Brantford, Ont.: W. Ross MacDonald School Resource Services Library.

van Manen, Max. 2014. *Phenomenology of Practice: Meaning-Giving Methods in Phenomenological Research and Writing.* Walnut Creek, CA: Left Coast Press.

Vie, Stephanie, and Jennifer deWinter. 2015. "Video Games and Surveillance." *Kairos* 20, no. 2. http://kairos.technorhetoric.net/20.2/topoi/beck-et-al/vie_dewin.html.

Virilio, Paul. 1986. *Speed and Politics: An Essay on Dromology.* New York: Columbia University.

Virilio, Paul. 2012. *The Great Accelerator.* Translated by Julie Rose. Cambridge, MA: Polity Press.

Walt, Vivienne, and Sebastian Meyer. 2018. "Blood, Sweat, and Batteries." *Fortune,* August 23, 2018. http://fortune.com/.

Walters, Keith, Andrea A. Lundsford, Helene Moglen, and James Slevin. 1990. "Language, Logic, and Literacy." In *The Right to Literacy,* 173–88. New York: MLA.

Watkins, Lee, and Dean A. Snyder. 2003. "Digital Hammurabi." *Digital Hammurabi.* John Hopkins University. https://pages.jh.edu/~dighamm/.

Weissman, Judith. 2016. "Serious Psychological Distress among Adults: United States, 2009–2013." In *Creating the Healthiest Nation: Ensuring the Right to Health.* Denver: APHA.

Wang, Feng, Ruediger Kuehr, Daniel Ahlquist, and Jinhui Li. 2013. "E-Waste in China: A Country Report." Rep. *E-Waste in China: A Country Report.* United Nations StEP Program (Solving the E-Waste Problem).

West, Geoffrey B. 2018. *Scale: The Universal Laws of Growth, Innovation, Sustainability, and the Pace of Life in Organisms, Cities, Economies, and Companies.* New York: Penguin Press.

"What They Know." *Wall Street Journal,* n.d. Web. 27 Sept. 2012. http://online.wsj.com/public/page/what-they-know-digital-privacy.html?mod=WSJ_topnav_na_tech.

Wolff, William I. 2013. "Interactivity and the Invisible: What Counts as Writing in the Age of Web 2.0." *Computers and Composition* 30, no. 3: 211–25.

Wood, Eileen, Lucia Zivcakova, Petrice Gentile, Karin Archer, Domenica De Pasquale, and Amanda Nosko. 2012. "Examining the Impact of Off-Task Multi-Tasking with Technology on Real-Time Classroom Learning." *Computers and Education* 58, no. 1: 365–74. https://doi.org/10.1016/j.compedu.2011.08.029.

Wysocki, Anne Frances. 2004. *Writing New Media: Theory and Applications for Expanding the Teaching of Composition.* Logan: Utah State University Press.

Yagelski, Robert. 2011. *Writing as a Way of Being: Writing Instruction, Nonduality, and the Crisis of Sustainability.* New York: Hampton Press.

Yancey, Kathleen Blake. 2004. "Made Not Only in Words: Composition in a New Key." *College Composition and Communication* 56, no. 2: 297. https://doi.org/10.2307/4140651.

Yoffee, N. 1995. "Political Economy in Early Mesopotamian States." *Annual Review of Anthropology* 24, no. 1: 281–311. https://doi.org/10.1146/annurev.anthro.24.1.281.

Yoffee, Norman, ed. 2015. *The Cambridge World History: Early Cities in Comparative Perspective 4000 BCE–1200 CE.* Vol. 3. Cambridge: Cambridge University Press.

Young, Richard, and Patricia Sullivan. 1984. "Why Write? A Reconsideration." In *Essays on Classical Rhetoric and Modern Discourse,* edited by Robert J. Connors, Lisa S. Ede, Andrea A. Lunsford, and Edward P. J. Corbett, 215–25. Carbondale: Southern Illinois University Press.

Zappen, James P. 2018. "Digital Rhetoric and the Internet of Things." In *Theorizing Digital Rhetoric,* edited by Aaron Hess and Amber Davisson 55–67. New York: Routledge.

Zurawicki, Leon. 2010. *Neuromarketing: Exploring the Brain of the Consumer.* Berlin: Springer.

ABOUT THE AUTHOR

Christian J. Pulver is assistant professor in the department of Writing Studies, Rhetoric, and Composition at Roger Williams University in Rhode Island. He teaches first-year writing and upper-level courses on narrative theory, the art of the essay, and multimodal and visual rhetorics. His research interests currently focus on developing materialist theories of writing that combine writing and rhetorical studies with the natural sciences, information theory, economics, media studies, historical and dialectical materialism, and environmental studies.

INDEX